The Sugar Casino

Jonathan Kingsman

Contents

Preface

"Why don't you write a book about the sugar business?" he asked.

"Because no one is interested in the sugar business", I replied.

I was sitting with my best friend from the business in a Thai restaurant on the Quai de Mont Blanc in Geneva. All the other clients had long since left. The restaurant manager kept coming over to our table and sighing.

"You couldn't be more wrong", my friend said. "There is a huge debate about sugar now; in all its aspects. And there are some fascinating characters in the sugar business – and some fabulous stories to tell".

I wasn't sure that I knew either the characters or the stories. I had started my career as a trader with a big American trading house but had spent most of my time there as a futures trader, managing their hedging book. From there I had moved to being a futures broker, then a physical broker and then a market analyst. Unlike most commodity traders I had spent little time "on the ground". I had never been kidnapped by rebels in East Africa nor been driven by a local mill owner in an armoured truck in Central America. My life had been one of telephones, first fixed and then mobile, and progressively telexes, faxes and emails; lots of emails.

"It will have to be interesting" he added, "Otherwise no one will read it".

"How can anyone make the sugar business interesting?" I asked him with what must have been a look of despair.

"That's your problem", he replied. "If I knew that I would write it myself".

One month later I was having dinner with a publisher in a Brooklyn restaurant. There was a loudspeaker blasting out music just above the table and I could make out maybe one word in three that he was saying. We had spent the evening talking about the cookery book that he was publishing for the restaurant. I tried to steer the conversation back to the sugar business. He was resisting.

"I need to make it interesting", I said.

"How can you make the sugar business interesting?" he laughed, taking a bite of his vegetable linguine. He put his fork down. "But you do have one thing working in your favour," he added. "Sugar is on trend".

I had spent my working life looking for trends in the sugar price, trying to identify them just as they were starting, then jumping on board and eventually trying to get out before the trend changed. I knew all about trends.

"Give me an example of a trend in your business", I asked.

"Cookery books", he replied.

"I can't believe everyone is so interested in cooking," I sighed. "Why are they?"

"We are in the final stages of this civilisation", he replied. "We are at the same stage now as the Roman Empire was when all they were interested in were Roman baths and Bacchanalian feasts. Think about it: spas are now on trend; food and wine are on trend. It's the same thing."

I thought about what he had said as the waiter

brought us our main course, describing in detail how each dish was prepared and what it contained. At least I supposed that was what he was telling us. I didn't hear a word of what he said above the music and the noise from the other tables.

"There is a book that has come out", the publisher continued. "It is called, "I quit sugar". It's going to be a best seller. Everyone is talking about sugar and health.

"So what's your angle on the issue of obesity" he asked, suddenly switching to interview mode.

The previous evening I had attended the annual Sugar Dinner at the Waldorf Astoria in New York City, an event that attracts well over 1,000 people from the industry. José Orive, the new head of the International Sugar Organisation had given the after dinner speech; it was short and, well, sweet. He had said how happy he was to be there, thanked all the usual people and then said that his daughter had told him that she wasn't going to feed her children, his grandchildren, any food that had added sugar.

"Are you going to feed them water melon," he asked her, "or fruit of any kind? Because they also contain sugar", he told her. "Sugar from cane or beet is the same as sugar from apples or melons. It is same thing; it is treated by the body in the same way".

José had gone on to warn the unusually subdued diners that health concerns were the biggest current threat to the sugar industry and that this threat had to be taken seriously. He called on the industry "to counter these spurious claims and to get the message out there that sugar is a healthy natural product, a cheap calorie and a source of pleasure for millions of people around the world". He sat down to rapturous applause.

"Would it surprise you," I asked the publisher, "if I told you that people were eating less sugar now than in the past: per capita sugar consumption has actually been falling in Australia and Europe. It has hardly budged in the past forty years in the US."

"Yes that would surprise me," he replied. "You would have to be sure of your statistics but if you are right then that is a message that deserves to be out there." He took another bite of his organic spinach soufflé and I picked at my organic saffron risotto.

"And giving up sugar does not necessarily lead to weight loss," I continued, warming to the theme. "I have a friend who hasn't eaten sugar, or anything sweetened with sugar, for more than three years now."

"How is that working out for him?"

"He has put on fifteen kilos," I replied. "He almost certainly over compensated for the lost calories by eating more of other stuff. He gave up deserts but over compensated with bread and cheese. You can't just pick on one ingredient or food and claim it to be the source of the problem. The issue is far more complicated."

"But not too complicated," the publisher said thoughtfully. "Readers don't like complicated."

"I agree," I replied. "People prefer a simple message to a complicated one. But sometimes the truth is complicated; things are not always just black and white. There is a lot of grey out there. Besides, science is progressing all the time. What was true yesterday may not be true today. And what might be true for one person, or in one instance, may not be true for another person or in another instance."

"Give me another sugar issue," the publisher continued, ignoring my waffling. "I want two more sugar issues."

"What about speculation?" I asked. "Most people think that traders manipulate markets, push up food prices and cause hunger and starvation among the poor."

"Well, they do, don't they?" he laughed.

"No they don't. High food prices rarely cause hunger. Low food prices cause hunger; low prices drive farmers off their fields and into the cities. What the world needs is food prices high enough to encourage famers to farm. If farmers can make money farming the world can easily feed a growing population."

"Good", the editor replied. "You are getting better at this". Now give me your third issue."

I thought about it while I took another mouthful of my risotto. It didn't seem to taste of anything. The diners at the next table got up and left; the noise level dropped a couple of decibels. My throat was sore from shouting.

"Did you know," I asked the publisher, "that when Bill Clinton was entertaining, or rather being entertained by, Monica Lewinsky in the Oval Office he interrupted what he was doing to take a phone call?"

"No I didn't," the publisher replied with a laugh. "But it must have been an important call. Was it from Hilary?"

"No, it was from a Florida sugar producer; he was calling the President to lobby for help over legislation that at the time was going through the state assembly concerning the Everglades."

"So why would Bill take that call?"

"Because the US sugar producers are major contributors to both political parties. Lobbying is part of the landscape of all major democracies nowadays and it is all perfectly legal. But some would argue that lobbying on that scale is really nothing more than institutionalised corruption."

"Are you saying that the sugar market is corrupt?" he asked, suddenly interested.

"Sugar has been described as the most political commodity," I continued. "There are a lot of cane and beet farmers and they vote, so governments always want to keep them on their side. But political parties also like to receive donations from the sugar mill owners – so governments have to do a political balancing act where they maintain cane prices high enough to keep the farmers happy but low enough to keep the mills happy."

"What about the consumers?" he asked.

"Do you know how much you pay for a bag of sugar in your supermarket?" I asked. He shook his head. "In the Western world most people don't know how much they are paying for sugar. Most of the sugar we eat in the western world is in the form of processed foods; the price really only matters to the manufacturers of those foods.

"However, the price of sugar is important in developing countries and can become a political issue. This is especially so in India and Pakistan where sugar is an important source of calories, usually taken in tea.

"Everyone gets upset if there is no sugar, if the shelves are empty. But in times of shortage politicians blame speculators or hoarders and put a couple of people in prison, or in the case of Iraq once, hang them from the lampposts on the road leading to Baghdad airport."

"I may not know how much I pay for sugar but I do know that it is given away for free in most coffee shops and restaurants," the publisher said. "It can't be much of a business where your final product is given away free", he added thoughtfully.

"But it does look as if you have identified three issues", he continued. "You must write about all three: health, governments and speculation.

"And when you write about speculation you should also explain how a commodity market works. Most people don't know. I certainly don't.

"Food is becoming increasingly important now. People want to know where it comes from, how it is produced and how it is transported. In the past most people didn't care; but they do now. You need to go into that in some detail.

"Wouldn't that be too much information?" I asked. "Remember, it will be tough to make that interesting."

"If a reader finds some parts of the book less interesting he will skip them," he replied. "Virtually no one reads all of a book these days," he added.

"But I do think you are missing the most important aspect of all this," he continued thoughtfully.

"How do people feel when they think about sugar?" he asked. I must have looked blank because he continued without a pause.

"They feel guilty," he said, answering his own question. "When I think about sugar I think about its history. I think about slavery and I think about exploitation. I also think about deforestation and the destruction of ecosystems. I think about all the cane that is grown to produce unnecessary ethanol. I think about global warming.

"And when I eat sugar," he continued, "I feel guilty: I know it is bad for me but I eat it anyway. I am addicted to the stuff.

"I don't want to feel guilty when I eat sugar," he said. "And nor does anyone else. Write me that book."

"I am not sure I can," I replied, pretty much to myself.

"Well think about it" he replied with a smile, "and let me know what you decide".

Four days later my wife and I were standing in line at Dockland in Bermuda, waiting to catch a ferry to St George's, a town at the northernmost tip of the main island. We had stopped over in Bermuda on the way back from New York and had spent the weekend with old friends whom we hadn't seen since they had moved to Bermuda from the UK some years ago. But now it was Monday morning and our friends had gone back to work and we had set out to explore a little more of this rather old fashioned, but charming, former British colony.

The previous Friday we had taken the bus from our hotel to Dockland where we had caught a different ferry to Hamilton, the island's capital. Dockland had been almost deserted and we had caught the ferry with ease. Today, as the bus had driven around the headland I had caught sight of two enormous cruise liners. Today was not going to be as easy as the previous Friday; each cruise liner would hold close to 4,000 people– and a good percentage of them would want to take the ferry to St George's.

The sun was hotter than I had expected and I had forgotten to bring a hat. I suggested to my wife that she sit in the shade for a while; there was no point in both of us getting sunburnt. In front of me in the line were two families from Savannah in the US. As I eavesdropped on their conversation I understood that a daughter from each family had recently graduated from teacher training college and the cruise was a graduation present from their proud parents.

The daughters were both pretty and obviously smart; they talked enthusiastically about their plans for the future. One had accepted a job as a specialised teacher in a school for handicapped children; the other in a school in a very poor neighbourhood. Both had a social conscience and obviously wanted to use their education and their skills to help others. You couldn't have wished for better examples of a younger generation, full of optimism and goodwill.

The problem, of course, was that both girls were obese. They were very red, obviously suffering from the Bermudan heat. One appeared to have trouble breathing and her words came out as a series of urgent gasps.

The ferry arrived and we filed aboard, climbing quickly to the upper outer deck so that we could enjoy both the fresh sea breeze and the view. We found a couple of places on one of the benches; another family, also from one of the cruise ships, settled in front of us. The couple were in their late thirties and had four children aged from, at a guess, six to fourteen. The four children were skinny, the mother was of average build but the father was enormous. His neck, just in front of me, would not have looked out of place on a bull elephant. I looked around the deck and realised that close to nine out of ten of the passengers on board were seriously overweight or obese.

Once off the ferry we walked around St George's for a while. It wasn't much of a place but the locals had done their best to make it attractive for what was evidently a cruise ship clientele. The main street consisted entirely of souvenir shops or fast food restaurants. With trepidation we went to an imitation English pub where we ordered mineral water and Waldorf salads. All around us everyone seemed to be ordering pizzas, sugar-rich cocktails, milk shakes and cheesecakes. We watched in horror as the waitress struggled to table after table with the biggest pizzas I have ever seen, each one for only one person.

The table next to us cleared and two elderly couples sat down. We gathered from their conversation that they weren't off the cruise ships but had come to Bermuda for a vacation. They seemed as concerned as we were with what we saw all around us.

"Something has gone wrong," one of the two ladies said. "It's just not normal that everyone has got so fat. Something must have changed. It's just not possible that all these people have suddenly and collectively decided to eat too much."

"I think I will try and write that book," I said, turning to my wife.

Sugar is the spice of life

1.1   A spoonful of history (1)

"A Spoonful of sugar helps the medicine go down;
The medicine go down, The medicine go down
Just a spoonful of sugar helps the medicine go down
In a most delightful way" (2)

Mary Poppins knew what she was singing about in the 1964 Disney Classic. Sugar has been helping the medicine to go down since the earliest of days - not surprising when you consider what medicines used to be made of in the Middle Ages. In her book "Sugar", Elizabeth Abbott lists a few of them: "animal faeces or urine, minced worms, gall from a castrated boar, roasted viper's skin and poisons such as hemlock". (3)

But sugar not only helped the medicine go down; it was also considered as a medicine in its own right. In the 13th century there was even a theological debate within the Church as to whether sugar was a medicine that could be consumed during fasting days, or a food that could not.

Thomas Aquinas ruled on the issue and wrote,

"Though nutritious in themselves, sugared spices are nonetheless not eaten with the end in mind of nourishment, but rather for ease of digestion; accordingly, they do not break the fast any more than the taking of other medicines." (4)

Sugar was also a spice. In the Middle Ages,

spices such as ginger, cardamom and ginger were believed to help the digestion. They certainly helped "spice" up a monotonous diet. Most importantly, at a time when it was difficult to keep food fresh, spices hid the taste of rotten fish and meat.

"At all events, whatever the reason, most dishes were smothered with spices, whether needed or not. As a rule, possibly because of its provenance from the East, sugar was classed with spices." (5)

Whether medicine, spice or food, sugar was a luxury when it first began to land on European tables. In the 13th century King Edward III ordered three pounds of it, but added, "If so much is to be had". (6)

The wealthy classes at that time were no different from the wealthy classes now: they liked to display their wealth. And what better way to show how rich you were than to display sugar as an ornament?

"A visitor to Persia in the 11th century had already reported that the Sultan's bakers had transformed 162,000 pounds of sugar into a life-sized tree and other replicas. And in North Africa the caliph, al-Zahir, kept sugar artists busy for weeks before Islamic feasts sculpting sugar art works for his guests. One such display featured 157 sugar statues and seven table-sized castles."

By the 16th century the fashion had reached England.

"On November 18, 1515, England's Cardinal Thomas Wolsey celebrated his installation at Westminster Abbey with extraordinarily lavish soteltes depicting castles and churches,

beasts and birds, fighting knights and dancing ladies, even an exquisite chess set, all made from "spiced plate" or hardened sugar." (7)

The fashion was not limited to England. When the Duke of Parma married Maria de Aviz in 1566 the City of Antwerp sent a wedding gift of 3,000 sugar sculptures. Even the candlesticks at the wedding were made of sugar. Back in England in 1591 the Earl of Hertford threw a "sugar banquet" (8) for Queen Elizabeth I. The feast lasted for four days and may have served as inspiration for Shakespeare's *Midsummer Nights Dream*. Two hundred gentlemen and their one hundred torchbearers paraded into the banqueting hall laden with sugar representations of castles, birds, animals, fish, soldiers and weaponry. Queen Elizabeth I was reputed to have had a sweet tooth and she evidently appreciated the banquet.

Seven years later, in 1598, when Elizabeth I was 65, the German lawyer Paul Hentzner had an audience with the Queen and wrote that she was

"very majestic, her face oblong, fair but wrinkled; her lips narrow and her teeth black, (a defect the English seem subject to, from their too great use of sugar." (9)

However Andre Hurault-Sieur de Maisse, the French ambassador to Elizabeth's court, had visited the Queen a year earlier and described her as follows (10)

"As for her face, it is and appears to be very aged. It is long and thin, and her teeth are very yellow and unequal, compared with what they were formerly, so they say, and on the left side less than on the right. Many of them are missing so that

one cannot understand her easily when she speaks quickly. Her figure is fair and tall and graceful in whatever she does; so far as may be she keeps her dignity, yet humbly and graciously withal."

It is not clear, therefore whether the Queen's few remaining teeth were yellow or black. However Hentzner blamed the black teeth that he saw on excess sugar consumption and this view has been passed down through generations of British school children. Their parents have told them, "Clean your teeth twice a day or you will have black teeth like Queen Elizabeth!"

By the reign of Queen Elizabeth I sugar had already made quite a journey from its humble beginnings in the jungles of Papua New Guinea where tribesmen had first discovered the sweetness and energy they could obtain by chewing on wild sugar cane (*Saccharum officinarum*), a member of the grass family. (11) The locals "harvested" the cane with axes made from volcanic rock and probably cut it into pieces before carrying it back to their villages.

Sugarcane is a grass and like all grasses has a jointed stem; its leaves and branches come from shoots at each joint. A tribesman in Papua New Guinea almost certainly discovered – and almost certainly by accident – that if you plant a piece of cane in the ground it grows into a new plant. Some 10,000 years ago sugar became the first crop to be cultivated anywhere in the world.

Sugar spread slowly west and by the time the armies of Alexander the Great had reached India in 325 BC it was already there. One of the Alexander's generals Nearchus described how

"A reed in India brings forth honey without the help of

bees, from which an intoxicating drink is made though the plant bears no fruit". (12)

One thousand years later the art of making sugar (rather than just juice) from cane was already well established in Persia, but whether the Persians or some other race discovered the process will probably never be known. In any case the discovery led to an acceleration in the speed with which both sugar and sugarcane spread around the world.

The growth of Islam also helped to disseminate sugar knowledge and by the end of the 6th century sugar was being cultivated all around the Mediterranean, or at least wherever irrigation was available. The Crusades in the 12th century introduced sugar to European palates and imports began into Europe, even if only in small amount. The Crusaders also indulged in what would now be called "vertical integration" and took over sugar plantations from the conquered Muslims; the Knights of Malta were among the first. (13)

The Venetians were big traders at that time and just as the Muslims had done before them, they reported on what they saw on their travels. Marco Polo (1254 – 1324) has been credited with bringing sugar refining technology back to Europe from China but at the time of his travels it already existed in Egypt. He acknowledged this when he wrote from the city of Fukien. (14)

"They have an enormous quantity of sugar. From this city the Great Khan gets all the sugar that is used at Court, enough to represent a considerable sum in value. You must know that in these parts before the Great Khan subjected it to his over lordship, the people did not know how to prepare and refine sugar

as is done in Egypt. They did not let it congeal and solidify in moulds, but merely boiled and skimmed it, so that it hardened to a kind of paste, and was black in colour. But after the country had been conquered by the Great Khan there came into the regions men of Egypt who had been at the Court of the Great Khan, and who taught them to refine it with the ashes of certain trees."

By the end of 16th century sugar was becoming more plentiful in Europe and was part of the middle class diet. In 1603 some Spaniards visited England and were astonished at

"This fondness of our countrymen and countrywomen for sweets...they drink nothing but what is sweetened with sugar, drinking it commonly with their wine and mixing it with their meat." (15)

Sugar had replaced spices as a means not only of preserving food but also of making it taste better.

The demand for sugar received a boost with the arrival of coffee into European markets. The first coffee shop opened in London in 1652 and by the end of the century there was one coffee shop for every thousand Londoners. To put that in perspective, there are now 1,552 chain coffee shops in London, one for every five thousand Londoners. A French visitor was so impressed by London's coffee shops in 1652 he wrote,

"You have all manner of news there; you have a good fire, which you may sit by as long as you please. You have a dish of coffee; you meet your friends for the transaction of business and all for a penny if you don't care to spend more." (16)

But they didn't have free WIFI.

By coincidence, the same year that our French visitor was enjoying his coffee by the fire, tea arrived in England from China. The first advertisement for tea appeared in an English paper in 1658 and when King Charles II married the Portuguese princess Catherine of Braganza in 1662 Catherine brought tea chests to England as part of her wedding dowry. She soon popularised the custom of taking tea at court. (Her dowry incidentally, also included sugar.) (17)

Fifty years later, tea drinking had become even more popular, once again, thanks to the Royal Family, when Queen Anne started drinking tea rather than beer with her breakfast. (In those days people drank beer because it was safer to drink than often-dirty water. Tea, because it involved boiling the water, played a similar role.)

By the 18th century the middle classes had taken up tea drinking and the first tea gardens opened in 1742. Well-to-do ladies would hold afternoon tea parties in their salons around a low table. Tea was relatively cheap compared to coffee and was slowly adopted first by the lower middle classes and then by the working classes. All this tea was sweetened with sugar. Per capita sugar consumption in England was 1.8 kg in 1700, 3.6 kg in 1729, 5.4 kg in 1789 and 8.2 kg by 1809. (18) By the middle of the 19th century it had increased to around 12 kilos per year and by the end of the century it would double again to around 24 kg per year (or about one pound per week). (19)

The Industrial Revolution was helping to drive this increase but at the same time tea and sugar were helping to drive the Industrial Revolution. Workers in the new factories drank tea with sugar during their "tea breaks", providing them with instant calories and a quick pick-up in energy, enabling them to get back quickly to their tasks.

When workers moved from the countryside into cities they worked in factories, earned more money but had less access to fresh food grown on their own land. Women increasingly worked in these new factories, leaving them less time to prepare food at home. This lead to a new meal, "high tea" that was served seated around a "high" rather than a "low" table and consisted of "tea with sugar, bread heaped with butter, jam preserves, cold meat, cheese or and egg." (20)

So popular was the new meal that the inmates of the Nacton poorhouse petitioned to forego their usual dinners of peas porridge and instead use the food money to buy bread and butter, tea and sugar. By the end of the 19th century, sugared tea had become the nation's "favourite dinner" and England had become the world's biggest sugar consumer. (21)

All this demand for sugar led to terrible human misery, but I will write more about that in the next chapter.

1.2   The sugar world today

This year (2015) the world's farmers will grow enough sugar beet and sugar cane to produce around 167 million tonnes of white sugar. (22) Of that amount, about 20% will come from sugar beet and the rest from sugarcane. There is chemically no difference between white sugar produced from beet and white sugar produced from cane. Some people argue that beet sugar has a residual odour when you open the bag but in reality that has never been proven. The two products are indistinguishable. They are identical products.

Consumers in developing countries prefer white sugar; it is viewed as more sophisticated and as purer than brown sugar. Consumers in developed countries often have a preference for brown sugar in the mistaken belief that it is somehow healthier than white sugar. Consumers in rich countries are often willing to pay more for raw sugar than for white sugar – so much so that some producers actually spray molasses back onto the refined sugar to give it a "healthier" look.

The world's estimated 7.125 billion people will eat and drink about 165 million tonnes of white sugar this year; on average that is about 23.2 kilos of white sugar per person per year – including, of course, babies and infants.

Out of the approximately 165 million tonnes of sugar that the world will eat this year, about one third will have been imported from another country. In the case of the EU that proportion is about 15%. That means that most of the sugar that EU consumers eat each year is produced within the EU, by EU companies and (relatively) affluent EU farmers.

World sugar consumption is increasing at around 2% per year, largely driven by the growth in both population and incomes. People in developing countries consume more sugar as their incomes rise, at least up to a certain income level. An Indian living in a rural area may find that as he earns a tiny bit more money each week he can buy his children a bottle of sugar-containing soda a month. When his children grow up and move to the city they will cook less and buy more of their food and drink from road stalls or fast food outlets. Prepared food usually contains more sugar than food cooked at home.

But once incomes rise above a certain level then

the growth in sugar consumption tails off. As they get richer the children of our Indian farm labourer may be able to afford more expensive calories such as grains or meat. And as they get even richer, health concerns may kick in; they may look to reduce their total calorie intake, including sugar.

In the developed world we have recently seen a slight reduction in per capita sugar consumption as consumers have reduced their calorific intake or moved from sugar to other sources of calories. Consciously or subconsciously consumers in the rich world are beginning to reduce their total sugar consumption. This can be part of a calorie-controlled diet that reduces their total calorie intake. Or it can be a reduction in the share of sugar as a percentage of their total calorie intake.

Indeed, in a move to encourage healthier eating, the World Health Organisation (WHO) recently (March 2015) recommended that people should limit their sugar consumption to 10% of their daily calorie intake. The WHO added,

"A further reduction to below 5% or roughly 25 grams (6 teaspoons) per day would provide additional health benefits." (23)

The sugar industry contests these recommendations, arguing that a calorie is the same whether it comes from sugar (a carbohydrate) or from other sources such as protein. However, many in the medical profession support the WHO recommendations. They argue that because the human body absorbs it so quickly,

"Sugar can lead to a surge in blood glucose that may place stress on the body's ability to maintain a stable equilibrium mediated by insulin"…When we eat sucrose we take in fructose that we do not need - and when we eat too much fructose we place an important metabolic burden on the liver." (24)

Despite the controversy, population growth and rising incomes mean that year after year the world as a whole continues to consume more sugar. And the world's producers need to expand to meet that demand. At current growth rates the world will need an extra 35 million tonnes of sugar in ten years time; some of the processing (factory) capacity to produce that has already been built but the world will still need more beet and cane to keep those factories running.

Some mills, particularly in Brazil, own their own farms and grow their own cane but most don't. The vast majority of cane mills and beet processing factories in the world buy their cane and beet from independent farmers. They coexist in a symbiotic relationship where they can't survive without each other.

Brazil is the world's biggest producer of sugar. In 2015, in spite of low world prices, the country will produce nearly 35 million tonnes of sugar: 20 million in the form of raw sugar for export and 15 million as white sugar for a mix of domestic consumption and export.

Of that tonnage, Brazil's 200 million people will consume around 12.5 million tonnes. The 21.5 million tonnes that they don't consume makes Brazil the world's biggest sugar exporter. But Brazil is also the world's biggest consumer of sugar on a per capita basis: on average every Brazilian gets through 62.5 kilos of sugar per year. And as that average figure includes babies and children it means that most Brazilian adults consume more than 62.5 kilos every year.

No one really knows why Brazilians eat so much sugar; perhaps it is for historical reasons; perhaps it is because sugar is one of the country's cheapest sources of calories. (Brazil has one of the world's lowest domestic prices of sugar.) With such a high level of sugar consumption you would expect Brazilians to have a high level of obesity. But they don't. The latest figures show that 12.5% of Brazilian men and 16.9% of Brazilian women are obese. These figures are obviously too high but are still relatively low compared to most developed countries.

In the US 33.3% of men and 35.8% of women are classified as obese; the comparable figures for the UK are 26% for men and 23.8% for women. (25) These figures suggest that factors other than sugar consumption may be driving the obesity epidemic, but more on that in a later chapter.

India is the world's second biggest producer of sugar with the last crop coming in at around 28 million tonnes; of that quantity India consumes around 24 million tonnes domestically. On average the country's 1.2 billion people consume about 20 kilos of sugar per year. (For what it is worth India has an obesity rate of 1.3% for men and 2.8% for women.) India's sugar production has in the past fluctuated widely, depending on the strength of the monsoon and the competitiveness of other agricultural crops. India has often swung from exporter to importer and back again.

In terms of employment India's sugar industry is the second largest in the country after the cotton textile industry. Sugarcane farmers and their families, numbering over 35 million, constitute more than 7% of the rural population. The sugar industry employs more than one million workers and also provides substantial indirect employment through various ancillary activities. (26)

All the sugar in India is produced from cane although there has recently been an experiment to also grow sugar beet; for the moment beets are only used for ethanol. The country has three, politically and geographically separated, industries; Uttar Pradesh in the north, Maharashtra and Karnataka in the middle and Tamil Nadu in the south.

Like most industries in India, the sugar sector was in the past bound up in government red tape: a myriad of often confusing, and sometimes conflicting, laws governed everything from how much sugar mills had to pay for their cane to how much sugar they could sell each month. These laws came not only from the central (federal) government, but also from the various state governments.

Many of these laws have now been abolished but there is still an on going dispute regarding the cane price. The state governments have an interest in setting the cane price high to keep their local cane growers happy, particularly in the lead-up to elections. At the same time the politicians have an interest in keeping the sugar price low for consumers.

The European Union's 27 member countries are the third biggest producer and consumer of sugar at about 15.2 million tonnes. The bloc's 503 million inhabitants consume 17.2 million tonnes, or about 33 kilos per person per year before you factor in any waste through food spoilage. For historical reasons the EU imports close to 3 million tonnes of raw sugar, mainly from former colonies. Under a 2006 agreement with the

World Trade Organisation the EU is only allowed to export a maximum of 1.3 million tonnes per year but this restriction ends in 2017.

Although some sugar cane used to be grown in Spain and Portugal, European sugar is now produced entirely from beet.

Continental Europeans – and in particular the French – have long mistrusted the ability of markets to match supply and demand; they have instead looked to manage markets by limiting production via quotas. Over history, these quotas have been variously set by committees or, in some cases, by dictators.

During the Napoleonic wars, when Britain's blockade of Napoleon's empire reduced the supplies of cane sugar reaching continental Europe, Napoleon encouraged the production of beet sugar, distributing production quotas to a number of families. Some of these same families still hold these quotas. Nicknamed "white gold", they are handed down from generation to generation like family jewels. Like all good things that come to an end, these quotas will be abolished in September 2017. From that date EU producers will be free to produce as much or as little sugar as they like.

Some commentators have expressed concern that Europeans are eating too much sugar. Rather surprisingly, however, European sweetener consumption has been falling over recent years, partly because of health concerns and partly because of the poor economy in the southern European countries.

China will be the world's fourth biggest producer this year at 10.5 million tonnes; the country's 1.37 billion people consume close to 14.75 million tonnes per year, with the balance coming from imports. The Chinese don't have a "sweet tooth" and on average consume around 10-11 kilos per capita per year, well below the world average.

China produces sugar from both beet and cane; the cane is grown in the sub-tropical south while the beet is grown in the north of the country. China has one of the highest costs of production anywhere in the world, largely because of the small farm plot size, often no bigger than a lawn in a small suburban garden in the Western world.

Rural poverty is a political issue in China and the government is doing its best to raise farm incomes while at the same time slowing migration to the cities. The government has had some success in the past in keeping farm prices high by maintaining commodity reserve stocks. Indeed the government has often made money by buying and stockpiling foodstuffs (and cotton) when domestic prices were low and reselling them when they rose again.

Since China joined the WTO, however, it has been less easy to do this. By maintaining high domestic commodity prices China has sucked in excessive imports and ended up storing the surpluses. This has happened most dramatically in cotton but also in sugar. As a result, the government is changing strategy and looking to directly subsidize farmers instead. Of course it will be tough to get the subsidies right: pitch them too low and farmers will plant other crops; pitch them too high and the country's warehouses will once again fill up to bursting point.

Under World Trade Organisation (WTO) rules China imposes a 5% import duty on 1.89 million tonnes of quota imports, with import licences allotted by the government. In theory anyone can import sugar outside of the WTO quota by paying a 50% duty. When world sugar prices are low traders can make money by importing sugar and paying the full duty – and it is this that has led to the current surplus. However the Chinese government has recently imposed restrictions on out-of-quota imports; they are no longer granted automatically.

Thailand's sugar production has been rising steadily over the years and it is now in fifth place among the world's biggest producers, at about 10.4 million tonnes this year. Of this quantity it exports about 7.0 million tonnes, making Thailand the world's second biggest exporter after Brazil. But compared to Brazil's 23 million tonnes, it is a long way behind.

The recent growth in Thailand's sugar industry has partly been a result of government initiatives to improve rural incomes through farm subsidies. It is also partly because the country's sugar millers have been reinvesting back into the industry the money that they made during an earlier period of high world prices.

Even without a subsidy, sugar cane is one of the most profitable crops for Thai farmers and the cane area has been expanding steadily. The government has been encouraging rice farmers to switch to sugar cane after an earlier government programme to set minimum rice prices pushed domestic rice production into a heavy surplus. Thailand's Agriculture Ministry has identified 640,000 ha of rice paddies suitable for growing sugar cane. That would represent an additional 4-5 million tonnes of sugar. Some rice farmers are in any case shifting to cane in areas that are currently too dry to grow rice.

The US comes in at number six on our list of the world's top ten sugar producers with about 7 million tonnes each year, about 55% from beet and

45% from cane. The cane is grown in Florida, Texas and Louisiana and the beet is mostly grown in Minnesota, North Dakota and Idaho.

America's 317 million people consume around 32 kilos of white sugar per year, nearly all of it "hidden" in processed foods and drinks. This is slightly less than Europeans consume but you have to remember that most of the soft drinks in the US, and a lot of the processed foods, use HFCS (High Fructose Corn Syrup) rather than sugar as a sweetener. Americans eat and drink almost as much corn sweetener per year as they do sugar – and this pushes their calorific sweetener consumption to around 60 kilos per year. That's not quite as much as the Brazilians consume, but it is close.

The US sugar and HFCS industries fight like cats and dogs but in reality there is no difference between sugar produced from cane or beet and the sweetener produced from corn. Both are about half glucose and half fructose and both are treated in the same way by the human body.

Obesity levels in the US began to take off in the early eighties at about the same time as HFCS began to take market share from sugar. There exists a strong correlation between the growth in obesity levels and the growth of HFCS consumption. It is therefore not surprising that HFCS has been repeatedly blamed for America's weight problem. However, as HFCS producers like to point out, correlation is not the same thing as causality. (27)

The US sugar and HFCS industries may fight like cats and dogs but that is nothing compared to the turf battles that are waged between the US and the Mexican sugar industries.

Having expanded their industry significantly

over the past decade Mexico is now the world's seventh largest sugar producer at around 5.6 – 6.0 million tonnes. Of that quantity Mexico consumes 4.2 million tonnes; they export the rest, mainly to the USA under NAFTA (North American Free Trade Association). Mexico's domestic sugar consumption works out at around 34 kilos per person per year.

However Mexico also uses about 1.5 million tonnes of HFCS that it imports from the US. (28) Once you add HFCS and sugar together, Mexico has an average calorific sweetener consumption of 47 kg per person per year, still a long way short of Brazil's 62.5 kg per person per year. However Mexico has obesity levels that are way higher than in Brazil: 26.8% for men and 37.5% for women.

Pakistan is the world's eighth largest sugar producer in the world with an annual production of close to 5 million tonnes of sugar. The country consumes most of what it produces. The small annual surplus of 250-500,000 tonnes finds its way across the country's borders, mainly into Afghanistan.

Pakistan occasionally suffers severe flooding that results in much loss of life and suffering among the country's rural poor. Despite the misery that these floods cause, they are usually beneficial for the country's sugar cane, bringing both water and much-needed nutrients with them. When the rivers flood Pakistan can become a significant exporter of white sugar onto the world market.

Russia is the ninth biggest producer of sugar in the world at around 4.5 million tonnes, all of it from beet. When the Berlin Wall collapsed in 1989/90 so did Russia's sugar sector: the country became the world's biggest importer of raw sugar. Slowly and surely the country has rebuilt its sugar industry behind strong import tariffs and is now almost self-sufficient.

Russia is one of the few countries in the world where total sugar consumption, as well as per capita consumption, is falling. Russia's population is declining but changing lifestyles also play a part. In Soviet times Russians used a lot of sugar to make home brewed alcoholic liquor; they now prefer to buy their vodka from a shop.

Australia is the world's tenth largest sugar producer and the third largest exporter after Brazil and Thailand. The Australian sugarcane industry is located mainly along Australia's eastern coastline, from Mossman in far north Queensland to Grafton in northern New South Wales. The country's 6,000 cane farmers grow and harvest around 30-35 million tonnes of cane each year, which the country's 24 sugar mills crush and process to produce around 4.0-4.5 million tonnes of sugar.

Of this amount the country eats and drinks about 1.2 million tonnes and exports about three million tonnes. Per capita sugar consumption has been declining in Australia but still stands at around 42 kilos per person per year once you take into account imports and exports of sugar containing food and drink products.

So those are the top ten sugar producers in the world. But if you were to ask your friends which country in the world produces and exports the most sugar, they would probably answer "Cuba".

Cuba did at one time dominate the world sugar market with production reaching 8.5 million tonnes in 1970 and 7.58 million tonnes in 1989. At one stage they even had a plan to increase production up to 14 million tonnes by the beginning of the 1980s.

However this depended on receiving large subsidies of oil and equipment from the Soviet Union. This, coupled with large quantities of fertilizer and pesticides, resulted in the Cuban sugar industry becoming highly inefficient. Cuba wanted to increase production via any means, rather than seeking to increase it through greater efficiency. Such an approach took no account of the costs of production and by the end of the century it was costing Cuba more than \$0.20 to produce one pound of sugar (or over \$440 per tonne). At the time other exporters were producing sugar for less than half that.

When the Soviet Union collapsed, Cuba just could no longer compete when it had to purchase oil and spare parts on the international market at prevailing prices.

This year Cuba is expected to produce around 1.5 million tonnes of sugar; that's an improvement on the 1.0-1.2 million tonnes that they were producing a few years back. Even so, with world sugar prices low and Brazil once again competitive (because of the country's weaker currency) it will be difficult for Cuba's sugar sector to get back on its feet.

Human rights

2.1   Sugar and slavery

"Daddy, did these slaves work growing sugar?"

We had taken the family for a short winter break in Senegal and were among a group of tourists visiting Gorée Island, a 20-minute boat ride off the coast from Dakar. The island is famous for its "House of Slaves", a museum and memorial to the Atlantic slave trade, as well as its "Door of No Return", the final exit point for the slaves from Africa.

The House of Slaves was reconstructed and opened as a museum in 1962 and is now a World Heritage Site. We were lucky to have the museum curator, Boubacar Joseph Ndiaye, take us through the site. He showed us the separate holding cells for men, women and young girls. He led us through the "Door of No Return" and showed us the iron shackles that the slaves wore as they were transported to the slave ships.

Historians differ as to how many slaves actually left Africa through the building. The museum's curator put the number at around one million. Some argue that only a few hundred slaves ever passed through the house. However, a Senegalese conference in 1998 found records from the French trading houses of Nantes that documented 103,000 slaves being sent from Gorée on Nantes-owned ships in a single year in the 18th century.

Whatever the truth, the island of Gorée is an important memorial to a trade that saw 11-12 million Africans wrenched from their villages and herded onto slave ships. Of those twelve million wretched souls an estimated two million died during the crossing. Among those that survived the sea voyage, six million worked and died in the cane fields and sugar factories of the Caribbean and of North and South America.

Slavery did not start with sugar. Slaves worked in the houses of ancient Egypt and Libya. At the time of Aristotle an estimated two thirds of the population of Athens were slaves of one kind or another. Rome also relied on slaves: at one point an estimated 500,000 slaves were bought to the city each year, most of which were prisoners captured in battle. And in Europe the Doomsday Book reported that there were some 25,000 slaves in England in 1086.

However it was with the growth of sugar that slavery became big business. Sugar is a very labour intensive crop and slavery provided that labour cheaply. In the 14th century slaves were transported to Crete and Cyprus to work in the cane fields (1) while historians believe that slaves were also used in the cane field in Morocco at around 1400. When the Portuguese colonised the Azores in 1445 (2) they transported about 1,000 African slaves to the islands to cultivate sugar cane.

Christopher Columbus is credited with taking sugar cane from La Gomera in the Canary Islands to Hispaniola on his second trip in 1493. His mother-in-law grew sugarcane on the island of Madeira. Within fifty years the first slaves were being transported to the New World, not to toil in the cane fields but to work in the gold mines. The work was originally done by the enslaved indigenous population but the local tribes became so decimated by disease and cruelty that by the middle of the 16th century they had largely died out. The first black slaves were shipped to Brazil in 1538 (3); by the second half of the century that trickle had turned into a tidal wave.

Up until the middle of the 18th century it took about 20 tonnes of cane to produce one tonne of sugar. The land had first to be prepared for planting by clearing and burning the existing vegetation. The work had to be done on windless days in July, usually the hottest season of the year. The cane had then to be planted. In the mid eighteenth century in Jamaica it took forty slaves one day to plant one acre of cane; the biggest plantations were more than one thousand acres. Plantations often subcontracted this work to planting (or "holing" as it was called in the Caribbean) gangs. Life expectancy in a holing gang was about seven years.

Once it had grown the cane had to be harvested and hauled to the mills where other slaves worked in terrible conditions. The cane had to be hand fed, usually by women, into huge rollers that, "easily caught a careless hand and pulled its owner along with the roller, crushing her to death." (4) After the cane was crushed the juice was piped to the boiling house where it was heated with lime to clarify it. To keep the factory running the slaves had to shovel tonnes of bagasse (the dried cane stalks once the juice has been squeezed out of them) and firewood into the boilers.

All this was done under duress. One Martinique planter declared that reason "is a language that the Negro does not understand; the music of the Negro is the whip."

In slave quarters everywhere the whip was the

music that began their day and gave rise to the expression "the crack of dawn" when the head overseer cracked his whip as a collective wake-up call". (5) In theory, "No rational man would beat, murder or maim a slave anymore than he would beat a cart horse beyond what was needed to make it work, for slaves and horses were property, and both cost money to replace". But unfortunately not all slave owners were rational. "Drunkenness from the abundant cheap rum, irritability caused by the tropical heat, even madness, led to actions that took a great toll of slaves lives". (6)

In addition, the slaves greatly outnumbered the white plantation owners in most plantation areas; the only way that the owners could be sure of controlling their slaves was through terror and cruelty. Some plantation owners were so worried about being so out-numbered that in 1774 the Jamaican House of Assembly petitioned the UK government to reduce the inflow of slaves by imposing a duty on them. The government refused, arguing,

"We cannot allow the colonies to check or discourage in any degree a traffic so beneficial to the nation". (7)

Two years later, in 1776 Adam Smith wrote in the Wealth of Nations,

"The experience of all ages and nations, I believe, demonstrates that the work done by slaves, though it appears to cost only their maintenance, is in the end the dearest of many."

That same year a motion to oppose slavery was defeated in the British House of Commons but the anti-slavery movement was already on the move before the British reformer William Wilberforce was elected to Parliament 1788. One incident (8) highlighted the cruelty of slavery and revealed it to a wider public, sparking the first real calls for the end of the slave trade.

In November 1781, the master of the slave-trading vessel the *Zong* threw 132 slaves overboard to drown. He then claimed insurance on them, arguing that a lack of water had left him no choice but to jettison them to save his crew and the remaining 440 slaves that were still on board. The Solicitor-General spoke for the owners in court, making the official and legal view of slaves clear:

"What is all this vast declamation of human people being thrown over-board? The question after all is, was it voluntary or an act of necessity? This is a case of chattels and goods. It is really so: it is the case of throwing over goods; for this purpose, and for the purpose of the insurance, they are goods and property: whether right or wrong we have nothing to do with it."

The anti-slavery lobby found support from an unexpected source: the East India Company, which by the end of the 18th century was producing sugar in India with hired, not slave labour. The East India Company viewed the slave labour in the West Indies as unfair competition and campaigned vigorously against it.

By 1792 the East India Company was claiming that a West Indies sugar slave's life cost 450 pounds of sugar. It said, "a family that uses 5 pounds of sugar a week will kill a slave every 21 months". (9) The company distributed sugar bowls with the legend, "East Indian Sugar not made by slaves".

The campaign worked and consumers began to

pay more for sugar that was made by freemen and not by slaves. In 1792 "slave" sugar from the Caribbean sold for 70-80 shillings per hundredweight while West Indian "non slave" sugar fetched 140 shillings per hundredweight.

Slavery was only abolished in the British Empire in 1833, and then only with a provision that slave owners could keep their existing slaves for a further twelve years. This provision was removed four years later but sugar plantation owners still kept tight control over their former slaves and working conditions scarcely improved.

In 1865 the Governor of Jamaica responded to a "black uprising" (and the death of some whites) by declaring martial law and hanging 400 blacks. Although applauded by the local (white) community the incident caused uproar in England with calls for the governor to be trialled for murder. The trial never happened.

Despite the end of slavery the sugar industry still desperately needed labour; it found it in "indentured" workers. This was a system where (mostly young) people paid for their passage to the New World by working for an employer for a certain number of years, usually five or seven. Once they had completed their "indenture" they were free to go off on their own.

The local employer purchased the indenture from the sea captain who brought the workers over. Both the worker and the employer were legally obligated to meet the terms, which were enforced by local American courts. Runaways were sought out and returned. About half of the white immigrants to the American colonies in the 17th and 18th centuries were indentured.

The system was often abused. Poor children

were kidnapped from their homes and sold into indentured labour in the Caribbean; some never attained their freedom. Once at destination employers had little interest in looking after their indentured workers. Indeed they looked after their slaves better; they owned a slave for life while they only had the indentured worked for five or seven years. Plantation owners worked their indentured workers harder than their slaves; they also gave them less sanitary shelter and fed them less.

It is hard for us now, in this age of cheap travel, to imagine that someone would have to work "like a slave" for five years to repay a one-way passage across the Atlantic. You can purchase a one-way flight now for the equivalent of a few weeks' work sitting in an air-conditioned office, not five years hard labour.

Indentured labour was already used in the sugar industry even before the abolition of slavery. Indentured Indian labourers had already been shipped to Mauritius as early as 1725. Indentured Chinese labourers were used in the sugar industries in Malaysia and Java. Chinese labour also operated the first Hawaiian sugar mill, built in 1836. Two years later, in 1838 the first Indian indentured labourers were recruited to work in the Caribbean. Of the 414 that left India, eighteen died during the voyage. Five years later a further 98 had died, giving a death rate of 27%. (10)

These death rates scarcely improved as the century wore on. Some 140,000 Chinese indentured labourers were shipped to Cuba between 1847 and 1880, many of which had been kidnapped. Of those numbers about 12% died on the voyage and 25% died in the fields and factories. Of the 4,551 Indians shipped to Jamaica between 1845 and 1847, some 1,805 died within ten years, mostly from cholera.

Indians were also shipped to South Africa as indentured labour in the second half of the 19th century, prompting a 24 year-old Indian lawyer, Mahatma Gandhi, to leave a law practice in Bombay, move to South Africa and work for the rights of the Indian sugar labourers there.

The sugar industry in Queensland, Australia, also needed labour, much of which was "recruited" from the New Hebrides (now Vanuatu), Papua New Guinea, the Solomon Islands and the Loyalty Islands of New Caledonia as well as Niue. These people were referred to as "Kanakas"; although officially called "indentured labourers" many were effectively slaves. Some travelled to Australia freely but others were kidnapped, or "blackbirded" as it was called.

Blackbirding was especially prevalent between 1847 and 1904; estimates vary as to the numbers of islanders that were blackbirded but they could have been as many as 55,000. The Queensland government tried to control the practice but the demand for labour was too strong. Blackbirding only died out in 1904 as a result of a law, enacted in 1901 by the Australian commonwealth, calling for the deportation of all Kanakas after 1906.

Mediterranean Europeans began to take the place of slaves and indentured workers in some sugar producing countries. By the time of the First World War about 30,000 Portuguese and around 7,000 Spaniards were working in Hawaii's cane industry. Australia began accepting Italians as workers in the cane fields and many Italian families are still farming the same land today.

"Yes", I replied to my son. "More than half of

the slaves that were transported from Africa worked to produce sugar."

"Does it still happen?" he asked. "Does slavery still exist in the sugar industry?"

"Most of the work that was once done by slaves is now done by machines", I replied. "Working conditions in the industry have improved enormously over the past one hundred years. But yes", I continued truthfully, "I am afraid there are still a few cases each year of people being forced to work in the fields, particularly at harvest time".

2.2   Human rights

A couple of years after our trip to Senegal we were back in Africa, driving down from the Kruger National Park to Durban where I was to meet up with friends from the South African sugar industry. On the way we drove through Swaziland where we were surprised by the poverty in the rural areas.

The sugar industry is one of Swaziland's main sources of foreign exchange and employment. Most of their sugar goes to the EU but with the EU reforms those exports are expected to come to an end after 2017. The EU is giving some aid to Swaziland to restructure the sugar sector and to make it more competitive but the amount being given is a mere drop in the ocean as to what is actually needed.

Back again in South Africa the poverty was less striking. The population was still poor but as we drove we noticed a definite pattern. Along the roadsides the houses would start to get a little bigger and more solidly built, the gardens better tended. A little further along we would start to see a few shops, then a school and then a medical clinic. We would then see the sugar factory, or at least the smoke from the sugar factory. We were there in August, the height of the sugar harvest.

Once past the factory the pattern would continue but in reverse. There would be fewer schools or clinics, shops would gradually disappear and the houses and land steadily less well attended. Then the pattern would start again as we approached the next sugar factory. This was the first time that I had realised the power of the sugar industry to raise rural incomes and to provide jobs in rural areas where there is little alternative employment.

The second time was in India where I had been invited to speak at a sugar conference in Goa. Shree Renuka Sugars (11) (a relative newcomer to the Indian sugar scene) invited some of the conference participants to visit their newly built Athani factory, a six-hour drive from the coast. As we drove inland into Karnataka the population became steadily poorer, especially once we were past the city of Belgaum. But then things picked up again once we approached the factory.

Shree Renuka had done something very unusual for that time; they had given the farmers shares in the company in exchange for them guaranteeing to produce cane for the factory. The farmers became rich when the company went public and the local area is now relatively prosperous. The company has since built schools and clinics and supplied medical equipment to the local hospital. None of that would have been possible if the company's founders had not decided to build a sugar factory in this isolated and poor rural area.

There is an old saying that "no one is perfect"

and this obviously also applies to the sugar industry.

The US Department of Labour (DOL), in conjunction with the Bureau of International Labour Affairs (ILAB) and the Departments of State and Homeland Security, is required by law to maintain a list of products and their source countries which it has a reasonable basis to believe are produced by forced or indentured child labour. The list is intended to ensure that U.S. federal agencies do not procure goods made by forced or indentured child labour. The initial list was published in 2001 and has been revised several times since then. (12)

The latest list details 54 cases that the Department believe involve forced or child labour, ranging from bricks to textiles and electronics. Two cases that involve sugar, one in Bolivia and the other in Burma are described on the DOL website:

"There are reports that children are forced to produce sugarcane in Bolivia. Based on the most recently available data from the ILO, it is estimated that almost a quarter of the migrants working in the sugarcane harvest are children under age 14, of which many are working in conditions of forced labour. Many children work with their families under conditions of bonded labour. Entire families, including children, live in accommodations provided by the employer; this dependence on the employer increases their vulnerability to forced labour. The families receive little payment if any, and lodging and food expenses are deducted from their paychecks. Some children inherit the debt of their parents if their parents pass away or stop working, and remain bonded and able to be sold to a different employer."

The DOL continues,

"There are (also) *reports that children are forced to work in the production of sugarcane in Burma. Forced child labour is found in the Thaton District, and particularly in areas near military camps. An NGO study documents villagers, including children, mobilized by the dozens each day from multiple villages to work during labour intensive times of the sugarcane production. The children are forced to cut trees and dig out the stumps to prepare the fields, plant the sugarcane, and then mill and boil the sugarcane after it is harvested. They are not paid for their work."*

I was brought up on a farm and I can remember helping to bring in the grain harvest. I started at a young age, probably eight, and was driving a tractor by the age of eleven. I was not the only child to be working on farms throughout Europe. It is no accident that the long school summer holidays coincide with the summer harvest period. They were designed that way specifically to enable children to help out on the farms during the busy harvest period.

I was not forced to work except perhaps through peer pressure from my two elder brothers. I really enjoyed helping out and I was paid extra pocket money for it. I was also, of course, well fed and well lodged.

In many developing countries the whole family still works together to bring in their sugarcane harvest. And even when they don't, a female worker will often bring her young children to the fields rather than leave them home alone. They may not officially be working but they may help out their mother to carry the cut cane to the waiting cane carts.

And as one mill-owner I spoke with told me,

"All it takes is for there to be a photographer in the field when one of those young children picks up a piece of cane and the picture goes viral and is on the front pages of all the newspapers the next day. It is a big problem for us. We encourage mothers not to take their children into the fields and we set up playschools in the villages, but they still do."

But this is not the same as the cases listed by US Department of Labor where the children are forced to work. These are genuine causes of concern. But having said that, the cases may be more country-specific problem than industry-specific. Nine out of the 54 cases listed by the DOL are in just two countries, Burma and Bolivia.

Human rights do not just concern labour; they also concern land ownership. In 2015, the National Human Rights Commission of Thailand accused the country's Khon Kaen Sugar (KSL) of human rights violations at its two Cambodian sugarcane plantations. In a report, the Commission found that the plantations

"Resulted in serious human rights violations, including the use of violence to evict villagers from their place of residence [and] impediments against the use of natural resources, which is fundamental to community subsistence." (13)

KSL denied any wrongdoing, arguing that it only bought into the plantations - originally secured by a Cambodian Senator - who then sold his stake to KSL - after the 2006 evictions. The Thai rights commission says KSL nevertheless bears responsibility.

"The impact of these human rights violations are a direct

responsibility of Khon Kaen Sugar ...due to the company's decision to receive and benefit from the land concessions which caused human rights violations, regardless of the fact that the company did not itself commit the act."

Two hundred of the displaced families have sued Tate & Lyle in London over the sugar the U.K. firm bought off the two KSL plantations in 2010 and 2011. At the time of writing the issue had not yet come to court. In their defence the Government of Cambodia has stated that the Economic Land Concessions were granted in accordance with the country's laws. It added that only 13 families were not compensated due to their inability to provide documentation or legal papers to prove they owned the land.

The issue was first brought to the public attention in 2013 when the NGO (Non Government Organisation) Inclusive Development published a report (*Bittersweet Harvest*) on the Cambodian sugar industry. (14) The NGO argued that the Cambodian sugar sector was developing as a result of the EU's "Everything But Arms" policy that removed import tariffs on goods from the world's poorest countries. The policy was specifically introduced to encourage development in those countries, something that seems to have resulted in unintended consequences.

In a report published in October 2013 *(Sugar Rush)* (15) the British charity Oxfam mentioned the issue, as well as two other land rights issues, this time involving indigenous groups in Brazil.

The first was in Ponta Porã, a municipality in the south of the Mato Grosso state, where two new sugar mills, including the Monteverde mill, started up in

2008. A number of farms started producing sugar cane to supply the mills, including in Jatayvary, an area claimed by the indigenous Guarani-Kaiowá communities. In 2004 the relevant federal agency, FUNAI, recognized the claim, starting a four-step administrative process of land demarcation. In 2011, the second step was completed when the Ministry of Justice recognised the Guarani-Kaiowá's rights over 8,800 ha of land. The Monteverde mill no longer buys cane from these areas.

The second case involved fifty-three fishing families who lived in an estuary on the coast of the north-eastern state of Pernambuco. In 1998, the local sugar mill Usina Trapiche obtained rights over the state land and the families were moved to the town of Sirinhaém where they now have access to electricity, water, sanitation, and schooling. Initially the courts upheld the families' rights to live in the estuary, but this decision was overturned in 2002.

We saw earlier how consumer pressure, and particularly consumers' willingness to pay more for non-slave sugar, helped to eradicate slavery in the 19th century. Oxfam is looking to repeat that success and believes that consumer pressure can help to resolve some of the few remaining issues in the sugar sector.

In 2013, Oxfam launched their *"Behind the Brands"* campaign that tracks ten of the world's biggest food and beverage companies and assesses their policies and commitments. These 'Big 10' are Associated British Foods (ABF), Coca-Cola, Danone, General Mills, Kellogg, Mars, Mondelez International, Nestlé, PepsiCo, and Unilever. Oxfam writes that,

"On the positive side, the companies gain credit for policies, commitments, and management of biodiversity and deforestation impacts in their supply chains. However, the scorecard reveals, by and large, that they have a poor awareness of key social issues."

However Oxfam does see some signs for optimism. It writes,

"Signs of leadership are already emerging as companies recognize the risk that land conflicts and land rights violations represent to their operations and reputations. As Mark Bowman, managing director of brewing company SAB Miller Africa, one of Coca-Cola's largest bottlers, put it, "Land purchases which ignore the interests of local communities and the local landscapes are both morally wrong and commercially short-sighted".

Oxfam also quotes Muhtar Kent, CEO of Coca-Cola, as saying,

"We recognize that the success and sustainability of our business is inextricably linked to the success and sustainability of the communities in which we operate. The strength of our brands is directly related to our social license to operate, which we must earn daily by keeping our promises to our customers, consumers, associates, investors, communities, and partners."

Coca Cola is by far the biggest buyer of sugar in the world and is a founding member of Bonsucro: but more on that in the next chapter.

2.3 Isara Vongkusolkit: believer in human dignity

Isara Vongkusolkit is now retired from active commercial life but remains Chairman of Mitr Phol Sugar Group.

With a production of 4.3 million tonnes in 2014 Mitr Phol Sugar Corp is the fourth largest sugar producer in the world and the largest in Asia. The company was founded in 1946 and remains family owned.

Isara is Chairman of the Thai Chamber of Commerce (TCC) and Chairman of the Board of Trade of Thailand and is a staunch defender of human rights, or what he calls "human dignity".

I began our conversation by asking Isara about his family history.

"My parents migrated from the southern part of China to Thailand about eighty years ago," he told me.

"My father, Juechai Vong left his native Canton province to join his cousins who were already farming in Banpong, Ratchaburi province. My mother, Noo-Far, joined him a year later. At that time there was much hardship in China. My parents had no education and no money. The relatives were farming all kinds of crops: corn, chili, and potatoes. My parents had seven children, five born before the war. I am the sixth. I was born in 1948.

"The war had been very tough on our family. At that time the government assumed that any Chinese aliens were a threat to national security. All Chinese schools were closed down. My family had to move from the farm and went to live with other relatives. They suffered just as all the Thai people suffered during the war. There was inadequate food and medicine. My parents did not have enough clothes for their children. In the wintertime when it was cold they dressed us in jute bags to keep out the wind.

"After the war things slowly got back to normal. My family resumed crushing cane, using cattle to turn the grinders. After squeezing the juice from the cane the family boiled it to make condensed syrup that they sold to the sugar factories. In 1947 the family started to make brown sugar for the first time. My family also had a small farm of about four hectares that was worked intensively.

"My father passed away in 1954; he was in his early forties. I was about seven years old. My mother had to look after all the children. My elder brother Kusol became head of the family and built our first sugar factory using modern equipment at Bangpong Ratchaburi province in 1956. We didn't have enough cane for the factory and had to expand the area to around 65 hectares. The factory employed about 70 workers – plus the family members.

"Kusol had poor health and a weak heart and he passed away in 1961, when he was in his thirties. My next brother Kamol took over a leading role and worked hard to grow the company. Growing up he was mostly self-educated and he recognized that the lack of schools in the community meant little or no educational opportunities for children. Because of that he established the Vongkusolkit Pittayakom School in 1975, which he still financially supports today.

"My mother had no education but she always strived for her children to go to school. Chinese families traditionally didn't push for the girls to go to school but my mother did her best to make sure we all went, girls included. My mother moved to the city where she rented a shop-house so that the younger children could complete higher education. My older brothers paid for my younger brother, my sister and me to study in the United States.

"But whatever we did, we had to think of our family and not ourselves. When we came back we had no choice but to work for the family business. I did not start the family business but I enhanced it from what I had learned during my education."

"But since you took over the company you have grown it enormously," I prompted.

"When I took over Mitr Phol we wanted it to be one of the best sugar companies in Asia in terms of quality and of management. When I took over as president of the company we all agreed on the philosophy and the vision of the company.

"To what do you attribute your company's success?" I asked.

"It comes from our family values: unity, integrity and honesty. We have developed these family values into a business concept.

"I think one factor in our success is the unity of the family members. We argue a lot in the meeting room but then that is what business is all about. Once we have made a decision we all work together to implement it.

"Hard work, sincerity and honesty are all important. The terms "sincerity and honesty" have deep meaning for me. Customers, suppliers and partners know that we have never taken advantage of them. Quality is also essential.

"But perhaps the most important factor in our success is that we believe in the value of human dignity."

"Could you tell me more about that?" I asked. "How do you fit human dignity and human rights into business?"

"Our business is deeply involved in communities and every member of those communities knows that their lives and their families' lives are respected and valued by us. They know we approach them with respect and treat them ethically."

"But it hasn't all gone right", I said. You have got caught up in Cambodia."

"We pulled out of Cambodia in late 2014. Back in 2009 the Cambodian government granted land concessions to us totalling about 20,000 hectares on which we intended to build a sugar factory and grow cane using a nucleus plantation concept; this would encourage and support local farmers to also grow cane. Our intent was to create economic activity in a very remote and poor area with difficult agricultural conditions.

"The project had difficulties from the beginning, including several years of problems between the Thailand and Cambodia governments that closed the border several times. In fact, it really never got started and we ended up building some roads, preparing some land for planting, and mostly experimenting by planting only about 200 ha of sugarcane to test the area. We did not build any sugar processing plant.

"There have been allegations that the Cambodian government illegally confiscated some of the land from villagers in breach of Cambodian laws before they granted the concession to us. We have seen most documentation ourselves and have been assured the process was according to the law, however, finally we decided to withdraw from the project while requesting that the government find a way to return any contested area to the community.

"We will continue to follow the issue and consider our responsibilities. For example, the EU and the Cambodian government are undertaking an audit of sugar industry concessions in Cambodia to examine if land acquisitions and evictions in projects were conducted legally.

"There have also been allegations of child labour in Cambodia. (16) How would you respond to those allegations?" I asked.

"In our Cambodian project area there has been very little activity and, in any case, we do not allow child labour in Mitr Phol operations in any country. As you know in general, child labour in agriculture is a complicated issue for most poor and developing countries.

"How do you balance the interests of your various stakeholders?" I asked.

"When we do business we involve five stakeholders: farmers, customers, employees, regulators and government, and company shareholders in order of our priority. We always emphasize that the farmer is the most important stakeholder. We were farmers ourselves. The sugar business is really about farming; it is not an industry. That's where I think people sometimes make a mistake.

"We honour cane growers because we were cane growers before. Cane growers and sugar mills depend on each other. We can't live without them.

"Our business means going out and making a contract with each farmer. We support our farmers with finance, technology and fertiliser. Each Thailand factory has about 5,000 cane growers so with our six factories we have a minimum of 30,000 contracts.

"We think of farmers as part of our family. Even in drought years we have never had a shortage of cane; our farmers have supplied us even if other mills were paying more. It is a long-term relationship built on trust, integrity and honesty.

"Our customer is our second most important stakeholder. We have to have a reasonable price, excellent quality and a good service.

"Our employees are number three on the list. In 1997 during the Asian economic crisis we increased our training for our staff to make them competitive. We also stepped up our training for our cane growers in terms of research and development support. During the crisis our company executives all agreed to cut their salaries. We got through the crisis without laying off a single employee and without cutting workers' wages.

"Our industry is still regulated so our fourth stakeholder is the regulator, the government. We always support government initiatives for economic development in communities and we recognize our responsibility to be a good corporate role model in all areas of governance; especially in being good taxpayers.

"Shareholders are our fifth stakeholders. We now have about eighty family members as shareholders, including nephews, nieces and grandchildren."

"What are your basic rules in life?" I asked.

"Our company is based on four important rules: we believe in the importance of leadership, the value of human dignity, standing firm in fairness and being accountable to society.

"What about sustainability?" I asked. "Isn't that also important?"

'We try to grow our business in a sustainable

manner while generating benefits for all stakeholders. We want to be a good corporate citizen, we want to improve cane growers' lives, serve both domestic and international customers with quality products and timely delivery, enhance staff capabilities and develop surrounding communities.

"Can you give me a few examples of what you are doing for farmers?" I asked.

'We have been promoting the use of drip irrigation. In the past our farmers used to pump the water and then let gravity take its course, but it used too much water. We have financed farmers to dig ponds for their own farms and use drip irrigation. So now we are actually using a third or a quarter of the water that was previously used; it is enough.

'Drip irrigation not only reduces water use but also increases yields as the fertiliser is efficiently applied through the water. The production for those farmers that have installed drip irrigation is up to 25 tonnes per hectare.

"Over the next few years we will see a lot more investment in this type of infrastructure. Normally farmers don't have pumping systems. We want to invest in bigger pumps and install the infrastructure in the farms.

"We provide technical services to cane growers to help them improve their yields, raise their revenues, and improve the quality of their lives. To do that there has to be a close cooperation between the farmers and our field staff. They are currently working together to ensure that the cane is cut more efficiently and without loss.

"We have also initiated a "cane clinic" for our farmers to disseminate technical knowledge and management techniques such as land preparation, early planting, irrigation systems and pest management.

"We are also working on the use of a Geographical Information System (GIS) and Global Positioning System (GPS). These should mean more accurate processing and effective planning in terms of soil and cane management, reducing costs and making sure the cane is cut at an optimum time.

"Many of these activities are built into a newer initiative called "Mitr Phol Modern Farm" that we started almost two years ago. This system is based on sustainability with best practices in agricultural management and our objective is to modernize sugarcane farming and improve farmer returns. It is very similar to Sustainability Cane in Africa and Smartcane BMP in Australia."

"That may be good for yields", I replied. "But is it good for the environment?"

"Preserving and protecting the environment is a way of showing our appreciation to the land we live in and where we work. We take this very seriously.

"Sugar production results in several waste or by-products such as bagasse and molasses. We have a "zero waste" mentality. For example, we burn bagasse to generate electricity but we also use it to make paper and particleboard. Particleboard can replace wood furniture while paper made from bagasse can replace paper made from trees.

"We use our leftover molasses to make ethanol for fuel and also believe that ethanol can also contribute to a sustainable future by reducing oil consumption and carbon emissions."

"Isara, many thanks for your time".

Sustainability

3.1 Sugar's challenges

The world's population is growing, incomes are rising and the demand for food is increasing. The FAO (Food and Agriculture Organisation) estimates that to feed the nine billion people expected to inhabit the earth by 2050, farmers will need to produce 60% more food than in 2005-2007. But how can they achieve that goal without depleting the world's resources or polluting the world's air or water?

According to a report from Harvard Kennedy School and "Business Fights Poverty" (1) agriculture already accounts for 70% of all freshwater use and 30% of all human-induced greenhouse gas emissions, a contribution comparable to that of the energy sector and far exceeding total emissions from transportation.

At the same time the report argues that agriculture is failing to support decent livelihoods for a significant percentage of those involved in it, especially small-scale farmers and farm workers. Approximately 2.5 billion rural people depend on agriculture for their livelihoods but as many as 80% of them may be living on less than $2 a day.

In addition, more than one third of the food that farmers produce today is lost or wasted. (2) This loss can occur while the crops are still growing in the fields, or when they are left in the fields unharvested. It can also occur post-harvest through inefficient storage, distribution and processing, mostly in developing countries. In developed countries food is often thrown away at the retail and consumer levels, mostly because it has passed its "sell-by" date. The FAO estimate the direct financial cost of food wastage at about US\$ 1 trillion each year. However add in environmental and social costs and that figure rises to US\$ 2.6 trillion per year.

No one knows how much sugar is lost through wastage but sugar has its own specific environmental challenges. Sugarcane is the third most water intensive agricultural commodity, requiring 1,400 to 3,000 litres per tonne. Sugar processing also requires water at several stages. Sugar mills generate approximately 1,000 litres of wastewater for each ton of sugarcane processed. Water intensiveness is often associated with water pollution, for example from fertilizer runoff and sedimentation from fields.

Sugarcane cultivation can reduce soil quality through loss of fertility due to monoculture and to erosion, especially when the cane is planted on slopes. It can also lead to a loss in biodiversity. Lastly, sugarcane is still often burned before harvesting (to get rid of the unwanted leaves and other vegetation), causing air pollution at harvest time.

But the sugarcane and beet industries face specific challenges if they are to meet the growing demand for their products. In addition to sugar for food, the cane and beet industries also produce ethanol for fuel and for industrial use, electricity for homes and factories, fibreboard for furniture and green plastics for (among other things) drink bottles and car dashboards. The demand for all of these products is also increasing.

How can the sugarcane and sugar beet industries sector meet this growing demand in a sustainable way? And what exactly do we mean by "sustainability"?

Sustainability means different things to different people. The International Institute for Sustainable Development define it as

"Development that meets the needs of the present without compromising the ability of future generations to meet their own needs." (3)

The FAO defines a sustainable agricultural value chain as one that is

"Profitable throughout, has broad-based benefits for society, and does not permanently deplete natural resources." (4)

Unfortunately, sustainability does not mean much to most people. In 2012, only 16% of the cane sugar that had been certified as "sustainable" was sold as certified. To put that in perspective, that is equivalent to 0.3% of global production and 1% of global exports.

Consumers are, in contrast, willing to pay more money for organic sugar: In 2012 an estimated 90% of sugar that had been certified as organic was sold as organic. The uncomfortable truth is that we as consumers are willing to pay more for our own wellbeing than we are for the wellbeing of others. Nor indeed, are we willing to pay more for the general well being of everyone, even if it includes ourselves.

The other evening I went out for dinner with a group of friends. We tend to meet up regularly, often at the same restaurant. Sometimes we split the bill equally, regardless of what we eat; sometimes we pay separately.

When we split the bill equally the total bill is always more than when we each pay separately. Consciously or sub-consciously we order more expensive dishes when we split the bill equally than we do when we each pay separately.

Unfortunately the environment works in the same way. We as inhabitants of the globe all split the environmental cost equally.

In 1833, the English economist William Forster Lloyd published a pamphlet which included an example of herders sharing a common parcel of land on which they were each entitled to let their sheep graze. He suggested that overgrazing could result because for each additional sheep, a herder could receive benefits, while the group shared damage to the commons. If all herders made this individually rational economic decision, the common could be depleted or even destroyed, to the detriment of all. (5)

In 1968, ecologist Garrett Hardin explored this social dilemma in his article *"The Tragedy of the Commons"*, published in the journal *Science*. The essay derived its title from the pamphlet by Lloyd, which he cites, on the over-grazing of common land.

This morning on the radio I heard France's Ecology Minister, Ségolène Royal, calling for a consumer boycott of "Nutella" because it is made from palm oil. Nutella is a leading brand of Ferrero, an Italian food company that has made considerable efforts to make sure that their ingredients are grown and sourced in a sustainable way. All the palm oil, for example, that goes into Nutella is certified as sustainable by the Roundtable on Sustainable Palm Oil (RSPO).

What is the point, you may ask, of companies

investing time and money into making sure that their products are sustainable if consumers don't care about sustainability or if politicians do not differentiate between sustainable and non-sustainable products?

There are two answers to that essential question. The first is that fashions change: what was unimportant yesterday may be important tomorrow. Consumers today may only be willing to pay lip service (rather than real money) for sustainable products but that may change tomorrow. Remember that it was the UK's sugar consumers that helped to end slavery in the 18th century by paying more for non-slave sugar. Consumers can be educated or shamed into acting responsibly.

Oxfam (through their Better Brands initiative) and Bonsucro (a sustainability certification agency) know that the best way to improve the sustainability of sugar production is by working through consumers and getting them to put pressure on producers. In the case of sugar the biggest buyers are the leading food companies. To date, eight of Bonsucro's buyer members have set quantitative targets for sustainable sourcing: Bacardi, Ferrero, General Mills, PepsiCo, SABMiller, Shell, Coca-Cola and Unilever. Six of these are aiming for 100% sustainably sourced sugarcane products by 2020-2022. The seventh, Shell, does not disclose its target publicly.

The second answer is that it is in the best interest of farmers to invest in sustainable practices if that investment reduces their production costs or increases the value of their land. In that sense, as far as the environment is concerned, a farmers' self-interest may be more closely aligned with collective self-interest than a consumers'. Farmers are custodians of their land for future generations. They know that they can only continue to farm if they act responsibly and not take short-term measures that damage their land and their ability to farm.

However self-interest can only go so far and governments are already playing an important role in avoiding the "tragedy of the commons". Through legislation they can ensure that community goods such as clean air and clean water are priced correctly, that labour and land rights are enforced and that health and sanitary conditions are respected.

So how does this all work out in practice? Let's start with Brazil. Progress in law enforcement, adoption of appropriate public policies, and the pro-activity of the private sector and civil society have led to a sharp decrease in the deforestation rate in the Brazilian Amazon rainforest over the last five years. The Brazilian government has created agricultural zoning across its territory and has signed, ratified and successfully implemented the main international treaties governing environmental policy, such as the Convention on International Trade in Endangered Species of Wild Fauna and Flora, the Convention on Biological Diversity, the Cartagena Protocol on Biosafety and the Kyoto Protocol.

Brazil is one country in the world that does have the room to expand its agricultural production and will play a major role in providing that 60% increase in food production that will be necessary by 2050. Most of the available arable land in Brazil is made up of, mostly degraded, cattle pastures that currently cover 198 million hectares. As the cattle industry has become more efficient the sector has "released" substantial areas of pastures each year; these areas are being used to expand the production of sugarcane as well as of grains and oilseeds.

A 2008 report by the Dutch University of Wageningen showed that between 2002 and 2006, 5.4 million hectares of Brazilian pastureland were made available for other uses while at the same time the cattle herd increased by 18,383 heads. (6) The Brazilian National Institute for Space Research (INPE) predicts that more than 60% of new sugarcane production will occur on pastures while the remaining 40% will be on cropland.

Direct expansion of sugarcane on degraded pastures previously used for cattle ranching or on land used for other crops can generate a benefit in terms of carbon sequestration. Sugarcane is a semi-perennial crop – it only needs to be replanted every five or six years with minimum tillage. As such it can capture larger amounts of carbon than the previous land uses. Empirical measurements have shown carbon emissions can drop when sugarcane replaces other agricultural activities.

Sugarcane is grown on only a small amount of Brazil's farmland, occupying 9.5 million hectares, less than 1% of the total land surface and less than 3% of the country's arable land. And contrary to popular opinion, none of that is anywhere near the Amazon jungle. Almost 90% of Brazilian sugarcane production takes place in South-Central Brazil, with the remainder grown in North-eastern Brazil. Both producing regions are located some 2,000 to 2,500 km away from the Amazon. That is roughly the distance between Paris and Moscow. The Amazon region simply does not offer appropriate growing conditions for sugarcane and would never be a target for expanded production, regardless of government regulation.

In 2009, the Brazilian government launched a "Zoning for Sugarcane" initiative to encourage the expansion of sugarcane production into suitable areas. This initiative has a stated goal "to expand production, preserve life and ensure a future" and is essential to guarantee the sustainable growth of sugarcane production.

Under the zoning rules sugarcane expansion or new ethanol production facilities are not permitted in sensitive ecosystems such as the Amazon, the Pantanal wetlands and the Upper Paraguay River basin. There can be no clearance of native plants to expand sugarcane cultivation anywhere in the country; this ensures the protection of the native Cerrado, a vast tropical savannah eco-region in central Brazil, particularly in the states of Goiás and Minas Gerais.

The new rules have identified suitable areas in the country where sugarcane could be prioritized. These areas include land with proper conditions for the use of mechanical harvesting, cattle breeding areas that are underused or degraded (more than 34 million hectares), and also regions with less need for water usage in production.

Another important government initiative was São Paulo's Green Protocol under which 164 signatory mills and 29 associations of sugarcane suppliers committed to protect and recover 280,000 hectares of land alongside streams and riverbanks.

Sustainability is not only good for the environment; it can also be good for business. In Sao Paulo State the Association of Cane Suppliers of Bariri (Assobari), in partnership with WWF (World Wildlife Fund) have created the Assobari Protocol to help its members, more than 300 farmers working an average of 50 hectares apiece, to comply with environmental and labour laws. So far 24% of Assobari members have implemented the Protocol, increasing productivity and revenue per hectare by 15% and 22% respectively. (7)

But Brazil is not alone in trying to reduce the environmental impact of sugar production. Australian sugarcane growers are also recognised for leading the way in sustainability. They regard best practice farming not as a cost but as a means of improving their productivity, efficiency and sustainability. Most importantly, they see sustainability as a basis for ensuring the long-term viability of the sector. (8)

Australia's cane growers have voluntarily introduced initiatives that have reduced the negative impact of their crop on waterways, the Great Barrier Reef, coastal ecosystems and biodiversity. These efforts began more than twenty years ago when the sector published a Code of Practice for Sustainable Cane Growing in Queensland which was later endorsed by the Queensland Government under the Environmental Protection Act 1994.

Sugar cane was in the past always burnt before it was harvested. The fire burned off the surplus vegetation and made it easier for either manual workers or mechanical harvesters to harvest the cane. (In the case of manual cutting the fire also drove any snakes out of the fields.) One of the biggest cultural changes in cane growing in Australia has been the replacement of pre-harvest cane burning by green cane harvesting and trash blanketing. In 2014, some 80% of the Queensland crop was cut green (without burning it before) compared with only 18% in 1987. Trash blanketing, or leaving the cane leaves and trash in the fields, protects soil from erosion during heavy rains and flooding and increases the amount of organic matter in the soil, improving composition and structure. It also assists in weed control and conserving soil moisture.

More than 60% of all cane produced in Australia is irrigated. Irrigation is costly, with water and associated pumping costs accounting for one third of all costs. Drip (or trickle) irrigation and low-pressure, overhead irrigation systems are being increasingly used, not just to save total volume but also to improve water use efficiency and productivity. "Tail water" dams are now commonly used to ensure that water run-off after irrigation is captured and reused. The effect has been to dramatically reduce off-farm movement of nutrients, thus protecting fragile environmental systems while increasing production and reducing costs.

Over the past twenty years the industry has brought new land under cultivation and this has meant clearing existing vegetation. Recent recognition of both the environmental and economic importance of riparian zones (vegetation adjacent to watercourses) means that trees are now being left adjacent to water ways on all new developments. Trees are also being replanted in already established areas, even though that replanting may reduce available area for cultivation. Riparian zones have a major role in the filtration of nutrient run-off, stabilisation and prevention of bank erosion, and the siltation of waterways. They also play a vital part in the provision of wildlife corridors and in vermin control. Planting trees on riverbanks eliminates undergrowth, weeds and grasses, greatly reducing rat populations around cane fields. In turn, this dramatically reduces the need for costly chemical controls. But progress is not just being made in Australia and Brazil.

In India, DCM Shriram Consolidated Ltd (DSCL), which operates sugar mills in the state of Uttar Pradesh in India, has developed the "Sweet Gold" project in collaboration with the International Finance Scheme (IFC) to improve the productivity of its 150,000 small-scale sugarcane suppliers in a sustainable way. (9) The project involves training based on a pictorial manual encompassing seed management, soil improvement, water use, planting techniques, and other practices. The 2,000 suppliers that participated in the first year of the project saw average productivity increases of 23% that year, and 86% the following year.

Still in India, NSL-Sugar Limited and Rajshree Sugars and Chemicals Limited (RSCL) entered into an agreement in June 2015 with Solidaridad (an NGO – Non Governmental Organisation) to collaborate on sustainable production of sugarcane, implementing measures to reduce water use and promote good agricultural practices. This effort targets 35,000 sugarcane farmers. The expected outcomes include 10-15 per cent yield improvement along with savings of 90 billion litres of irrigation water and a reduction of 16 per cent energy consumption.

With funding from the Netherlands Ministry of Foreign Affairs, Solidaridad's Farmer Support Program works with mills in seven countries to train farmers in better crop management practices, reaching 230,000 farmers working 195,000 hectares of land between 2012 and May 2014. In South Africa, the South African Sugar Association (SASA) is working with the government and local mills across the country to provide small-scale farmer training and facilitate access to improved sugarcane varieties suitable to specific climactic and soil conditions. One impact study showed that these efforts helped improve yields, reduce vulnerability in low rainfall years, attract more people to sugarcane farming, and increase sugarcane income in the community.

These are just some of the examples of what the sugar industry is doing in the more than 100 countries where sugarcane is grown. Sugar companies and associations are making real and genuine efforts to be more sustainable and to set up systems and processes that will help them meet growing demand without damaging the environment or trampling on human rights. In the process, sugarcane is bringing development and electrification to rural areas and creating jobs.

3.2   Does ethanol have a role to play?

Ten years ago, back in the summer of 2005, I was sitting in a meeting room discussing the future of the cane industry.

"Is the future sugar or ethanol?" my client asked.

At the time, oil prices had just touched $70 per barrel and, although we did not know it then, were set to double to $140 per barrel within the next two years. The global financial crisis and the mortgage crisis were, with a few notable exceptions, unimaginable. The threat of global warming was, however, on the front pages of all the newspapers; everyone was working out their global carbon footprint on specialised websites. I personally had begun to take the bus, rather than drive, to work, in a futile attempt to offset all the international travelling that I did.

"Ethanol", I confidently answered. "It's a no-brainer.

My client nodded his head politely but did not seem convinced. But I was: back in 2005 I really believed that "ethanol was a no-brainer". At the time ethanol – and biofuels in general – had the support of three powerful constituencies. Iraq was in chaos and US commentators were beginning to question their country's involvement in the Middle East. Politicians were looking for a way to reduce the US's dependence on imported oil; ethanol produced at home was an obvious way to do that.

America's farmers added their weight to the debate, arguing that they could help fuel the nation's cars by significantly increasing their corn production without impacting food production. Environmentalists also added their support, arguing that that ethanol was a "green", renewable energy that would reduce CO_2 emissions and slow global warming.

My optimism was short-lived. Ethanol met resistance first from oil companies, concerned that they would lose market share to a non mineral oil product. It also met resistance from the big food companies who were worried that it would push up their input costs. A couple of bad weather years and reduced crops ignited the "food versus fuel" debate and gave the anti-ethanol lobby some good ammunition. At the same time scientists began to question whether ethanol, particularly ethanol from corn, was really "green"; did it really reduce CO_2 emissions? Amid the noise and the confusion many environmentalists reversed their positions, arguing that biofuels "were bad for the planet".

All this negative publicity began to eat away at the support of the farmers. Farmers, in developed economies such as the EU and US each year receive billions of dollars in direct and indirect subsidies and are heavily dependent on political support. This political support is in turn based on public support; if the public turns their backs on farmers then the politicians will do the same. As a result the farming lobby scaled down its support for ethanol, preferring to be seen as part of the solution to global hunger, not part of the problem.

Lastly, and perhaps more importantly, high oil prices and rapid technological innovation gave the US an alternative "home grown" energy source in the form of shale oil. The subsequent over-supply eventually led to a collapse in world oil prices, removing one of the last arguments in favour of ethanol. It was no longer cheaper to "grow" ethanol than it was to pump oil. Meanwhile rising costs in Brazil had already begun to erode the economic benefits of sugarcane-based ethanol. The government's policy of keeping gasoline prices below international levels (to help control domestic inflation) further eroded ethanol's economic advantage.

At the time of writing world energy prices are low and likely to remain low, capped by the cost of producing shale gas and oil in the US. Ethanol will have a hard time to compete pricewise with gasoline.

But wait a minute – aren't things about to go around full circle? After a short lull global warming is once again hitting the front pages. Indeed, low oil prices may aggravate the problem as they could reduce the incentive to conserve energy, resulting in greater CO_2 emissions. Ethanol could see a revival of interest, or a reduction of opposition, from environmentalists.

Food prices have fallen dramatically over the past couple of years and ethanol has dropped off the radar screen of public concern. Biofuels were an easy scapegoat when food prices were skyrocketing but with food prices now falling there is little blame to attribute.

The fact that corn prices are currently stable, even though 40% of the US corn crop is now used to produce ethanol, takes the sting out of the food versus fuel debate. As long as the weather holds good food prices will stay low and food company lobbyists will remain silent. Ethanol is an important alternative outlet for corn when food prices are low. Farmer support for ethanol may once again grow within the US.

This swing in perceptions has already begun. In an editorial (10) entitled *"Biofuels put more food on the table"* José Graziano da Silva, Director-General of the FAO wrote,

"The choice cannot be between food and fuel. We can make good use of both. Given the right conditions, biofuels can be an effective means to increase food security by providing poor farmers with a sustainable and affordable energy source.

"Flexibility is key to efforts to leverage the world's growing reliance on biofuels to boost agricultural productivity, accelerate rural development, and increase food security. For example, policymakers must defuse the competitive pressures between food and fuel by designing schemes to counter price volatility for basic foodstuffs. Authorities could require that the percentage of biofuels blended with conventional fuel be increased when food prices drop and cut when they rise. This would serve as a sort of automatic stabilizer. Poor farmers would continue to enjoy robust demand for their products even when food prices dropped, and consumers would be protected from rapid or excessive price increases."

Sugarcane is a much more efficient converter of sunlight into energy than any other crop. Producing ethanol from sugarcane results in 9.3 units of renewable energy for every one unit of fossil fuel that is used as an input. (11) This compares to 1.4 units for ethanol produced from corn and 2 units for ethanol from wheat or sugar beet. This means that one hectare of sugar cane can produce 7,000 litres of ethanol. This compares to 3,800 litres from a hectare of corn, 2,500 litres from a hectare of wheat and 5,500 litres from a hectare of sugar beet. Depending on how you calculate it, this means a reduction in greenhouse gas emissions of between 61 to 91% for cane, 0 to 38% for corn, 16 to 69% for wheat and 52% for sugar beet.

The California Air Resources Board (CARB) has said that ethanol from sugarcane can reduce greenhouse gas emissions by 87% compared to gasoline. In a 2009 report used to develop the standard, the California Energy Commission concluded:

"Currently, Brazilian sugarcane ethanol has the lowest carbon life-cycle rating of all of the different types of ethanol that are currently being produced at commercial-sized facilities."

But why does sugarcane reduce greenhouse gases so much more than other crops? About 60 tonnes of carbon are stored in each hectare of a sugarcane field. (12) As sugarcane only needs to be replanted about every six years, this reduces the tilling of land that releases carbon dioxide. The carbon stays in the ground and is not released into the air. No-till techniques are also beginning to be used, considerably lowering the amount of fuel necessary to run agricultural machinery in the field.

The application of pesticides in sugarcane fields is low and the use of fungicides practically non-existent. Sugarcane growers also apply relatively few industrialized fertilizers, due to the innovative use of organic fertilizers from recycled production residues. All of this reduces the demand for fossil-based products, improving sugarcane ethanol's greenhouse benefits.

Sugarcane mills are energy self-sufficient. They burn bagasse (the cane stalks that are left over after the cane has been crushed) in boilers to produce enough bioelectricity to power their operations; they often sell any surplus energy back to the grid.

As each hectare of sugarcane produces more than 7,000 liters of ethanol, more energy is produced with less input, including fossil fuel input, boosting the greenhouse gas reduction benefits of sugarcane-based products. UNICA (a producers' association) estimates that since 2003, Brazil's use of sugarcane ethanol has reduced that country's emissions of carbon dioxide by more than 300 million tonnes. That's as good for the environment as planting and maintaining 2.1 billion trees for 20 years.

As I mentioned in the previous section, sugarcane is grown on only a small amount of Brazil's farmland, occupying 9.5 million hectares. Of that amount, 4.6 million is used to grow cane to be processed into ethanol. Using just 1.4% of the country's arable land, Brazil has managed to replace almost 42% of its gasoline consumption with clean and renewable ethanol.

Brazil's ethanol can be used in two ways. Anhydrous ethanol (ethanol with less water content) can be blended with gasoline at levels ranging from 5 to

27% to reduce petroleum use, boost octane ratings and cut tailpipe emissions. Hydrous ethanol (with a higher water content) can be used as a pure ethanol in specially designed engines. Ethanol adds oxygen to gasoline which helps reduce air pollution and harmful emissions in tailpipe exhaust. It is a high-octane fuel that helps prevent engine knocking and generates more power in higher compression engines.

In 2013/14, Brazilian ethanol production reached 24 billion litres (6.34 billion gallons). The domestic market where it is sold as either pure ethanol fuel or blended with gasoline absorbs most of this production. All gasoline sold in Brazil includes a blend of 18 to 27% ethanol.

The country first began using ethanol in vehicles as early as the 1920s, and the trend gained urgency during the oil shock of the 1970s. However, sugarcane ethanol's popularity really took off in 2003 with the introduction of flex fuel vehicles that can run on any mixture of gasoline and ethanol, both hydrous and anhydrous. More than 90% of the new cars sold today in Brazil are flex fuel, and these vehicles now make up about half of the country's entire light vehicle fleet – a remarkable accomplishment in less than a decade.

As a result, Brazilian consumers have a choice at the pump when they fuel their cars and most are choosing sugarcane ethanol for its price and environmental benefits, making gasoline the alternative fuel in the country.

Sugarcane ethanol today is made from the sucrose found in sugarcane juice and molasses. This current process taps only one-third of the energy sugarcane can offer. The other two-thirds remains locked in leftover cane fibre (called bagasse) and straw. While some of this energy is converted to bioelectricity in Brazil, scientists are discovering new techniques to produce ethanol – known as cellulosic ethanol – from leftover plant material. This complex process involves hydrolysis and gasification technologies to break down lignocellulose – the structural material found in plant matter – into sugar. While cellulosic ethanol can be manufactured from abundant and diverse raw materials, its production requires a greater amount of processing than traditional sugarcane ethanol and is therefore currently more expensive.

A couple of industrial sized cellulosic ethanol plants are now in operation in Brazil and if engineers and technical experts perfect commercial-scale manufacturing, production costs will come down. Cellulosic ethanol might then double the volume of fuel coming from the same amount of land planted with sugarcane.

Sugarcane ethanol therefore does have a role to play in sustainable development, in reducing green house gases and in providing fuel security, while at the same time supporting farmer incomes at times of low food prices and, in the words of the FAO, putting "more food on the table".

3.3 Sunny Verghese: concerned citizen (12)

Sunny Verghese is Co-Founder, Group Managing Director and Chief Executive Officer of Olam International Limited, responsible for the strategic planning, business development and overall management for the Olam group of companies worldwide.

"Good morning Sunny. You mentioned that you wanted to talk about some of the challenges facing us today?"

"I believe that the world is facing four key developmental challenges: food security, water security, energy security and the impact of climate change. Policy makers are focussing on these four development problems as if they were isolated. They are not; they are interrelated with interlocked causes. For example, energy makes up 47% of the cost of mechanised large-scale farming. When energy prices go up so do the costs of fertiliser, irrigation, storage and transport."

"So let's start with the food security issue", I prompted.

"We all know the drivers on the demand side. The first driver is that population is growing: 75 to 80 million people are being added to the world each year and they all need to be fed. Africa is growing its population at 2.2% per annum while world population is growing at 0.9% per annum. Africa is going to double its population to two billion people by 2050 versus one billion now. Of the predicted 2.2 billion growth in population by 2050, one billion will be in Africa and 1.2 billion in Asia.

"The second factor that is driving this increased demand is higher incomes. In the past thirty years the world added about 750 million people to the middle class. In the next 20 years we are going to add another 3 billion people to the world's middle classes. Ninety per cent of that growth in the middle class will happen in Asia: 2.7 out of the 3 billion will happen in Asia.

"It took Britain 154 years between 1700 and 1854 to double per capita income, from $1,300 to $2,600. The US took 54 years to double its per capita income. Both countries started that process with a population of about 9-10 million each. Germany took 64 years to double their per capita income from a population base of 28 million. Japan took 33 years from a population basis of 48 million to double their per capita income. Korea took just 16 years. China is taking 12 years. That's 12 years on a population of 1.3-1.5 billion people. India has taken 16 years on a population base of close to 1.3 billion. This has never happened in history. This is happening at a speed that is ten times what happened in the British Industrial Revolution and at 200 times the scale.

"This rise in income results in a significant change from a cereal carbohydrate diet to a protein and fat based diet. In the mid-eighties China used to consume 15kg of meat per capita; today it consumes between 52 and 55 kg of meat per capita. To put that in perspective, the US consumes between 110 and 120 kg of meat per capita. In the past we have said that for cultural reasons the Chinese could never eat as much meat as in the US. However, Taiwan and Hong Kong today consume between 90 and 100 kg of meat per capita per year. It is all about incomes and affordability.

"Urbanisation is another driver. Brazil has already reached 80% urbanisation rate. China this year reached 50% urbanisation rate. India is at 30%. When you live in an urban area in China you consume 3.5 times more meat, 3 times more eggs, poultry and diary products than the rural population. Increased urbanisation increases demand.

"At the same time we have diverted more of our food crops to produce fuel. In the past there were three sources of agricultural demand: food, feed and fibre. Now you have to add fuel to the mix. In the US last year 40% of the corn harvest was used to produce ethanol. Half of Brazil's sugar cane crop is used to produce ethanol. Ten per cent of the world's oilseed production goes into biodiesel production. Ten per cent of the world's acreage is now producing fuel.

"How do you feel about the food versus fuel debate?" I asked. "It is certainly controversial".

"You have to take a nuanced approach to determine whether it makes sense to convert food crops into fuel. It makes a lot of sense to convert sugarcane into ethanol in terms of energy efficiency. Where there is good input-output energy savings then you should do it. Converting corn into ethanol has a less efficient input-output efficiency."

"So the demand for agricultural crops is constantly increasing," I said. "Can supply keep up?"

"These increases in demand mean that we will have to grow food production by 70% between now and 2050. At the same time we are seeing a decrease in agricultural land through urbanisation and soil erosion and salinization, as well as over-tillage. If the first problem is a decline in agricultural land the second problem is a decline in agricultural productivity growth rates. Between 1960 and 2000 agricultural productivity grew about 2.2% per year. Between 1990 and 2000 that growth rate had halved to about 1.1%. One forecast that I have seen is that that growth rate will decline further to about 0.8%.

"We have to make a distinction between large-scale agriculture and small-scale agriculture: 85% of world agriculture is small scale. You can stand on your head but you are not going to get to the level of efficiency seen in large-scale holdings.

"In India you have 600 million people engaged

in agriculture, in China 500 million people. Just imagine telling all the Chinese and Indian farmers that they have to leave the land because their farms are being mechanised and consolidated and then tell the government that it has to find jobs for all the people streaming into the urban centres.

"The Chinese government today is trying to bridge the gap between rural and urban incomes and is paying prices across almost the entire agricultural complex that are between 10 and 20 per cent higher than international prices. They are doing that because they want to transfer wealth from urban to rural centres. They don't want more people coming to urban areas.

"But it is not just a question of producing the food", I prompted. You also have to transport it to the people that need it."

"We currently waste between 30 and 50% of the food we produce. There is so much infrastructure investment that needs to be done. The FAO has estimated that we need 4 trillion dollars of investment. They say the multilateral inter-government agencies can provide 250 to 500 million dollars of that. The rest of the money is not going to come and we will have to live with the fact that there will be constant food wastage.

I don't think most policy makers believe these problems will really happen in our lifetime; they prefer to let someone else deal with it. But these trends should wake us up. It is not all despair: there is a lot of hope as well. But we need to add our voice to find the solutions.

"But governments are not just intervening in China", I argued. "They intervene everywhere."

"It may come as a surprise to you that about 55-60% of global agriculture is unviable, only supported by government subsidies and transfers from taxpayers to the farmers. In 2012 the thirty OECD countries paid out US$387 billion in farm subsidies. The rest of the world paid out around $615 billion. The total value or GDP of the global economy was estimated for 2012 at $72 trillion, of which about $1 trillion is in subsidies. This does not include tariff barriers – these are direct farm subsidies.

"I think governments in most developing countries would like to give even more subsidies, as they are sure vote winners. India would like to make more transfers to farmers but they can't afford it. The OECD countries can afford it. But India has a lot of indirect subsidies for fertilizer, for irrigation, for diesel, all kinds of subsidies go to the farmer. And some cases there are minimum support prices. The government wants to make sure that the rural and farming populations are prospering and improving their lot. At the same time they have to make sure that food price inflation is kept under control.

"In China's case this is driven by a wish to encourage domestic consumption at a time when a large portion of the population is in rural areas. To reduce the disparity between rural and urban incomes and make direct transfers to rural areas by having high support prices for crops, even if it means domestic prices above international prices.

"Some commentators blame speculators for rising food prices and shortages", I said. "Do you think speculation has played a role?" I asked.

"At the peak of the food price crisis in June 2008 the G8 held a meeting in Hokkaido Japan and they were looking to find someone to blame – and they blamed speculators. I remember Olam was invited to present at a subsequent G20 meeting on the role of speculation in agricultural prices. Olam is fairly unique in that over half of the 44 agricultural commodities in which we deal do not have a derivative or a futures market. Our company has price series data for the 23 years that we have been in business on the non-futures traded agricultural commodities.

"This data shows very clearly that the volatility in the non-futures traded commodities has been statistically significantly higher than in the futures traded commodities. But there are few, if any, speculators in the non-futures traded commodities.

"Food prices increases have a disproportionate impact in different countries. In India 60% of the consumption basket is spent on food. In Africa it is between 70 and 80% and it is about 45% in China. In Europe it is 9% and in the USA it is about 10%. The World Bank estimates that in the 2008 world financial crisis 100-150 million people fell below the poverty line. The number of under or mal-nourished people in the world remained static around 900 million.

"What do policy makers do when food prices rise? They ban exports and impose price controls. But price controls are precisely the wrong reaction when you want to induce a supply response: you need high prices as a cure for high prices. But if 70% of your population's consumption expenditure is on food, high food prices can result in unstable political conditions.

"So how do resolve the dilemma that you need higher prices to induce a supply response but higher prices will affect the poor people the most?" I asked.

"My answer is simple: you transfer all the subsidies - the $387 billion that the rich world gives to farmers who don't actually need the money – subsidise food costs for the poor. We need to start to try and use those subsidies to ensure that people below the poverty line are not impacted by high food prices.

"What about water?" I asked.

"Today we use about 4.5 trillion cu m of water. To meet the water requirements of a population of 8.4 billion people by 2030 - and assuming no change in water use efficiencies - we will need to increase our water consumption from about 4.5 trillion cubic metres now to about 6.9 trillion cubic metres. About 70% of this water goes into agriculture, 22% goes into industrial use and the balance goes into household consumption. As you industrialise and urbanise, the share of water use that goes to household and industrial use increases.

"In India it is estimated that household water use will treble by 2020 and that industrial use will double by 2020. In China in late 80s and early 90s eighty per cent of China's water went into agriculture; today it is about 60 per cent. If you are to produce one tonne of wheat you will need 1,500 litres of water. If you use that same quantity of water for industrial use you will get 50 times the amount of revenue. So the priority will go to industry.

"Today I tried to calculate the amount of water that was used to produce my breakfast. One toast requires 40 litres of water to produce; one tomato requires 13 litres of water; one potato requires 25 litres of water; a cup of coffee requires 140 litres of water; a glass of milk for my cereal requires 200 litres of water; two strips of bacon requires 320 litres of water; two eggs sunny side up, requires 240 litres of water. That's about 1,000 litres that I used this morning for my breakfast. As a rough rule of thumb we use one litre of water for every calorie that we consume.

"The challenge is clearly to improve water use efficiency. At Olam we look to maximise crop per drop of water for all our upstream plantation operations. We don't want any flood irrigation; we want to move into drip irrigation as much as possible. We also want to select drought resistant varieties. Nor do we want to grow crops that have poor water efficiencies, even if it might currently be economic to do so. Although something might make money in the short term it may not be sustainable in the long run. So when we invested in almond plantations in Australia, 70% of the investment value that we paid was to secure high performing permanent water rights. The other 30% went to the value of the orchard.

"The UN estimates that there are 500 million people living in water scarcity and that number will according to the UN go up to 3 billion people by 2030. If we could fight wars over oil we could definitely fight bigger wars over food and water.

"Lastly," I asked, "What about climate change?"

"Even the most hardened sceptics are now coming around to the view that there has to be a catalyst for these recent recurrent episodes of drought and floods. Scientists in the UK looked at the last seven major climate episodes and concluded that six of them are attributable to climate change.

"The IPCC, the Inter-government Panel on Climate Change, put out a very controversial report saying that the Himalayan glaciers would melt by 2035. Those glaciers support seven major river systems and about 1.3 billion people engaged in agriculture. Maybe that report was flawed but climate change is a real deal that cannot be ignored".

"Thank you Sunny for your comments."

Speculation

4.1   Everyone is a speculator

"Can you ride a horse?"

The year was 1974 and I was sitting on a bed in the YMCA in Perth Australia. That day I had just disembarked from a passenger ship that had sailed in from Singapore. The ship had broken down two days out of Perth and had had to be towed in. I had flown to Singapore on a twin prop Dan Air (colloquially known at the time as "Dan Dare") from Luton in the UK. My mother had burst into tears when she saw the plane, but I wasn't sure whether it was just the fact that I was leaving home or whether she had been afraid that the plane wouldn't make it all the way.

The plane made its first refuelling stop in Tehran, but once it arrived in Delhi the plane was arrested. Apparently Dan Air hadn't paid for fuel the last time it had stopped there. We were kept in the plane for seven sweaty hours while the situation was sorted out. During this time all the food went off and the leg from Delhi to Singapore was memorable by the long queues for the plane's two toilets; food poisoning on a plane is never a pretty sight.

I had just won a place at one of the UK's top universities and was at the start of a nine-month "Gap Year" that was due to take in both Australia and New Zealand. I had enough money to get to Australia, and enough money to survive for a couple of months, but I didn't have enough money to get home again.

Despite the difficulty of the trip out to Perth my

spirits and self-confidence were high. All this had prompted me to ask my YMCA roommate for advice on finding a job in Australia. His question as to whether I could ride a horse took me by surprise. I could do differential maths equations; I knew what a J-curve was in Economics and I could write an essay on the role of foreign capital in developing economies. But I couldn't ride a horse. I had ridden one once when I was eight, but not since. I shook my head.

"Can you mend a fence?" I shook my head again.

"Can you shear a sheep?" Embarrassed, I mumbled something about possibly learning but he cut me short. "You're no bloody use to anyone then" he snorted and left the room.

Forty years later I was again in Australia, standing in a sugar cane field in Nikenbah, near Hervey Bay on the coast of Queensland. The sugar cane was in beautiful condition, lush and green, largely as a result of the low-pressure pivot irrigation system that the Petersen family had installed a few years earlier. The Petersens have been growing cane in this area for four generations and had long ago learned how to live with the vagaries of Australia's fickle and sometimes violent climate.

One of the things I love about being in the sugar business was that you meet such a wide range of people, from a simple cane farmer to a sugar mill owner to a sophisticated hedge fund manager. However Ashley and David Petersen were far from simple cane farmers. They were well educated and prided themselves on using the latest technology, the "best practice" possible.

Before a farmer decides which crop to plant –

or whether to plant any crop at all – he has to form an opinion as to what return he will get from that crop when it is harvested. If the farmer is an Australian cane grower like the Petersens he may be able to sell his crop in advance, something that is called "hedging". Or at least he may be able to fix the price of it, something that is called "pricing". But even if he does hedge or price his expected production he is still taking a risk.

If the weather is bad or if his crop is hit by disease his production will disappoint and he may have to buy back some, or all, of what he already sold. The trouble is that if he produces less than expected it is likely that other farmers in the area will also produce less. They may also have to buy back their hedges (sales) at prices that could well be higher than when they sold originally. If that happens, not only will they have less revenue (because of less sugar) but they will also have to pay back the loss on their forward sales.

Before they make their planting decisions the Petersens will try to assess all the available information – and use all their experience and training. They will ask themselves a number of questions. Have they planted cane on this area before and, if they have, how did it do? How much fertiliser and pesticide will they need – and what will it cost? What about the long-range weather forecast: are the weather experts predicting a dry or wet growing season? And how will the weather affect the different crops that they could plant?

Most importantly, however, the Petersens will try to guess what the price of their crop will be at harvest time. In their estimations they will probably do what everyone else does: take the current price as a reference and then try and work out what factors might move that price over the coming months. Are their neighbours planning to grow cane this year – and if they are, how much? Are they looking to increase their acreage under cane and if they are, what is the risk of over-supply and lower prices? The two brothers will talk to their friends in the business and to the mill owners, asking for their varied opinions in an attempt to get as good a picture as possible of all the various factors that could impact price.

The Petersens will also have to take a view as to what will be the cost of harvesting their crop and getting it to market. Will the on-going crisis in the Middle East lead to higher oil prices and make it more expensive to buy fertilisers or run their harvesters? Is the government planning on a change in transport regulations that might take the bigger trucks off the road and raise the cost of getting their cane to the mill?

None of their information will be complete: the Petersens will therefore have to make their planting decisions based on incomplete information. The Petersens will be speculating about the future. In doing so they will be also evaluating the downside risk if they get it wrong. Will the crop be totally ruined if the weather is bad or will they be able to salvage some of it? If prices fall, how low could they fall: what is their downside risk?

How much money the Petersens have in the bank at the start of the season may influence the amount of risk they will be willing to take. Should they plant a crop like sugar cane that they can be sure of selling even if the prices are poor? Or do they have enough financial capital to take the risk of planting a crop such as pineapples that should give a better return, but might not?

Sugar is an unusual crop in that both sugarcane

and sugar beet require processing in a factory before the sugar can be consumed. It is for this reason that it is called an "agro-industrial crop".

Unless a cane or beet farmer is in an area where there is more than one cane mill or beet factory he will only have one potential buyer for his crop. This adds another level of uncertainty. What happens if for some reason the factory owner refuses to buy his production or if he squeezes him down on its price? What recourse does the grower have? What is his relative bargaining power?

In reality, the relationship between the mill and the farmer is not as asymmetric as it may seem in sugar. The factory owner has invested capital in his production facilities and needs the farmer's beet or cane as much as the farmer needs the factory to process it. The factory cannot work without raw materials – and the factory owner will try to maximise factory throughput in order to reduce his unit costs. The two parties therefore have a mutual interest in a similar outcome: producing as much sugar as possible and selling it at the best possible price. In theory, at least, it is a true "win-win" situation.

In practice, and human nature being what it is, the farmer / processor relationship can sometimes be a source of conflict. The farmer wants to sell his cane or beet at the highest possible price while the factory or mill owner will want to buy it at the cheapest possible price. To avoid this conflict many countries have legislation governing how much of the final selling price of the sugar the farmer gets and how much the factory gets. It usually runs at about one-third for the factory owner and two-thirds for the farmer.

Some argue that the mill or factory owner is

merely providing a service to the cane or beet farmer. The mill converts a crop that has only a limited number of buyers into a product that has an almost infinite number of buyers. The factory owner could theoretically charge a fee for this service but in almost all cases the factory owner assumes at least one third of the price risk. The system works better – and is more likely to result in a "win-win" outcome - if the factory or mill owner has "some skin in the game".

In some countries, most notably in Russia and Ukraine, the beet factories used to not pay the farmers for the beet but to give them back the processed sugar (minus a percentage that the mills kept as a service fee) for the farmers to sell themselves. However the farmers were usually desperate for money by the end of the harvest and they all wanted to sell their sugar at the same time. As a result sugar prices collapsed at the end of each harvest. Eventually all parties decided that it was more efficient for the factories to buy the beets from the farmers, sell the sugar over the course of the year and to split the proceeds.

Some governments, most notably in India, fix a minimum price for cane or beet so as to ensure that the farmers get a guaranteed minimum return on their crop. In a period of over-supply the mills can get "caught between a rock and a hard spot"; they can be forced to pay a minimum price for their raw material while selling the finished product at a loss. If losses build up then the mills may run out of money to pay the farmers. In the worst of cases the factory could go bankrupt, leaving the farmer with no outlet for his crop.

By agreeing to buy beet or cane from a grower, the factory is hoping that it can sell the sugar that it produces at a profit. It is therefore not just the growers who have to speculate; factory owners will also have to speculate as to how the sugar price will move in the future. They will need to form an opinion as to how much they should sell in advance and how much to leave until the sugar is actually produced. It all comes down to one basic question: Will sugar prices be higher or lower in six months time than they are now?

Each individual grower or mill owner will take his own individual decision as to how much to produce. However these individual decisions can have unexpected outcomes once they are aggregated together. For example, in a period of low prices one would expect both factories and farmers to reduce production. However a farmer may focus on total revenue rather than on price and actually expand production in a period of lower prices. Similarly a factory will try to maximise throughput so as to reduce unit costs. This could also lead to higher production. Of course this can only last for a limited time. If everyone expands production prices will fall; factories will eventually go bankrupt and farmers will plant an alternative crop. However the process can be surprisingly slow. Farmers may be reluctant to change crops and even more reluctant to give up farming altogether.

The "ratoon" nature of sugarcane further complicates the issue. Most crops are grown from seed. Sugarcane is rarely planted from seed; instead farmers cut up harvested cane stalks into small pieces and then plant the pieces in the ground. This process is expensive but once the crop is in the ground it can be harvested for a number of years. Sugarcane is a grass that, like a lawn, can be mowed many times. Unlike a lawn, however, the cane cannot stay in the ground forever. Well it could, but the size and quality of the cane deteriorates over the years. In most countries growers replant cane after four years but some keep the same cane in the ground for up to seven years. In India the cane is replaced every year – or every other year. In Hervey Bay Australia, the Petersens usually keep their cane in the ground for four years.

Sugar beet, however, is an annual crop, planted in the spring and harvested in the autumn. As such, beet farmers tend to react more quickly to changes in the price of sugar and, more importantly, to the price of sugar relative to alternative crops such as wheat or corn. But in all cases everyone involved has to speculate on, and take a risk on, the future.

"What do you think of the market?" asked David Petersen as he leaned back against the cane harvester that he had just bought. It was the question that I had been dreading.

"I am bullish," I replied. (You are "bullish" if you think prices will rise and "bearish" if you think they will fall. A "bull market" is one where you expect prices to rise; a "bear market" is one where you expect prices to fall.) David looked pleased with my answer; a little too pleased.

"But you should never bet the farm, or your family's wellbeing, on what I believe prices will do", I continued. "You should use a prudent hedging strategy, selling a little of your expected production everyday. You should only speculate with a small percentage of your production and never risk your financial wellbeing".

David began to fiddle with something on the harvester. He had heard it all before.

4.2 Are all speculators alike?

When I arrived in Minneapolis in September 1979 raw sugar was trading on the world market at 13 c/lb ($286 per metric tonne). Within a year the price had tripled to over 44 c/lb ($1,000 per metric tonne) and by the time I left in September 1981 the price had fallen again to 13 c/lb. Those were crazy times, but not just in the commodity markets: Jimmy Carter was in the White House; Americans were being held hostage in Iran and the world thought that it was running out of oil. (The world thinks that from time to time.) The sugar market was going crazy but so too was pretty much everything else, particularly copper. And when markets go crazy, traders make money.

Being in Minneapolis protected me somewhat from all the craziness of that period but as a young trader I did spend some wild times in New York. Sugar traders at that time used to congregate after the market closed in a bar called St John's. You could always be sure of meeting someone from the sugar business there of an evening.

After a volatile day the bar would be packed with floor brokers from the floor and traders from the offices. I was in the bar after a particularly wild day when one of the biggest and most prominent locals on the floor took me outside and pointed at the skyscraper opposite.

"I made enough money today", he said proudly, "to buy that building". Although he was pretty drunk at the time I knew that he was telling the truth.

Years later, perhaps twenty years later, I was on my way to a client meeting in New York and popped into a deli on Lexington Avenue to buy a sandwich for lunch. I was shocked when I thought I recognised the man serving behind the counter. I was sure it was the local who had made enough money in a day to buy a skyscraper. When I got to my meeting I was still in a state of shock and asked my client about him. He replied,

"No, that's not him. But the guy you are thinking of does by coincidence work in a deli in the Bronx. He got into bad habits and fell onto hard times. He's lucky to be alive. A lot of the guys from that era couldn't handle it. Some couldn't cope with getting rich so quickly and went mad on drugs. Others couldn't cope when the markets slowed down. They had thought they were making money because they were smart but they weren't any smarter than most people on the street. They were just in the right place at the right time."

Each week the CFTC (Commodities Futures Trading Commission) publishes the COT (Commitment of Traders) report that gives a breakdown of the positions held by different categories of players in each market. The report splits the "non commercial" (i.e. speculative) participants in the futures markets into three categories: index funds, large speculators and "unreportables" (small speculators). The index funds tend to be "long only": they buy and hold commodities as if they were equities; at the time of writing they are long of sugar futures contracts to the tune of nearly 14 million tonnes of sugar. (I will write more about the index funds in the next chapter.)

Large speculators, as defined by the CFTC, can be short as well as long in the market. Indeed, at the time of writing (June, 2015) the large speculators are "short" about 90,000 futures contracts, representing almost four million tons of sugar. The small speculators are "short" about one million tons.

It is often difficult to grasp the concept of "selling something short" - selling something that you don't have in the hope that you can buy it back later at a cheaper price. After all, if you don't own something, how can you sell it? The answer is that you can't sell it if you have to hand it over straight away. However, if what you are selling is something that you plan to deliver sometime in the future then you can sell it without owning it first. You should have time to buy whatever it is at a later date and deliver it to your buyer when the time comes.

A sugar miller can, and often does, sell sugar for future delivery, sugar that has not yet been produced. The miller will not usually sell more than he expects to produce but if weather is bad and his production disappoints the miller may be "over-sold". If that happens he will have to either buy back some of what he has already sold or buy in what the difference from someone else.

It is not just a miller that can sell sugar that he doesn't have. A trader that is looking to sell a cargo of white sugar, say, to West Africa, for delivery in three months time may take the view that the price of sugar will fall between the time he makes the sale and the time he has to deliver the sugar. In such a situation he could sell the sugar without having bought it first; he could sell short.

An investor or speculator that is not involved in the physical sugar market may also believe that sugar prices will fall in the future. If they have a futures trading account they could sell futures now and buy them back later. If they are wrong - and prices rise instead of fall - then they will lose money. If they are right and prices do fall they will make a profit.

In the equity markets "selling short" is considered more risking that "going long". If an equity investor buys a particular share then he can hold on to it for as long as he wants. However if the investor sells a particular share that he does not already own he will have to borrow it from someone else. The short-seller knows that at a prearranged time he will be asked to deliver that share to the buyer. He will be forced to buy it at the then prevailing price and could be "squeezed".

On the other hand an investor that is long of a share cannot be forced to sell it and can never be squeezed. The risk of being long or short of equities is therefore asymmetric: there is more risk in being short than in being long.

The same does not apply to commodities. Of course if our short seller runs out of time he also risks being "squeezed": at some stage he will have no choice but to buy the sugar at whatever the prevailing price is.

However if he is "long" a commodity he also risks being "squeezed". Once the delivery (or shipment) period arrives he will have to charter a vessel to load the sugar he has bought. If he doesn't, he will be classed as being in default and have to pay severe penalties.

If, once he has loaded the sugar on to the vessel, he still does not have a buyer he can store the sugar on the vessel. However, he will have to pay daily charter rates to the vessel owner, sums of money that quickly build up. The risks are roughly the same therefore whether you are long or short commodities; they are symmetric.

In traders' jargon, a cargo for immediate

delivery that has not already been sold is called a "distressed" cargo. Potential buyers of that cargo will know that the owner of the sugar is "squeezed"; they know he will eventually have to sell the cargo at any price just to get rid of it.

The sugar futures contracts in both London and New York are what are called "FOB" contracts. The deliverer is obligated to deliver the sugar "Free on Board" (loaded onto) a ship and the receiver (buyer) is obligated to present a vessel for loading. If either party fails to meet their obligations, then they are in default.

Some commodity contracts, however, are what are called "warehouse" contracts (examples include coffee or cocoa) where the receiver (buyer) takes delivery in a warehouse designated by the futures exchange.

You could argue that as the receiver can keep the product in the warehouse (and pay the warehouse owner a storage fee), these warehouse contracts are more similar to equities: that it is less risky to be long than short. However, each commodity is different and each futures contract has its own defined rules as to what the receiver and the deliverer have to do.

As I mentioned earlier, at the time of writing large speculators are net short of four million tons of sugar futures while the small speculators (the "non-reportables") are net short of about one million tons of sugar futures. However these "net" figures are made up of large gross positions: some large speculators are long 8.5 million tons while others are short of 12.5 million tons; some small speculators are long of four million tons while other small speculators are short of one million tons.

But why is there this disparity of opinion? Why

are some speculators betting that sugar prices will rise while others are betting that they will fall? The answer is that different speculators have different ways of trading: some may look at price patterns on a chart while others may look at fundamental supply and demand data. But even within those two categories, different traders may interpret the charts or the data differently. Some may think that a particular chart pattern is "bullish" (suggesting that prices will rise in the future), while others may interpret it as "bearish" (suggesting that prices will fall in the future).

And as for fundamental traders, one may be looking at a short-term over-supply and expect prices to fall; another may be predicting a shortage further into the future and expect prices to rise. And, to make matters even more complicated, most traders will look at both the charts and the fundamentals, applying different weights to each.

Anyone looking to speculate on the price of sugar, or on the commodity markets in general has a number of alternatives. They can seek out a "Commodity Trading Advisor" (CTA) at a brokerage house or bank who will advise them on the markets and recommend various strategies within those markets. Alternatively they could look for a fund and hand their money over to a manager (or group of managers) to manage it for him.

But what are the different types of commodity funds?

"Value Funds" are those that use fundamentally based trading strategies based on detailed statistical analysis of supply and demand, usually operating on a medium- to long-term timeframe. They will usually look at each market separately, searching for opportunities where price may be over-, or under-, valued. They may also look at the wider commodity board and, for example, go long of a basket of commodities in the expectation that the US dollar might weaken – or short a basket of commodities if they expect the US dollar to strengthen.

"Event trading funds" may look for particular "events" that may impact price. For example, an outbreak of "mad cow disease" could lead to drop in demand for animal feed and a fall in the corn price.

A long-term fundamental fund may bet on longer-term trends; they could for example bet that corn prices are on a long-term uptrend due to increased usage of ethanol.

Algorithmic funds have received a lot of attention over the past couple of years. They have been blamed for a couple of "flash crashes" on the US stock markets and been criticised for "front running" customer orders. Think of them as Mr Smith in the Matrix, weaving in and out of the software that runs the various electronic exchanges. These funds (controversially) pay the Exchanges to allow them to place their computers as close as possible to the exchange computers and in the process gain an advantage of a fraction of a millisecond over other market participants.

By doing so, these computer programmes can "see" buy or sell orders before they are executed. This gives them an advantage over other market participants as it allows them either to "front run" an order or to cancel the other side of an existing order. In the first case the programme can, for example, see a large buy order hitting the market and then take advantage of their speed to buy whatever is on offer in the market before the other person can. They can then turn around and sell what they have bought to the original buyer at a higher price.

An algorithmic fund may leave multiple standing orders in the market, both on the buy and sell side. If, for example, the market begins to move higher and the fund's standing sell orders start to get executed then the computer will cancel those standing orders and buy instead. The same would happen in the other direction if prices begin to fall. It is for this reason that these algorithmic funds are blamed for exaggerating market moves and sometimes causing flash crashes.

However, in their defence, most of these programmes are looking for multiple small short-term changes in the price rather than long term big moves. A programme that buys in front of another buyer will quickly turn around and sell what it has bought at only a couple of points higher.

What this does mean, however, is that most orders these days are traded twice; this has led to a near doubling of trading volumes on the futures exchanges. And, as the exchanges are paid a fee for each lot, they can hardly be blamed for not pulling the plug on those algorithmic programmes.

Supporters of algorithmic funds argue that by increasing traded volumes on the market the funds increase liquidity and make it easier for other participants to trade. This would be true if the funds were to take the other side of orders and then trade out of them afterwards. But they don't do that; instead they front-run genuine orders and can make trading for everyone else as difficult as catching that slippery bar of soap in the shower.

Many fund managers are "technical traders";

they ignore the supply and demand fundamentals completely and just trade based on patterns on the price charts. They argue that there are too many unknowns to correctly predict future physical supply and demand for a particular commodity and even if they could, the correlation between price and physical supply and demand is too loose. Technical traders argue that all the market information is available in just one element: the price. They prefer to try to predict future price movements by interpreting how prices have moved in the past.

The fact that so many traders use technical trading suggests that it works at least part of the time. But how can it work? In a way, the answer to that question may be circular. It is possible that technical analysis works because people believe it does. The power of positive thinking has long been demonstrated and it sometimes seems that just believing in something can make it happen. However, the power of positive thinking has its limits. Many people believe that aliens already live on our planet but that does not mean they do.

The power of belief does go some way to explaining why charts work. By studying chart analysis and accepting some basic rules of the game, technical traders may behave in similar ways in response to different patterns and formations. The more people that believe in technical analysis, the more the whole business can become self-reinforcing.

However, a better answer may be found in the nature of human psychology and behaviour. Human beings are irrational and emotional. No matter how well you think you know someone, it is difficult to predict how that person will behave in response to a particular event. However, if you put a number of individuals together, human behaviour becomes repeatable and predictable. There is an old saying that there is nothing new under the sun. Although at first sight this is obvious nonsense, if you narrow the saying down to apply solely to human nature, then it makes more sense. Human behaviour does not change.

Taking the argument further, if human behaviour does not change, it must repeat itself. And if it repeats itself, it must be predictable. To put it another way, consciously or subconsciously, humans use their experiences of past events to show them how to react to current ones. If you put enough human beings and enough of those experiences together you get a pattern. If the sample size is big enough you may be able predict the future just by looking at that pattern.

Psychologists have distilled all human behaviour down to two driving forces. The first is the seeking of pleasure. The second is the avoidance of pain. In markets, this can be translated into the infamous "greed" and "fear". Traders seek pleasure from monetary gain or from knowing that they got the market right. And they seek to avoid the pain of losing money or looking a fool in front of their friends and industry peers.

So, although you may think that you are a unique individual, you respond in similar ways to similar situations and your behaviour follows certain rules that can be identified. You are a social animal that seeks to be accepted by the herd and to go with the crowd. In that crowd, your behaviour is repeatable and predictable.

4.3   Robert Kuok: Sugar King

Born in October 1923 in Johor Baru Malaysia, Robert Kuok (or RK as he is known) is a major figure in the world of sugar and has been nicknamed "The King of Sugar". He has been an extraordinarily successful businessman and apart from sugar he is best known as the founder of the Shangri La Hotel chain and the owner of the South China Morning Post. Like many successful Asian businessmen, he is media-shy and rarely gives interviews.

I met RK at his new offices. He welcomed me and apologised for his terrible cold and cough. He had caught it on a recent trip to London where he had been visiting the latest addition to his hotel chain, the Shangri La in the Shard Building. I started by trying to explain my book project but he seemed distracted by his telephone.

"I see I have four messages but I don't know if they are important", he said. "Ah yes, last night's sugar market close."

"You are not still trading the sugar market?" I asked, astonished.

"I watch the market every day" he replied. "I started in 1955 and this "topping up" takes seconds; if I stop I can never get on to it again. I still trade the sugar market for my claret money; so that I can afford Petrus 1989. Otherwise you would be mad to buy it. But if you are winning at the sugar casino; then why not continue? And the days I lose money, I look sadly at my wine and I tell myself, "Tonight you don't deserve it". I open the bottle and drink only one glass as a punishment to myself for trading badly."

I did a quick sum in my head. RK had started in

the Rice Department with Mitsubishi in 1942, the year the Japanese Army occupied Singapore and Malaya. That meant that he had been in the commodity markets for 72 years and trading sugar for 60 years; that had to be a record. I shared my mental arithmetic with him and he smiled.

"Have the markets changed much since you first started?" I asked.

"No," he replied. "The change has mainly been the speed of information dissemination or gathering, but you have to adapt to that. So my trading volume today is one per cent of what it was. I used to trade 4,000 lots (200,000 tons) in one go; now I trade 40 lots (2,000 tons). Today I am 40 lots long, but my trading pays for the Petrus!" he said with a laugh.

"Let me tell you how I started," he offered. "Before the Japanese army invaded Malaya and Singapore the whole world, particularly South East Asia and India, was still reeling from the Great Depression. Economies were just beginning to recover because the war excited production of raw materials, for example rubber for tires.

"In late Dec 1941 we were told to pack the essentials and leave town. Japanese invaders in plain clothes had infiltrated the area where we lived and it was getting very dangerous. So we packed a few things. The Japanese launched an assault on Singapore on about 8th February. Singapore fell on 15th February. It took them a week. We did not come back for almost three months. We went to a pineapple plantation on about 1000 acres of rolling land. And when we came back to our house there was a big hole in the middle of it.

"It was a very impoverished world that the

Japanese invaded and once they took over they dominated domestic trading: Mitsubishi had a monopoly on rice and tobacco and Mitsui controlled sugar and salt.

"One morning a Taiwanese officer in Japanese army uniform barged into our home and spoke to us in our local dialect. "Close the door!" he said. "He explained that he missed his own people - and the food. He asked if he could stay for lunch; my mother cooked a bit extra and he befriended us. He was a bit of a rough character but decent with us. On his fifth visit he told my mother that the head of the local Japanese Gestapo lived 150 yards from our house and he would soon find out that my two brothers and I were not working. For him that would mean only one thing, that we were anti-Japanese.

"He told us that he knew a senior manager in Mitsubishi in Singapore who was looking for someone to help start a representative office in Johor Bahru. He asked which one of us brothers wanted to work. My eldest brother Philip turned it down. William also turned him down. I said I would do it. I was the first employee. I had never worked in my life and I started as chief clerk of the rice department. A few months later they added tobacco to my responsibilities. My father was a rice trader but there was nothing left for him to trade. The Japanese had a monopoly on rice. My father had to buy rice from me.

"Did you continue to trade rice?" I asked.

"After the war I joined my father's business and worked for him for three years and two months before he suddenly died. I continued the business after his death.

"When did you get your first big break?" I

asked.

"In the spring of 1963 I had a hunch and I decided to fly to London. A Malaysian friend who travelled with me had the use of an apartment in the Grosvenor House Hotel.

I asked RK if he was easily accepted into that world of English traders.

"Quite easily. The monkey in me meant that I could pick up accents easily - many people thought I spoke good English. I enjoyed mixing with people. I am totally non feudal. I don't like social dos and don'ts. I can't stand snobbery; I lived under colonialism and I felt that was more than enough. Someone once said that I have half a Chinese mind and half a British mind. That opens doors. In business you have to succeed through intelligence, not through gimmicks. If you rely on gimmicks then you lose the essence of things."

"But in early autumn 1963 the sugar market went down and you almost went broke," I prompted.

"I had enough cash, thank God, to meet margins. In the autumn of 1963 Hurricane Flora hit Cuba and the market rallied; I was saved. August that year was very difficult. But somehow I can always manage. I was 40 years old and at my best. Although it worried me I never felt like jumping off a building. Still, the position was large for me, maybe 250,000 tons of sugar, part physical sugar and part futures - a huge position for me. Anyway the market turned around. I took some profit and then more profit."

"How did you know when to take profits?" I asked. "I find the biggest difficulty about trading is knowing when to take profits".

"Not knowing when to take a profit is the Achilles' heel for a trader. Take profits! Don't wait. If you have a profit you have to take it. If you wait it will be your downfall. Also, have the wisdom to realise that you can't take it in one go or you destroy the market for the balance. If you are a big trader it takes 10, 20, 30 days to unload, depending on how big your footstep is.

"If you are a big trader you had better start even if you are in minus territory if the market is going up. You are long and you have been suffering: a big minus, a small minus, and then a negligible minus. At that point start liquidating. Even if you sell only 3% you still have 97% to go. You have to shed weight. Waiting to take profits is dangerous.

"What about taking losses?" I asked.

"Well," RK replied with a sigh. "It is wonderful to take losses when you have profits under your belt. So you need some luck to build up some profits first. You have to start on the right leg. And everything, including quantity must be according to your size.

"In 1963 I took a big position," he continued. "I was very confident. I felt that sugar was worth more than it was. But you know the sugar market. There is always over production. There is no point hoarding sugar. There is always a bumper crop coming up.

"The biggest sugar market ever was in 1974: vast fortunes were made and lost. Can you tell me a little bit about that?" I asked.

"There were three main trade houses at the time, Sucden, E.D.&F Man and Tate & Lyle. I was more of an absentee player. We were long hundreds of thousands of tons of sugar, whites and raws, bought before the rise. The market went limit up (1) for 15 to 20 days with no trades. We all knew that no one should touch it.

"But then tension got to us and we started to

put on hedges, to sell out our long positions. We sold blocks of sugar to Iran and to Russia at the highs of the market but when the sugar went to Iran they refused to unload it and the demurrage bills wiped out all the profits. The ship owners looked to the charterers and finally with the help of the Foreign Offices of France and Britain Iranian assets overseas were frozen. The Iranians came to the negotiating table to settle and pay part of the demurrage bills; they cut off 30-40%. I think at one time we must have been looking at £300-400 million profit. In those days that was huge.

"So what happened in the end?" I asked.

"You are talking of Britain's might and France's might," he replied. "Iran was shaky because Khomeini had just come into a plundered country.

"But you know with sugar there is always over production. It is like my hotel business. I don't know why I go into feast and famine business. As soon as you make money in hotels every Dick, Tom and Harry builds a hotel and then there is oversupply. And then you all cry for seven to eight years before you start to make a bit of money.

"Have the skills you learnt trading sugar helped you in the hotel business," I asked. "The hotel industry also has cycles".

"No it is different. The hotel business is all about brand building. The hotel brand is my Aladdin's lamp and I have to build that brand up and polish it all the time. It is little things that are important."

"You are perhaps better known now for your hotel chain that for your sugar trading. Can you tell me a little bit about how it started?" I asked.

"I joined three other investors looking to build a hotel in Singapore. At that time I had 10% of the investment. There were three other owners and they thought how lucky they were to find an idiot, a moron, like me willing to take on all the worries of building and launching a new hotel.

"One day when the hotel was under construction I had a visit from a sugar trader from Sucden's office in Tokyo – a Frenchman. I took him to Raffles Hotel, the Elizabethan Grill. We talked sugar a bit and then the lunch was over. He said, "Mr Kuok my only purpose in coming to Singapore was to see you. What am I going to do with my time?"

"I said that was up to him. "What are you doing now?" he asked me. I said I was going to see my hotel that was under construction". "Let me come along", he said. I could hardly refuse. He jumped in the car with me. From there to Orchard Road is a barely a mile. As we got closer he said, "What's the name of the hotel?" I replied that I hadn't thought of it but the road on which the land sits is called "Orange Grove". Maybe I will call it "Orange Grove Hotel".

"Stupid" he replied. (Frenchman you see!) But luckily I was built small so I couldn't pick a fight with him and all I could do was swallow my anger. "What would you call it?" I asked. He thought for a moment and said " Shangri La". That's a good name, I said. I took it to the board but they didn't like the name. The number one owner spoke no English. He said, "You know in Bangkok I go to a massage parlour called Shangri La, how can we call our hotel that?"

"We could not decide on a name so we went on without a name. We hired Westin International Hotels in Seattle to come and manage it. They sent a two-man team and they asked me what we would call it; I told them I liked the name "Shangri La". We had a meeting with the other investors. I kept quiet. The two men suggested Shangri La and all the board said, "Very good; very good name". I nearly spat out like a machine gun the four-letter word. But it became Shangri-la Hotel, Singapore. The hotel opened in March 1971.

"The early 1960s were wonderful for me in the sugar market. I was hunting in a lake just teeming with salmon trout. There were only three or five predators; these sharks could eat their fill. I would swim past them and they weren't even interested in me. Today you go to the same lake: there are giant crocodiles, giant sharks. There is not enough fish to feed these giant predators. You have to think twice before swimming in the lake.

"A lot of traders are arrogant", I ventured. "They have big positions and have to convince themselves that they are right and therefore have to convince other people that they are right."

"You have to be humble because you are never always right. You don't need to convince anyone. You can trade as a very humble man."

"Is speculation and risk taking an integral part of all life?" I asked.

"An emphatic yes!" RK replied. "When you get into your car and leave your home you are taking a risk. In the modern world there is no back-to-back trading where you can make a simple margin on a physical sugar transaction. Those days are long gone. Those opportunities when they come are like golfing holes in one. I have been playing golf since 1947 and I have never scored a hole in one. So where there is no back to back trading it means you have to lift a leg: you have to sell before you buy or buy before you sell. You have to take a risk. But you can still make good money trading."

"You have a reputation for being close to

China," I asked. "How did that start?

"In 1973 the Chinese called me in Singapore and I flew to Hong Kong to meet them. They told me that China needed sugar but the government didn't have enough money to pay for it. They knew that if they stepped in to buy what they needed from the world market the price would explode. They asked me to help them make money from the futures market. I laughed at them. I told them that they were brilliant; they had left me no option but to say, "Yes". I knew their secret and if I didn't serve them I would serve myself; there was no third way out. I am no hypocrite. I made a joke of it but all my life I had wanted to help China, especially Mao's China.

"Are you a businessman who started as a trader or are you a trader who applied your trading skills to business?" I asked.

"I have been asking myself that question for the past 50 years. Let's take soccer as a parallel. You can train someone to play football but you never produce a Pele, a Ronaldo or a Messi. You have to have natural verve. We are not born equal. You either have that attribute in you, call it genius if you like, but of course different degrees of genius, and then circumstance or fate gives you the playground to exercise your skills. If you are born in the wrong community and your parents force you into the armed forces, well then how do you become a trader? But traders are born, not taught."

"Footballers often have particular styles, as do traders", I prompted. "What is your style?"

"When you play poker the secret is to never let the other players guess your next move. I can play a contrarian game but I can also flow with the current. I even involve superstition. In my early days I would look at a fellow trader to see if he had a lucky glow on his forehead. If he did I would spend more time with him that day."

"Commodity trading is based on trust," I said. "You have to start a relationship offering trust. But what do you do when someone abuses that trust?"

"Well that is just too bad. You just have to cut your losses; you have no other choice. If you want, you can keep that person as a friend but do so at arm's length; no more business dealings. But it is better to just cut the cord and part company. If you bear a grudge you are just hurting yourself; you are not hurting the other person. It is like throwing good money after bad. Keep your wits, keep your humour and if you are a good man, luck will come your way again. You will see another opportunity and you will grasp it. I have always believed that.

"But business is about taking and not just giving. I came up the hard school. In an arena where no holds are barred you have to win. Giving is for my charity side. I had wanted to build a charitable foundation with $10 billion in cash.

"A big American financial company did the dirtiest thing to me. I lost more than two billion cash with them in 2007-2008. They sold me toxic derivatives. One day a senior staff member of the company came to me. He came from a very poor family. My heart went out to him. He came to me one day, at this table, and said he was off to London that evening. "I want you to take up this type of trading", he said, and for more than one hour I couldn't understand what he was trying to sell me. It still makes no sense to me. I asked him what was the most that I could lose, give me the bottom line and he lied. The worst as it turned out was a 1,000 times worse. I said no but eventually I gave in.

"To get me out the company sent a team to Hong Kong to extract me from hell. We kept paying and paying up cash. I tried to get lawyers but you don't know how ugly American capitalism can be. They had sown up every top financial lawyer in Hong Kong; none would work for me against the company. They had signed up every lawyer against me. I now regret sending my children to US universities.

"But did they receive a good education there?" I asked.

"What is education? I never finished my tertiary but I can write a good business letter and do mental arithmetic sums quickly."

"Out of all the great people you have met," I asked, "Who is the one that you most admire?

"Deng Xiaoping. That was real greatness", he replied. "I never met Mao."

"You have known a few dictators," I ventured tentatively, not sure how he would react. "Does absolute power corrupt?" I asked.

"There is some truth in that statement. But do not only use the word "power". Enormous greed corrupts the soul even more. Anything excessive has strong deleterious effects. Then again, it is an over-simplification if you apply it to every happening. It is obviously true if you apply the word "corrupt" in its dictionary sense. But if you use the word "corrupt" to mean "takes bribes" then it is not necessarily true. Some political leaders I have known have never taken a bribe in their life. But they became dictatorial; they would hound their political enemies all the way.

"One piece of advice: never hug the high and mighty; they electrocute you. Keep them at arms length.

And always adhere to moral practices and nothing can stop you. If someone asks you for a bribe you should say that neither you nor your company could do that. But stay very polite. Don't stand on your high horse and preach morality at that moment. Just turn them down nicely. If you get a chance later at a meal or something you can pontificate a little, but not then - they are not in the mood to be listening to moral truth.

"I have a simple motto in life: everything single material thing that I have in life can be traded. It is for sale. It is a question of, when, where, to whom and price. The first three are more important. If you like a person the price becomes unimportant.

"Business is quite a game but at the end you want to use your money to help those that need help. We have a very good charitable foundation that is opening the darkened skies above a little more than 30 poor and backward villages in China and adding."

"What is the thing that you are most proud of in your life?" I asked. It was my penultimate question.

"I have never indulged myself in pride. I don't understand that feeling. I really don't. I can understand some people luxuriating in the thought that they created something. For me it is always work, a job that needs to be done."

"Finally, Robert," I asked. "What advice would you give to someone starting out in business today?

"I would tell them to go east and make their fortune. What you are seeing in China is still only the beginning."

Food prices

5.1 Markets are not perfect

The U.S. Commodity Futures Trading Commission (CFTC) defines a speculator as

"A trader who does not hedge, but who trades with the objective of achieving profits through the successful anticipation of price movements."

On a macro level commodity trading is a zero sum game; if a speculator correctly predicts prices - and in the process makes a profit - that profit has to come from somewhere. It may come from a farmer who receives less income for his sugarcane or from a consumer who has to pay more for his sugar. Alternatively, it may come from other actors in the supply chain, a refiner, distributor or wholesaler. It may simply come from another speculator; one person's loss is another's gain.

However speculators in the commodity markets do add value to the supply chain; the game is not as zero-sum, as it may seem at first sight. A speculator plays an important role in bearing some of the price risk in the market. A sugar producer may think that prices will increase but he won't want to "bet the farm" on it. He may be willing to carry some price risk but he will want to lay off some on someone else. A speculator may be happy to absorb that price risk. The speculator can therefore add liquidity to a market by buying when a producer wants to sell or selling when a consumer wants to buy.

Speculators sometimes drive prices higher or lower more quickly than they would otherwise move; this allows the price signal to get more quickly to the producer or the consumer. An earlier price signal will give a producer more time to expand or contract production and it will give a consumer more time to adjust his sugar use.

Speculators can sometimes drive prices higher or lower than they would otherwise be – or at least should be. This is what the CFTC calls "excessive" speculation, defined as *"harmful to the proper functioning of futures markets"*. However a speculator will usually lose money if he buys something at a price higher than its "fundamental" value or if he sells it below its "fundamental" value. If he or she persists in doing this, he or she will go broke. In theory, therefore, markets should rarely go to excessive levels. But who determines what are "excessive" levels – and what is "excessive" speculation?

There is an old saying in the commodity markets that "trees do not grow to the sky". If there is a shortage of a particular commodity the price will rise to encourage producers to produce more and for consumers to consume less. If corn prices rise farmers will react by planting more corn. As a result of this increased production, corn prices will fall. If soybean prices fall, animal feed manufacturers will use more beans in their feed mix and less, say, wheat. The same applies to metals: prices go up and more mines open; prices go down and they close.

Of course there is a time lag in all this, a variable one depending on the commodity. If corn prices rise farmers can increase production within a year. If rubber prices increase it could take a few years for the rubber trees to be planted, mature and produce rubber. And if copper prices rise it could take even longer to get all the environmental permits to open, or reopen, a mine.

Commodity prices fluctuate continuously as the market moves to match supply with demand. Markets are usually pretty good at their job and it is unusual for them to get it wrong. (There is an old saying in the markets that "the price is always right".) Although price nearly always makes sure that supply equals demand, that price may be unacceptable (or at the least uncomfortable) for many in the market. The price may be too high for some consumers to be able to buy that commodity – or as much of that commodity as they would like. On the other hand the price might be too low and drive a farmer to bankruptcy.

Speculators can distort markets by exaggerating the supply and demand. As we saw in the previous chapter, at the time of writing the speculators are short of (have sold without owning) around four million tons of sugar futures. Having sold this quantity they have in the short term temporarily increased the supply of sugar futures. It is almost certain that prices would have been higher if they had not sold so much.

Speculative activity can exaggerate price moves in the short term. Speculators can push prices both too high and too low and this can send misleading or incorrect signals to both producers and consumers. In the case of sugar, during the price spike in 2011 to nearly 35 c/lb (US$ 770/tonne) speculators were long of (owned) more than 11 million tons of sugar futures on the New York ICE sugar market. This massive position almost certainly help prices to move higher than they otherwise would have and almost certainly encouraged farmers to increase production over and above what was needed to satisfy demand. In the same way during the recent price collapse to 12 c/lb the speculators were short (had sold without already owning) about 6.5 million tons of ICE futures. It is unlikely that prices would have fallen so far or so fast if the speculators had had no position.

However these price exaggerations are almost always short-lived. In the long term prices revert to what economists call the "equilibrium price", the price at which the marginal supply of a commodity equals the marginal demand for that commodity. The equilibrium price is usually said to be the cost of producing an extra (or marginal) unit of that commodity in the most efficient producer; economists call this the "marginal cost of production". No matter how high or how low commodity prices go in the short term they should revert in the long term to a price equal to the marginal cost of production in the most efficient producer.

Equity (share) prices do not follow the same laws. Equities can "grow to the sky", increasing in value in line with the general growth in the economy. There may be good years and bad years (and the occasional crash) in equity markets but if you hold on to them long enough, equities should increase in value in line with economic growth. This is not the case in commodities.

There is therefore a fundamental difference between equities and commodities. Equity "investors" buy shares in a company and hold on to them; commodity "speculators" bet that a particular commodity price will move up or down in the short term as a result of some weather event or political upheaval.

Winston Churchill once said that democracy was the worst form of government, except for all those other forms that have been tried from time to time. He could have said the same thing about markets.

Markets are imperfect; they always have been and always will be. Over time various governments – and international agencies - have tried to find a better solution than price to match supply and demand. Their preferred method was to first try to work out what the demand was for a particular commodity and then set a system of production quotas to make sure that supply was in line with that perceived demand. A price was then set for that production at a level that was perceived as "fair" for both consumer and producer.

One of the problems with this system is that it is difficult to work out what the actual demand is for a commodity, especially on an international level. However the main difficulty is in deciding at what level to set the price. Set it too low and production may fall below what is needed; set it too high and the producer extracts a "quota rent", paid for by the consumer. If the price is too high production quotas can become extremely valuable and, if they are tradable, can be sold at a good price.

Another thing that is wrong with production quotas and fixed prices is that they often result in all the benefits of technological change going to the producer and none to the consumer. Over the past thirty years there have been considerable improvement in beet yields and processing efficiency and this has significantly lowered production costs. Within the EU at least sugar prices have been consistently raised in line with inflation. This significantly increased producer margins and made production quotas extremely valuable. During the 1990s French farmers called sugar production quotas "white gold".

However the biggest problem when government committees, rather than markets, set prices is that the system is rigid and unresponsive. When production is affected by bad weather – as it often is - prices don't change and demand does not react. Demand therefore stays the same while supply falls and this can lead to shortages. By fixing prices the government can cause shortages. It is ironic therefore that governments often blame a shortage of something on speculators.

There have been various attempts over the years to fix sugar and other commodity prices on a global rather than a national level. In the case of sugar, and under the first International Sugar Agreements, each sugar producing country was given a fixed production or export quota. If prices fell below a certain predetermined "fair" price, then each country had to hold back a certain percentage of their production as stocks. When prices rose again, those countries were supposed to release their stocks and dampen prices.

In practice producers were reluctant to hold stocks when prices fell; they needed the money to pay their beet or cane farmers. When prices increased the stocks that should have been there weren't there. In the end the various sugar agreements created more price volatility than would have existed without them. Fixing a price that is "fair" to both consumers and producers is a lovely idea but it simply does not work in practice.

5.2 Commodity Index Funds

A commodity index fund is similar to an equity index fund; the money in the fund is invested in futures contracts based on, or linked to, a commodity price index. The value of these indexes fluctuates based on their underlying commodities, and this value can be traded on an exchange in much the same way as stock index futures. The price index can either be representative of the broad commodity asset class or can be a specific subset of commodities, such as energy or agriculture.

The S&P GSCI (formerly the Goldman Sachs Commodity Index) is probably the best known and the most widely followed of the indexes. It was created by Goldman Sachs in 1991 but was sold in 2007 to Standard & Poor's, a division of McGraw Hill Financial. At the time of writing the S&P GSCI is made up of 24 commodities from all commodity sectors - energy products, industrial metals, agricultural products, livestock products and precious metals. The wide range of constituent commodities provides the S&P GSCI with a level of diversification that reduces the impact of individual market events, which have large implications for the individual commodity markets but are minimised when aggregated to the level of the S&P GSCI.

The Bloomberg Commodity Index (BCOM) is probably the second most widely followed commodity price index. The index was originally launched in 1998 as the Dow Jones-AIG Commodity Index (DJ-AIGCI) and renamed as the Dow Jones-UBS Commodity Index (DJ-UBSCI) in 2009, when UBS acquired the index from AIG. The index was rebranded under its current name in July 2014. The BCOM currently has 22 commodity futures in seven sectors. No single commodity can compose less than 2% or more than 15% of the index, and no sector can represent more than 33% of the index (as of the annual weightings of the components). The weightings for each commodity included in the BCOM are calculated to ensure that the relative proportion of each of the underlying individual commodities reflects its global economic significance and market liquidity.

The Thomson Reuters/Jefferies CRB Index (TR/J CRB) was first calculated by Commodity Research Bureau, Inc. in 1957 and was originally composed of 28 commodities, 26 of which were traded on futures exchanges and two in cash markets. Its components and formula have been periodically adjusted and it is currently made up of 19 commodities.

The Rogers International Commodity Index (RICI) is a broad index of commodity futures designed by Jim Rogers in 1996/1997. The index tracks 38 commodity futures contracts from 13 international exchanges and is divided into three sub-indices: RICI Agriculture, RICI Energy and RICI Metals.

Although these indexes have been around for a while they initially attracted little interest from the investing public. Commodities were largely viewed as both too speculative and too specialised for an outside investor. You really had to be an expert in sugar to invest in sugar – and you had to be an expert in pork bellies to invest in pork bellies. The price of each commodity, whether it be sugar or pork bellies, depended on a whole range of commodity-specific fundamental information that needed to be analysed on an individual basis: pork prices could go down because of changing eating habits and a decrease in demand for bacon; sugar prices could go up because of a drought in Thailand. There was little to no correlation between the two commodities.

In addition, each individual market was relatively small compared to the equity markets, too illiquid to absorb large inflows of investor money from, say, a major pension fund. Most importantly, however, commodities were not considered worthy of investor (as opposed to speculative) interest as they were "mean-reverting": they reverted over time to the marginal cost of production in the most efficient producer.

This way of thinking was fundamentally challenged in 2005 when Gary Gorton (then of Wharton) and Geert Rounwehorst (of Yale) published *"Facts and Fantasies About Commodities Futures"*. (1) The abstract of their paper reads as follows:

"We construct an equally-weighted index of commodity futures monthly returns over the period between July of 1959 and December of 2004 in order to study simple properties of commodity futures as an asset class. Fully collateralized commodity futures have historically offered the same return and Sharpe ratio as equities. While the risk premium on commodity futures is essentially the same as equities, commodity futures returns are negatively correlated with equity returns and bond returns. The negative correlation between commodity futures and the other asset classes is due, in significant part, to different behaviour over the business cycle. In addition, commodity futures are positively correlated with inflation, unexpected inflation, and changes in expected inflation."

In other words, if you look at a basket of commodities, rather than just one particular commodity, the authors found that commodity prices are inversely correlated with the prices of bonds and equities and positively correlated with inflation. The report was like an electric shock to the investment industry. It had particular significance for the pension funds that were looking both for a hedge against inflation and a hedge against those horrid years when bond and equity prices fell. When equity prices fall, the report basically concluded, the losses on your portfolio would be offset by increases in commodity prices. (Of course no one thought too much about the years when equity prices rise but commodity prices fall and when portfolio gains on equities are offset by portfolio losses on commodities. But that's another story.)

Pension funds reacted quickly to the report; they loved the idea that commodity indexes could be used as a hedge both against inflation and against a fall in bond and equity prices. The pension funds also loved the idea of investing in commodities as a way of taking part in the China growth story. The study hit the financial press at about the same time as the world generally was getting excited about China and the country's apparently insatiable appetite for commodities. Iron ore and copper was needed to build skyscrapers and roads, while soybeans were needed to fatten the pigs to meet China's growing demand for meat.

After a decade or more of price stagnation and under-investment, commodity producers were ill equipped to meet this enormous surge in demand from China; supply bottlenecks built up everywhere. New mines had to be dug. More oil had to be discovered. More land had to be cleared for agriculture. All this took time. And in the meantime prices surged higher.

Rising demand from China was a game changer for the world's commodity markets and caused something approaching near panic among the world's concerned classes. To give just one example, Chinese per capita meat consumption in 1980 was 20 kg per year but by 2007 it had risen to 50 kg per year. "Just imagine if the Chinese end up eating as much meat as Americans (125 kg per year)", the concerned classes argued. "The world will not be able to produce all the grains required to feed those farm animals. Prices will have to rise to ration demand".

Pension funds rushed into commodities and a whole industry quickly grew up around commodity index fund management, most of it within the banks. The banks built up large commodity trading desks that not only managed the investment flows but also traded around those flows.

The most common way banks did this was by anticipating "the roll". A bank would know in advance that their index fund clients would have to "roll" their long positions from the spot futures contract (that was about to expire) to the next futures contract. They could easily and legally put on positions ahead of that role.

Index fund investors often lose money when they roll from one futures contract month to another. By pushing forward prices higher than they might otherwise be they encourage extra production that depresses prices once those crops hit the market place. As index funds buy forward and sell spot they often buy high and sell low. This is called a "roll loss": the money that is lost when they have to sell out their longs in a month that is expiring and replace (buy back) those longs in the next, higher priced, futures months.

In a "surplus" market where the supply of a physical commodity exceeds the demand for that physical commodity, the excess has to be stored until sometime in the future when it might be needed. But people will only store a commodity if they can think they will be able to sell it at a higher price in the future than they can now. If sugar is in over-supply the price needs to be higher in the future than it is now to offset the cost of storing the excess sugar until it is needed. This market "structure" is called a "contango" or "carrying charge".

In times of shortage the people that don't need the commodity straight away can run down their stocks and delay their purchases until the shortage is over. But people with no stocks will have no choice but to pay up and buy now. This can result in a market structure where spot prices are higher than forward prices; it is called an "inverse" or a "backwardation".

As most commodities are in oversupply most of the time, forward prices are usually higher than the spot prices. This means that index funds usually lose money when they roll their positions forward; in the jargon this is called "a negative roll return". To offset this negative roll return commodity index fund investors need outright prices to rise to make money. They lose money if outright prices remain unchanged.

The CFTC first differentiated the Index Funds from the other speculators in their COT (Commitment of Traders) report in January 2007. At that time the index funds were already long (owned) 7.8 million tons of sugar futures on the NY ICE exchange. Over the next few years they continued to buy and their position peaked in May 2008 at just below 20 million tons of sugar futures.

All this began to attract the attention of the media and the general public, especially as it coincided with rising food prices. Well-meaning commentators naturally blamed the increase in food prices – as well as the ensuing food riots in a number of countries - on speculators, most particularly on the arrival of index fund investors into the commodity markets.

But were commodity prices rising because investors were holding supply off the market and pushing food prices out of the reach of a hungry population? Or were investors flocking to the commodity markets because prices were rising because of increased demand and supply bottlenecks coupled with a run of bad weather and poor harvests? Public opinion went with the first explanation, arguing that speculators (and index funds in particular) were pushing up food prices. Many called for the futures markets to be closed (markets were closed in India even though India doesn't have any commodity index funds) and pressure was put on the banks to stop investing in commodities (and some did).

In 2010 an article in Harper's magazine accused Goldman Sachs of profiting while people went hungry or even starved. The article argued that Goldman's large purchases of long-options on wheat futures created a demand shock in the wheat market, which disturbed the normal relationship between supply and demand and pushed up prices.

However a report in 2010 by the Organisation for Economic Co-operation and Development (OECD) found that there was

"no convincing evidence that positions held by index traders…impact market returns".

The OECD argued that there was no correlation between the size of index fund positions in particular commodities and the price rise for those raw materials.

The OECD also pointed out that commodities without futures markets – and hence without any index fund involvement - also saw price increases during the period.

However, others have argued that the commodities without futures markets saw their prices rise as a consequence of the rising prices of commodities with futures markets: for example there is a case to be made that the rising price of wheat caused the price of rice to subsequently rise. The UN Conference on Trade and Development (UNCTAD) said index traders

"Can significantly influence prices and create speculative bubbles, with extremely detrimental effects on normal trading activities and market efficiency."(2)

Some academic research bore this out. Ke Tang of Tsinghua University and Wei Xiong of Princeton University found that "financialisation" made ostensibly different commodities such as grains and oil more closely correlated after 2004. Prof Wei wrote that the trend was

"related to large inflows of investment capital to commodity index securities during this period",.

Having said that, commodity index investing is different from equity index investing. When investors hold equities, either individually or via an index fund, those equities are removed from the market. As a result there is a reduced supply of those equities available for others to purchase: the mere fact of holding those equities off the market can, if demand remains constant, result in higher prices.

When a commodity index fund buys and holds commodity futures the supply of those futures is reduced and prices can rise as a result. However while an equity fund can hold a particular equity forever, a commodity fund can't. As the futures contract (or month, as it is often called) approaches expiry, the fund will either have to take delivery of the underlying commodity or it will have to sell out their longs in the expiring futures contract and buy them back in the next futures contract.

Contracts expire in the raw sugar futures market at the end of February, April, June and September; at each expiry index funds have to sell out their longs in the nearby contract and replace those longs further down the board (in other words, buy a futures contract for a later delivery). If anything, this process results in index funds pushing down the prices of commodities for nearby delivery and pushing up the prices of commodities for future delivery.

Farmers react to high forward prices by planting more, thus increasing supply. And then once that extra supply is produced, the index funds that have bought it forward have no choice but to "dump" the extra production and push down the prices for immediate delivery. (Remember a commodity for immediate delivery is called "spot". The market for commodities for immediate delivery is called a "spot market".) Consumers rarely buy forward and usually buy "spot". For this reason, the index funds are inadvertently part of the solution, rather than being part of the problem: they increase prices for producers and reduce prices for consumers.

When the sugar market peaked at 35 c/lb in February 2011 the index funds owned slightly more than 8.3 million tons of New York ICE sugar futures. By the time the sugar price had fallen to 12 c/lb in February 2015 the index funds owned 11.6 million tons of sugar futures. In spite of their buying of 3.3 million tons of futures over the period the price of sugar had been divided by three. It is almost certain that if the price had risen during that period the index funds would have been blamed for some of that rise. But it is difficult to say that the index funds have influenced the price of sugar given the way prices have fallen.

But how have those index fund investors fared over the past few years? Remember the rationale for investing in an index fund was that it offered similar returns to equities but moved out of step with both stocks and bonds. After the 2008 financial crisis commodity prices crashed with equities and traded tightly in line with the stock market over the years that followed, providing no diversification. When they finally parted company, commodities tumbled while stocks roared ahead. At the time of writing, the Bloomberg Commodity Index has lost 37% on a total return basis since early 2011.

In response to negative criticism, Gary Gorton and K Geert Rouwenhorst published fresh research supporting their original, controversial conclusions. (3) The new paper acknowledges that after 2005 commodities did move more closely in line with other asset classes and with each other, especially during the financial crisis. The correlation between commodities and stocks — negative before — became strongly positive after 2005, which was just when asset owners most needed some protection from the crash in equities. This was disastrous for risk managers; institutions' commodity investments had failed to spread or reduce their risk as intended.

Lately, correlations have returned almost to zero. This is true even though index investors still make up 24% of the open interest in major commodities. (4) The authors argue that the return to low correlations suggests commodities are once more driven by supply and demand in their own markets, and not by fears in the stock and bond markets. Therefore, they do offer some hedge or diversification for big asset managers.

However investors remain sceptical as to whether investing in a broad range of commodities is a good idea. It seemed to be when the tide from China's rapid industrialisation was lifting all boats, just as it was when South Korea and Japan were going through rapid industrialisation in the 1970s. But with China's growth rate slowing the tide has long since ebbed.

The last year that investors pumped net cash into commodity index swaps was 2010. A trickle of outflows since then became a torrent in 2014, when investors pulled out $24.2 billion, reducing the value of commodity assets under management to $67 billion from a pre-crisis high of more than $150 billion. In 2015 the $36.4 billion Harvard University endowment cut its target portfolio for commodities to zero. It had been as high as 8% in 2008.

It is therefore probably best not to buy commodities as some sort of hedge against bonds, inflation or equities. Rather you should only buy them if you think they will go up in price.

5.3 Food price inflation

Although the media and the general public only really pay attention to food prices when they rise, high food prices are not bad for everyone. High food prices favour rural areas but penalise the urban poor. City dwellers in poor countries are among the worst affected by high food prices. In Nigeria, for example, food accounts for a third of total consumer spending while in China the figure is 25%. In the UK food accounts for around 7% of total consumer spending and in the USA it accounts for around 5% - enough to moan about but not enough to provoke a riot.

Back in 1798 the English clergyman Reverend Robert Malthus wrote his famous *"Essay on the Principle of Population"* in which he argued that the world's population would eventually be checked by famine. Malthus argued that the world's food supply grew arithmetically while the world's population grew geometrically. He wrote,

"The power of population is indefinitely greater than the power in the earth to produce subsistence for man".

He believed that God had made it thus to teach mankind "virtuous" behaviour. Malthus believed that the increase in the world's population would be limited by the means of subsistence and he predicted a future of "misery and vice".

Luckily for all of us he was wrong (so far at least). There is no limit to man's ingenuity (when tested) and there has been a massive increase in agricultural yields since Malthus wrote his treaty. Farming and crop breeding techniques have improved significantly and food production per hectare is now way above what it was 200 years ago. The mass starvation that he predicted has not happened.

That is not to deny the global tragedy that an estimated 870 million people in the world go to bed hungry every night. The question that has to be asked is why that should happen when the world as a whole has never recently been short of food – and when a large percentage of the world's population is suffering from too much food. What is going wrong?

As I mentioned in Chapter Three, the FAO estimates that each year about one third of all food for human consumption, around 1.3 billion tons, is wasted, along with the energy, water and chemicals needed both to produce it and dispose of it.

In the developed world, much of the waste comes from consumers buying too much and throwing it away once it is past its sell-by date. In developing countries the wastage is mainly a function of inefficient farming (particularly harvesting) and a lack of proper storage and logistics facilities.

The FAO has estimated that in 2013 the cost of wasted food, excluding fish and seafood, at $570 billion - based on producer prices.

Wastage through poor farming techniques and inefficient supply lines is part of the problem but ill-advised government policies can also negatively impact food supply. Well-intentioned governments often try to fix food prices at a level low enough for the poorest people to be able to buy what they need. The problem is that these prices are often too low for a farmer to be able to grow and harvest his crop. If the price at which he can sell his production this year does not cover the cost of producing it he may not farm next year.

But the blame cannot be laid solely at the door of naïve but well-meaning governments in developing countries. The rich world heavily subsidises it own agriculture. This often leads to over-production that is then exported, often with even more subsidies. These exports can reduce world food prices, discouraging food production in the less efficient agriculture regions in developing countries. They can drive farmers off their fields and into the cities. This increases the number of urban poor, exacerbating the problem.

The same can sometimes apply to food aid – food that the rich countries give to poor ones. The aid agencies do a tremendous job in helping to tackle starvation caused by war or a localised crop failure. However, long-term food aid can depress food prices in receiving countries and discourage local farmers from planting crops again once the weather turns better.

The only long-term solution to global hunger is not to drive food prices lower but to raise the incomes of poor people through sound government policies that promote education, medical care and economic growth. Low food prices only result in less food being produced, they aggravate the problem. And food prices are returning to previous low levels. At the time of writing (June 2015) the FAO Food Price Index (5) stands at 166.8 points, down 20.7% on June 2014 and its lowest level since September 2009.

Between 2005 and 2008 Mexico suffered a serious of bad harvests and by 2008 there were demonstrations in the streets of Mexico against high food prices. By 2013 the weather and the harvests had improved and it was the farmers' turn to take to the streets, protesting against low food prices. What goes around comes around.

From Farm to Fork

6.1 What do traders do?

I began my career as a trainee commodity trader in September 1978. My employer's UK office was in Maidenhead, a pleasant but nondescript town on the River Thames. After a three-month training period I was allocated to the soymeal desk, given a list of farmers throughout the UK and told to call them up and sell them soymeal for animal feed.

What the other traders on the desk didn't tell me was that the company had in one way or another upset all the clients on the list; they had all sworn never to buy soymeal from the company ever again. My success was, as you might imagine, limited.

But the problem was deeper than that. I had grown up on a farm and was familiar with the grain merchants that used to visit my father to either sell him animal feed or to buy the wheat or barley that we grew. (My father said the merchants were all crooks, but that's by the by.) I had gone to university to escape from the farm and in my new job I suddenly found myself back there again, even if on the other side of the fence. This was not what I had had in mind.

In addition, my girlfriend at that time lived in London and it was pretty much impossible to do a daily commute from London to Maidenhead. When you are 21 years old these things matter a lot.

After a couple of frustrating months I heard that there was a position open for a trainee on the company's sugar trading desk in the City of London. I applied for the position, along with another graduate, and we journeyed up to London together. I can't remember the name of the other applicant but he had been doing quite a bit of research into the sugar business and seemed even more desperate than I to get out of Maidenhead.

The interview wasn't much of an interview. It consisted of the head of the trading desk taking us both out to lunch and getting us drunk. (Remember that this was 1978: it wouldn't happen now!) He then found an excuse to send us both back, but at different times, to the office. The other applicant left first but never made it back to the office. Somehow I did. I got the job by default.

I moved to London but once there I found out that my girlfriend had one boyfriend for the week and one (me) for the weekend. I told her that she had to choose between the two of us and she chose the week rather than the weekend. She left me but I was stuck with the sugar business for the rest of my life.

Commodity trading is usually defined as "storing and/or transporting and/or processing a commodity from when, when, or in what form it is not needed to when, where or in what form it is needed". (1) That definition is quite a mouthful.

A more fun definition, at least in the world of sugar, is "selling something that you don't have to someone that doesn't want it."

Commodity traders and commodity trading companies (or "trade houses" as they are called) have been around since mankind started to plant crops.

Anyone who bought grain from a farmer, transported it to a local village market and then resold it on to a consumer was a commodity trader.

The miller in Chaucer's *Canterbury Tales*, written in the fourteenth century, was a commodity trader. He processed something that nobody could use in its current form (wheat) into something that they could use (flour). Incidentally, the miller was drunk when he told his tale on the road to Canterbury, a story of extra-marital sex and general debauchery. So even back then, traders had quite a reputation.

The role of trade houses is to transport, store and process commodities. In addition they may provide finance, advice and risk management services to their clients. They may, for example, lend money to a sugar mill before the harvest starts, enabling the mill to pay the farmers for their cane and to pay the workers to run the factory. Trade houses may also advise the sugar mill owners on how and when to sell or price their production, as well as manage any futures position that the mill might have.

Contrary to what you might imagine, trade houses like to limit their exposure to the outright, or flat, price of a commodity. They usually hedge their flat price risk, preferring to make their money elsewhere, namely on "differentials".

These differentials may be the difference between the price of the physical commodity relative to the underlying futures contract. They may be the difference between the price of a commodity in one region compared to another. Or they may be the difference in price between one quality and another; an example would be the difference between the price of the raw material and the processed product.

They may also be the difference in price at different times. At harvest time farmers are keen to cash in their crop and may depress the price when they all try to sell at the same time. When this happens traders can lock in a margin by buying the crop from the farmer, storing (and financing) it and then selling it on to the consumer or processor at a later date.

Virtually all commodities are processed before they are consumed: sugar, produced from either sugarcane or sugar beet, is no exception. Admittedly you can chew on a stick of sugarcane to obtain the sucrose containing juice - and this is still common practice in many countries at harvest time. As far as I know, however, no one chews on sugar beet directly, although it is often fed as winter fodder to cattle.

Sugarcane needs to be processed before it can be consumed and it needs to be processed as soon as possible after it has been harvested. Cane is a perishable commodity that cannot be transported over long distances or stored for long periods: as such it is only traded locally between farmers and mills - and almost never internationally.

Sugar beet has a longer "shelf life". Farmers harvest the beet in winter, often racing to get the crop harvested before the ground freezes. Once the farmers have harvested the beets they often "store" them in piles (called "silos") at the sides of their fields; they then gradually transport them to the factory for processing. As long as the weather stays cool and dry the beets deteriorate little in their silos. However alternating periods of freezing and warm weather can turn the beets into mush, making them difficult if not impossible to process. Like sugarcane, beets only tend to trade locally – and almost never internationally.

International traders, therefore, trade sugar, not sugarcane or sugar beet. Sugar can be transported long distances and can be stored for up to (usually) eighteen months without deteriorating. Sugar from cane goes through an intermediary "raw" stage before being processed (refined) into white sugar. White sugar is produced directly from sugar beet without going through an intermediary "raw" stage. Raw sugar, because it is transported and stored in bulk (and not bags), is not usually considered fit for direct human consumption. White sugar is usually stored and transported in bags (which are often now placed in shipping containers). However white sugar is also often now transported in bulk in "food grade" (usually aluminium) tanks, trucks and railcars.

In the sugar market, therefore, sugar traders are usually either "white sugar" traders or "raw sugar" traders. Most big trading companies trade both raw and white sugar but usually on separate trading desks. Although the prices of raw and white sugar are correlated, they are different markets with different participants. In any particular importing country there may be multiple buyers of white sugar but only a limited number of raw sugar buyers.

Many commodities undergo multiple transformations between the farm and the final consumer. Soybeans need to be stored, transported and crushed before they are consumed. Crude oil needs to be refined before it can be used as a fuel in a car. Sugarcane needs to be crushed and the resulting juice crystallised (and then usually refined) before it can be burnt as fuel in a body. Trading companies add value in the supply chain by storing, financing, transporting and processing crops.

Although that sounds easy, it isn't. During harvest time there may not be enough trucks to move the sugar to the ports or enough warehouse space to store it in once it arrives at the ports. In the case of raw sugar there may be insufficient elevator capacity to load the sugar onto the ships that are waiting at the port. If it is white sugar there may not be enough space on the container ship to take all the sugar that a trader may want to ship.

Commodity trading companies have to operate within a myriad of different laws and regulations that often change without warning. Governments may set import quotas – or in some cases ban imports – to protect their own farmers and keep domestic prices higher than world prices.

Without an import licence a trader can't take advantage of the arbitrage between world and domestic prices. And even if governments don't restrict imports by quantity they may set quality restrictions: Japan's insistence (until recently) on importing only low quality raw sugar was based on a desire to protect their domestic refining industry.

Commodity trading companies also have to operate within financial constraints. A trade house may see a profitable opportunity to ship Brazilian raw sugar to China but not have the bank lines (the finance) to do as much as they might like.

Traders may be constrained by their internal risk management departments. A trader may see a profitable opportunity to (again) sell Brazilian raw sugar to a Chinese refinery but the trading house will want to limit their financial exposure to any individual company in case that company goes out of business or does not honour its contracts. In addition, a trading house's risk management department will almost always place risk limits on the amount of financial exposure to any particular country.

To be able to take advantage of profitable trading opportunities – and to add value to the supply chain – the trading company will have to know how and where to find those opportunities: in fact, not only to find them but to anticipate them. Information and analysis is the lifeblood of trading. It is almost impossible to succeed in the commodity markets without a global information network and an experienced group of traders and analysts to interpret and understand that information.

In addition, it is almost impossible to make money in the physical commodity business without a network of clients. To take our earlier example it is no use knowing that you can make money exporting raw sugar from Brazil into China if you don't know anyone in Brazil to buy sugar from or in China to sell sugar to. Traders have to keep regular contact with their networks, even if it means trading the occasional business at a loss. Traders often rightly argue that you have to be in it to win it.

One of the major difficulties that trade houses now face is that information is widely and freely available. It also travels incredibly fast. Back in the 1980s traders had little way of knowing how the Russian or Brazilian crops were progressing without physically going there – and even then they could never physically cover the whole growing area. Now they can get the latest information just sitting in their offices in London or Singapore. This means that a trade house's office in Sao Paulo or Krasnodar becomes less of an advantage and more of a cost.

Although it is hard to imagine now, a trader who wanted to make a telephone call from London to Moscow back in the 1980s had to book the call a week in advance. Similarly, up until the advent of fax machines, Indonesian sugar importers received price indications by mail, posted from London on a Friday evening and arriving a week later. Compare that to now when anyone can get the latest prices instantly. Technological change has reduced the potential for traders to profitably arbitrage between geographical regions.

The world is also better educated. Back in the 1980s a sugar importer in a developing country would probably have left school when he was twelve; he would have had little understanding of world markets. Today the chances are that she will have been educated at Harvard or Yale and have as good an understanding of the world sugar market as a trader at an international trade house. Having better educated clients has reduced the ability of the international trade houses to make money from contract terms, particularly from tolerances on the shipped tonnage and on the shipment periods.

In the 1980s it was common to have a 5-10% tonnage tolerance for shipping purposes. Traders who sold sugar on a cost and freight basis to destination would often sell, say, 25,000 tonnes plus or minus 10% at seller's option. The seller could at his discretion ship any tonnage between 27,500 tonnes and 22,500 tonnes. In theory this was to make it easier for the trader to find a suitably sized vessel in which to ship the sugar. In reality, the trader would decide on the quantity to ship depending on what the market price did between the moment he made the contract and the time he shipped the sugar. If the price fell during that interim period the trader would maximise the shipment quantity, buying in the extra sugar that he needed at a lower price. If the price rose he would minimise the shipment quantity and sell out, to another buyer, the unshipped quantity at a higher price.

It was effectively a free option around which the trader could trade risk free. And with any luck the market price would fluctuate many times either side of the sale price between the time of the sale and the time of the shipment. This would allow the trader to repeatedly buy the extra quantity when the market price was below the sale price and sell out the surplus quantity when it was above – all risk free.

The most famous example of this in sugar was when a major US trade house sold 600,000 tonnes of raw sugar to China with a tolerance of plus or minus 10%. The Chinese understood this to mean that each shipment of (at the time) 25,000 tonnes would have a tolerance of 10%. The trade house interpreted the contract as meaning that they could sell at their choice – and depending on what happened to the market price – either 540,000 tonnes or 660,000 tonnes.

It is perhaps not surprising that sugar importers no longer accept shipping tolerances and only buy on "min/max" terms where the quantity is fixed at the time of the contract.

In the 1980s it was also not unusual for producers to sell long shipment periods of up to six or even, occasionally, twelve months. This gave the trade houses flexibility as to when they shipped the sugar. If prices for nearby shipment were lower than for deferred shipment then the trade house would ship the sugar at the end of the shipment period. If prices were higher at the beginning of the shipment period than they were at the end then they would ship it as early as possible.

The other major change – and this one is definitely for the good - is that governments and government agencies have largely got out of the commodity business. In the 1980s governments were usually responsible for ensuring an adequate supply of sugar for their population and would import (or export sugar) accordingly. This led to an enormous opportunity for corruption. Low paid government officials were easy targets for unscrupulous traders; official buying or selling tenders were often rigged in favour of the traders that paid the biggest bribes.

Happily the world sugar trade has now largely been privatised and these opportunities have disappeared. Private importers or refiners now meet import needs, not government agencies. These private companies have no interest in accepting a bribe. And even if a salaried employee of one of these companies did take a bribe (to sell sugar at a lower price than the market or to buy sugar at a higher price than the market), the market is sufficiently transparent that he would be quickly found out.

All these changes have reduced arbitrage opportunities and made it harder for traders to make money. Some trade houses have embraced and adapted to this new environment and thrived as a result; others have continued to do the same thing in the hope of a different, better outcome – Einstein's definition of madness.

6.2 How have traders adapted?

Over the past twenty years trade houses have sought out alternative and additional sources of revenue by investing both upstream and downstream. At one end of the scale a trade house may have a small factory in an importing country that repacks white sugar from the 50 kg bags that are used for international trade into one kg retail bags. At the other end of the scale a trade house may have a significant investment in sugar mills and cane plantations. In the middle they may own warehouses at strategic distribution hubs or truck and rail companies, port loading refineries, shipping lines, sugar refineries and sales networks.

Probably the first upstream investments that the sugar trade houses made were in port loading terminals in Centre South Brazil. In the early nineties the region became a major sugar producer and exporter and the ports became bottlenecks. In 1993 sugar that was delivered against the expiring May futures contract in New York was still being shipped in September. Vessels waited for months to load, racking up huge costs for the trade houses involved.

A second surge in investment was made in refineries in importing countries or regions. Al Khaleej's Dubai refinery was the first of its kind and the model was quickly copied with refineries being built in Saudi Arabia, Syria Algeria, Nigeria, China, India and recently Iraq and Bahrain. The economics of destination refineries are relatively attractive. First, it is (usually) cheaper to transport raw sugar in bulk and refine it at destination than to transport white sugar in bags. Second, selling white sugar locally gives a refinery more flexibility in terms of timing and quantities than shipping it from an exporting country. Third, refineries usually have large warehouses for both raw and white sugar, allowing them to take advantage of time (calendar) spreads on both raw and white sugar. For example, a refinery can import raw sugar during the harvest when prices are lower, store it and then sell the white sugar locally throughout the year.

It was unsurprising that some of the bigger international trade houses should want to get into the refining business. Owning a refinery gives a trade house a captive home for raw sugar and a steady supply of white sugar. It is "a home of last resort" in case the trade house had to find somewhere to put a "distressed" cargo of raw sugar, one that is afloat, or soon to go afloat, unsold. Owning a refinery means owning storage capacity, enabling the trade house to profit when the market is in "contango" – a market structure where the price of forward delivery is higher than for prompt ("spot") delivery. Having this storage available can also help the trader make various "plays" on the futures markets. (But more on this in the next chapter.)

The third big wave of trade house investment was into sugar production, most notably in Brazil but also in Australia. Ethanol was the catalyst for the move into Brazilian production, spurred on by a rising oil price and environmental concerns over global warming. With the benefit of perfect hindsight the trading house investment into Brazilian sugarcane crushing has been a disaster. But why did it go so wrong? The answer is "part bad luck, part bad strategy".

The rapid expansion in the Brazilian cane sector led to a shortage of skilled workers and a sharp increase in the costs for building new mills and operating existing ones. Engineering firms could not keep pace with the demand for machinery and software and wages for engineers and technicians skyrocketed. This resulted in an inflow of inexperienced workers from other sectors; mistakes were made and efficiency lost.

On an agricultural level this inexperience led to the misuse of fertilizers and herbicides and a resulting drop in yields. This was exacerbated by a legally enforced move away from manual to mechanical cane cutting. Inexperience and a lack of training led to harvesting machines being badly adjusted. If the cutting blades were set too high they left too much cane (and sucrose) in the fields; if they were set too low they damaged the ratoons for the next harvest. In addition the heavy machines compacted the earth in the fields, making it harder for the moisture to penetrate the soil.

Some of the new mills were built in new cane areas such as Mato Grosso du Sul rather than the traditional cane areas in Parana and Sao Paulo states. These new areas had little history of cane growing and had markedly different soil types and weather patterns. The cane varieties that grew well in traditional areas often grew badly in new areas; yields disappointed.

Even when new mills were built in traditional areas they found themselves competing for cane with mills that were already there. Anyone who has ever run a factory knows that the secret to success is to run it at as close to full capacity as possible, reducing the fixed cost per unit. In every business plan that I saw at the time the new owners made their forecasts on the basis that they would have enough cane to run at, or close to, full capacity. But a series of poor weather years made planting cane difficult – as did a shortage of skilled agricultural labour.

The new entrants also underestimated the cost and difficulty of planting new cane. The cost, often running into hundreds of millions of dollars, soaked up the trade house financing and dwarfed anything that the trade houses could make in their traditional trading activities. Insufficient cane area coupled with poor yields meant there was not enough cane to keep the mills running at anything close to full capacity. This sharply increased unit production costs to a level that made them uneconomic.

The new entrants also underestimated the importance of the private growers. In Brazil an extended family would often own the mill while individual family members grew the cane. Once the mill had been sold to a trade house the family members had no particular loyalty to the buyer and felt free to sell their cane to another mill, or to plant another crop. The same applied to non-family members. Traditional mill owners realised the importance of the cane supply and cultivated their relationships with the growers. The new owners were slow to realize the importance of those relationships.

Many trade houses went into milling sugar in the belief that it was similar, say, to crushing beans or grinding flour. Bean crushers or flour grinders do not produce their own raw materials but buy them in: feedstock supply is almost never an issue. This is not the case in sugar milling: cane cannot easily be transported over long distances and mills are almost entirely dependent on local supply

There is another problem: most mills traditionally grow a significant proportion of their own cane. By getting involved in cane crushing the trade houses became involved in farming. There is an old joke about a farmer who wins the lottery. When asked what he will do with his winnings he answers, "I guess I will keep farming until they are all gone".

Farming requires a completely different mind-set than trading: farmers farm through good years and bad years. They know that they have to take a long-term view to their business. If the weather is bad one year they know that there is little that they can do but sit it out and hope it gets better. Traders however traditionally take a short-term view to their business. If they have a position that is losing money they will usually liquidate that position and move on. You can't do that with farming – or even with cane crushing. In the short-term sugar millers have little choice but to keep planting cane and maintain their machinery, even if it means putting good money after bad. Sugar traders make bad sugar millers.

Traders do however like the "optionality" that the Brazilian cane industry offers them in terms of finished products. Within the limits of their installed capacity - and the prices of the finished products - a Brazilian cane mill can choose whether to produce sugar or ethanol from their cane juice. Not only that, the mill can chose – again within the limits of the installed capacity - whether to produce anhydrous or hydrous ethanol.

Just as a reminder, anhydrous ethanol is "drier" than hydrous ethanol; it contains less water and so can be used in most petrol engines without adjustment. Hydrous ethanol contains more water and can only be burnt in specially adapted engines. More than 90% of all light vehicles sold in Brazil are now "flex-fuel": they can burn any mixture of hydrous or anhydrous ethanol or gasoline without damaging the engine.

This production flexibility gives sugarcane millers a free option. If ethanol pays more than sugar they produce more ethanol and less sugar. If sugar pays more than ethanol they produce more sugar. A lot of the new investment into the sector over the past ten years has gone into increasing the flexibility of the existing mills to choose between the two end products.

Foreign trade houses invested heavily in both "crystallisation" and "distillation" capacity: the former to "crystallise" the cane juice into sugar; the later to distil the juice into ethanol. In addition, trade houses spent heavily on dehydration columns to give them the ability to produce more anhydrous ethanol should it pay more than hydrous ethanol.

Ten to fifteen years ago, production costs in Brazil were low and mills made money. The ensuing rapid expansion of the industry, coupled with a series of poor harvests and insufficient cane, increased costs sharply, making it uneconomic for most mills to operate. At the same time a strong Brazilian economy strengthened the Brazilian Real, reducing export returns.

The strong domestic economy in Brazil also led to inflation. As part of its campaign to control inflation the Brazilian government capped domestic gasoline prices. This had two consequences. First, Petrobras (the country's petroleum company) had no choice but to import gasoline and sell it at a loss in the domestic market. Second, the low gasoline price imposed by the government meant that domestically produced ethanol could no longer compete. The country's cane sector lost money on every litre of ethanol that the mills sold.

Brazil's cane sector also had the weather against them: heavy rain slowed or prevented cane planting; dry weather in the growing season slowed cane development; a couple of severe frosts killed some cane and encouraged early flowering in other cane. (When sugarcane flowers it stops producing sucrose in the juice and uses its energy to produce the flowers.) And in the really bad years, heavy rain at harvest time slowed or prevented harvesting while washing/diluting the sucrose content of the cane.

The conclusion is that traders – or at least sugar traders - make bad farmers. However they do make good logistics operators.

6.3 Chris Mahoney: logistics maestro (2)

Chris Mahoney is Director of the Agricultural Products Business Segment at Glencore International PLC, overseeing all global farming, logistics, processing and marketing businesses, responsible for both strategy and operations.

Chris joined Glencore in September 1998. Prior to joining Glencore Chris spent 17 years with Cargill where he held various management positions in sugar and grain, gaining expertise in the agricultural products industry and marketing operations.

Chris holds an MA degree from Oxford University. He won a silver medal for rowing in the British eight in the 1980 Moscow Olympics. I caught up with Chris in Dubai and asked him how he had got into the commodity business.

"I entered this industry straight from university in 1981 and it was a pure coincidence that I became a commodity trader. I was a keen sportsman at that time training many hours a day and had no time and not much desire for job interviews. The Oxford and

Cambridge Boat race in which I participated was held in the spring, so a spring interview was out of the question. All the investment banks interviewed in spring but Cargill interviewed later in the summer. I was doubly lucky. For that reason not only did I join the commodity industry but perhaps more fortuitously I did not become an investment banker."

"How was the business then different from what it is today?" I asked.

"Certainly thirty-two years ago the sugar business was not what it was today. In those days it was, or at least it could be, primarily a business of buying FOB (Free on Board) from an exporting country and selling it CIF (Cost, Insurance, Freight) to an importing country; the business was to a large extent based on relationships and information. Back then governments were often our clients. Today, for Glencore, and the same is true for Cargill, Bunge, ADM and for others, it is the business of procuring, storing, processing, transporting, and distributing the raw materials that provide us with food. It is thereby a business of addressing deficits, and certainly not one of creating them as some might suggest.

"Companies such as ours buy, build and operate upcountry silos and warehouses, port facilities, oilseed crushing plants, wheat, rice, corn and sugar refineries and biodiesel and ethanol production facilities. Some in the industry go further down the value chain to produce eggs, poultry or meat. In the agricultural division of Glencore, just as an example, we employ 13,000 people; operate 22 port facilities; 280 silos; and 40 processing plants of different types."

"That seems very "asset heavy," I remarked. "Are assets now so important in trading?"

"In our view there is no asset-less trading model today and maybe not even any asset-light trading model of any scale that is sustainable or viable. When Glencore looks at potential acquisitions we are seeking either individual assets or asset rich companies. These are companies where the majority of earnings come from logistics, storage, port and processing activities and not from trading or marketing. We already have marketing expertise that we can leverage; we don't feel the need to buy it. One obvious distinction between an agricultural business and, say the mining or the petroleum business, is that the supply enters the market within a short harvest period, usually a matter of weeks. Demand on the other hand is more or less spread throughout the year."

"You make it sound as if you have to be big now to be successful," I suggested.

"Farmers do not wish to – or may not have the means to – carry their crop until the consumer shows up. Consumers meanwhile are seldom willing to buy their entire annual consumption at harvest time. So not only is the infrastructure large in our business but given the need to carry inventory, the working capital requirement can also be very significant. In addition, a global reach and a global book enable the big companies to spot areas of deficit and move products there quickly, as well as to arbitrage one geographical area against another.

"There is also some advantage in being multi-commodity in that diversity helps smooth earnings. Operating across multiple regions reduces political risk while having a network of offices and people that can represent a company's diverse interests does of course provide some cost saving. Scale itself can be an advantage. When looking critically at their lending portfolios banks prefer to lend to larger, more diverse customers where they rightly perceive the risk profile to be lower. All of this then favours large companies. A regional player can succeed of course but it is not quite the same game."

"So you are optimistic that trade houses have a role to play in the future?" I asked.

"We are optimistic. Agriculture is underpinned by good demand growth, driven by population growth, urbanisation, and the switch to poultry and meat based diets. Global oilseed demand is growing at just over 3.25% per year; corn is growing a little less. Wheat, rice and sugar demand are all growing at or just below 2% per year. The demand side of the equation is predictable and clear. But this demand growth largely needs to be met by yield gain, not by additional planted area. And the true potential for yield gain is perhaps known by only a few, the companies researching and manufacturing the agricultural inputs themselves.

"Having said that, who would have thought 15 years ago that global grain production would have been able to accommodate close to 130 million tonnes of additional corn demand for conversion to ethanol as is mandated in the US today – a tonnage equivalent to almost one and a half times the global seaborne traded quantity. One thing for sure is that in just seven years the world will need not only to produce but also to move 20% more food than it does today. We will need to store, transport and process it. Without the build-up of transport and logistics infrastructure and additional processing capacity, production will be unable to reach the consumer even if it keeps pace with demand. Ensuring that infrastructure grows at the same pace as production is both the task and the opportunity for a company like Glencore."

"Do you think further consolidation is likely in the industry?" I asked.

"For competition reasons I think it is unlikely that one of the largest food companies such as Cargill, ADM or Bunge would be able to buy each other. What is certainly possible is that an industry outsider could buy one of these companies. The combined market capitalisation of ADM, Bunge, Wilmar, Noble, GRAINCORP, the Andersons and a theoretical value for Louis Dreyfus is less than that of the fourth largest mining company.

"It would not be a big ticket therefore for a petroleum or mining company or a sovereign wealth fund - or a conglomerate such as Berkshire Hathaway - to buy the largest company in our industry. A change of ownership of course does not represent consolidation. I believe it is likely that there is further consolidation among the second or third tier companies. But there are not that many public or private companies of this type left to buy today. There are a number of cooperatives that would make attractive consolidation targets – candidates in Australia or the US are obvious, but the owners will first have to decide that they are for sale."

"What about sugar?" I asked. "Where does sugar fit in this grand scheme of things?"

"As mentioned earlier, diversity helps and sugar fits well within a grain and oilseed and broader soft commodity business. In terms of production and trade sugar is relatively small. Global sugar production at 180 million tonnes compares to grain, rice and oilseed production at 2.6 billion tonnes, or around 7%. Global seaborne trade of sugar at around 50 million tonnes compares to grain and oilseed (but excluding rice) at 530 million tonnes, or around 9%.

"Sugar processing, or at least milling and ethanol production and not refining, is different from most types of agricultural processing in that it is essentially a processing and a farming business combined. It is not a straight conversion business as it would be for oilseed processing for example. Indeed sugar milling is in a way more akin to mining as its profitability at least in part relies on the flat price component.

"Both grain and sugar of course are used as a feedstock for biofuel production, primarily ethanol: 150 million tonnes of grain globally is used to produce ethanol. That's about 9% of global grain production, excluding rice, but 17% of global corn production. And I am told that if the millers in Brazil stopped producing ethanol and produced only sugar an additional 25 million tonnes of sugar would add 15% to global production and about 50% to seaborne trade.

"The demand for ethanol today is largely mandated and unless crude oil and gasoline prices rally substantially it is unlikely that this demand will grow significantly - certainly not as it did in the early 2000s. Conversely we think it is also unlikely that these programmes will now be torn down. In the grain markets the ethanol producer has become another customer - albeit a very large. Sugar I think is a bit more complicated.

"If the global demand for ethanol is unlikely to grow very significantly and the US and the EU continue to favour and support domestic biofuel production then even if Brazil is the low cost producer of ethanol, which it undoubtedly is, the future outlook for the

Brazilian miller and ethanol producer may be more conditional on the Brazilian domestic market, on domestic policies and domestic politics."

"You talked about assets and their importance in the supply chain. What about agricultural assets in sugar?" I asked,

"I would say there are different types of assets. The mining business and the sugar and ethanol business in Brazil are similar. You dig stuff – or you grow stuff - out of the ground. You try to do that as efficiently as you can; it is very much price related. Other assets such as silos, warehouses, port facilities, and oilseed crushing plants are more logistic assets. In an oilseed crushing plant - where the beans come directly from the farm and then come out in product form onto a vessel - the plant plays a similar role to a warehouse.

"We believe that if you don't have the means to procure directly from the farmer, face to face from the farmer, to carry the stuff, to move the stuff, you can't really be in the trading business. So we have no choice. We cannot choose to be in the trading business and not invest in assets. For us they are the same thing. You cannot have one without the other."

"Glencore went public a few years back", I commented. "When I started in the business there was a general view that neither farming nor commodity trading were suited to the stock market. The investments were too long term and the returns too volatile, too dependent on the weather and commodity prices. Stock markets like continual growth."

"I am not sure that it is true. I think when you have a company that is diverse, handling different commodities in different geographies - and when your business is essentially a procurement and logistics business supported by assets - then although prices can be volatile and crop sizes can be volatile, your earnings can be relatively stable. And it is after all a growing business in terms of demand. It is a business that is volume driven and certainly the volumes will continue to increase."

"We all agree that we need increased scale to feed a growing population but the general government and public perception is that the trade houses are too big and are controlling the market", I said.

"It is partly a matter of education. The industry does not speak with one voice. It has not made much of an effort when it comes to the media and education. When I look at what Glencore does - and it is the same for other companies- it is clear we are building up the infrastructure necessary to carry the stuff as production grows. Somebody has to do that and the governments themselves are not going to do that. History has proven that. The good that we do and the fact that we are needed are fairly obvious. We are not conveying that message clearly."

"Chris", I said, "that is one reason why I am writing my book. Thank you for your time."

Traders and markets

7.1 Greg Page: the price of responsibility

Greg Page is Executive Chairman of Cargill Inc. The company has 152,000 employees in 67 countries and in fiscal year 2014 generated $134.9 billion in sales and earnings of $1.87 billion. I heard Greg speak at a Financial Times conference in Lausanne in 2013 and he kindly agreed to let me use a shortened version of that presentation in this book.

This is Greg's presentation:

"Trading has long been a fundamental of life. To quote Libanius, from his "Orations III, written in the 4th Century:

"God did not bestow all products on all parts of the earth, but distributed his gifts over the different regions, to the end that men might cultivate a social relationship because one would have need of the help of another. And so he called commerce in to being, that all men might be able to have common enjoyment of the fruits of earth, no matter where produced"

I am not sure that markets are necessarily divine, but I am convinced Libanius was on the right path. Cargill has not been in business that long, but in 2015 we are celebrating 150 years of our company's role in this ancient practice. Trading, or exchanging goods, has long underpinned human progress, and the interdependence that comes from trading creates the real capacity to raise living standards.

Trading across national boundaries is a necessity, not a luxury, if the world wants to better serve the needs of its citizens. And as we face into a global population reaching 9 billion by mid-century, an even greater proportion of the world's food will need to move across oceans to feed the people. National self-sufficiency in food will not suffice. So trading has always been important, and will always continue to be so.

But something has happened in recent years: perceptions of trading have changed, and not for the better. The term "trading" has become wrapped up and confused in the public perception with speculation, hoarding, market fixing, monopolies, cartels and bad practice. There is increasingly little differentiation in perception between trading and the worst excesses of banking – the massive points of difference being misunderstood or ignored.

We should not be afraid to point out the difference. We should not ignore or underestimate the significant value we bring to people's lives every day through moving food and crops from places of surplus to areas of deficit, or providing safe and efficient storage, minimising waste, maximising productivity, or supporting farmers with crop inputs, pre-financing or access to markets, managing risks or trading coal, electricity, natural gas, petroleum, iron ore and basic metals.

All these connected, basic commodities are fundamental to life and essential contributors to the global economy. So fundamental are they that we should question whether the term "trading" is even the correct descriptor for those of us dealing with physical products rather than purely abstract financial transactions. Because as the term becomes discredited and confused, so abuses by a minority of "traders" at any extreme of the "trading" spectrum impact negatively on the broader industry. And we all become tarred with the same brush – and suffer from the erroneous perception that trading is somehow "bad".

Just looking at our own businesses - we trade with more than two million smallholders around the world, giving access to markets, paying them promptly in cash so they can invest in planting, support their families, improve their livelihoods and invest in their futures. Is that "bad"?

Is providing training to tens of thousands of cocoa farmers, helping them improve their yields, raise the quality of their crop and increase their income "bad"? Is ploughing more than US $13 billion into physical infrastructure, transportation and logistics in the developing world alone to allow raw materials to be gathered, stored, moved and shipped safely "bad"? Is championing the need for open and free markets to allow true price discovery "bad"? Is improving shipping standards on all freight charters "bad"? Does innovation in improved efficiency and cost reduction in moving oil, metals, or energy, allowing billions to have power, phones and jobs because they have become affordable at ever diminishing real prices describe a "bad " profession? Is conserving finite materials, valued for their scarcity, a "bad" thing? We in Cargill do not think so.

So when does it go bad? It goes bad when trading becomes divorced from the management of the supply chain and becomes driven by a short-term horizon. When the management of risk and the seizing of opportunity become detached from its consequences. When it moves to become a purely abstract point of speculation and an outcome in its own right.

That is when it ceases to have a noble purpose. Cargill has always believed in a noble purpose – our vision "to be the global leader in nourishing people" speaks to our belief. We have long been at the forefront of such behaviour: storing crops and minimising spoilage; painting the bottom of ships to reduce energy use in propulsion; championing the use of green technologies to harness the wind in ocean transportation; sourcing responsibly; developing supply chains that respect people and human rights; using and promoting the most responsible practices across all our businesses; demanding and expecting the highest behavioural standards from all our people. Constantly being innovative, and working to meet the existing, evolving and often unspoken needs of customers and consumers around the world with physical products and tangible actions.

"Commodity merchandising" was the term we all used to use to describe what we do – and perhaps we should again. It speaks more to the relationships inherent in our world – we are a service industry first and foremost, providing essential lubrication for the global system with liquidity, mitigating risk, meeting the needs of our customers and our suppliers, helping them, and the world at large, thrive. They are lofty words, and highbrow principles, all of which are fine, but let me bring it down into some detail.

Fundamental to the "system" working is the supply chain. That's not something that can be left to chance. Companies like Cargill, Glencore, ADM, Shell,

Exxon, have long ago moved down, through and into the detail of the supply chain. Investments made on the ground in physical infrastructure for the long term both create and underpin the symbiotic trading relationships that Libanius referred to all those years ago.

As an example when we, Cargill, invest in vehicles and roads in Indonesia which allow smallholder farmers to have their palm fruit carefully and safely transited from their plots, and when we support and encourage the development of community cooperatives, and they, in turn, create and develop local cooperative banks, who in their turn support the cooperatives' long term reinvestment plans for the commercial smallholders, while we continue to provide access to not just market knowledge, but transportation to markets, and full and fair market price. Those interdependent elements are what we believe are important – and what I think Libanius was talking about.

There is a belief that the trading houses are secretive, totally opaque, manipulating markets and fixing prices in the same way a small number of bankers fixed Libor. There is a belief that there is no transparency.

That could not be further from the truth. Back in 1974 when I started, things arguably were opaque. There was no Internet, no cellular phones, no instant communication or flash commentary or opinion – and of course no email. (Sometimes I yearn for those days). The information was available on the ground and competitive advantage came from how quickly you could gather it and do something with it. Cargill was the first company in the world with its own private worldwide wire system, introduced to try and give us the edge on the one thing that mattered – speed.

Today every one of us has every piece of information available and at our fingertips, instantaneously. There is no time and date advantage. Everything is totally transparent - and the skill today is in the analysis, interpretation and the insight derived from that openly available mountain of knowledge. So far from being opaque, the reality of today's technology, instant information, and public opinion shaping global acceptability, means there is nowhere to hide– and neither should there be.

A 'Noble Purpose" needs nowhere to hide. The world needs what we do, and what we bring, today more than ever. We should all recognise the huge behavioural responsibility the industry carries, and we must all hold ourselves, and each other, accountable to it."

7.2 How do traders make money?

The phone was ringing. It was pitch dark but I knew what time it was without looking for my watch: 4.30am in Minneapolis was 10.30am in the UK, the opening of the London sugar futures market. My girlfriend at the time rolled over with her back to me and pulled the covers over her head. She would go back to sleep; she was used to these early morning phone calls.

I had arrived in Minneapolis in September, four months earlier, and the first snow had fallen in early November. The other traders in the department had warned me to find a girlfriend before the winter set in "because you won't be able to find one afterwards." But don't worry", they added, "you'll split up with her once the ice melts on the lake; everyone does". Someone had obviously given my girlfriend the same advice and we did indeed split up in the spring. It was a relationship of convenience: no one wants to look for a partner when it is -20°C outside.

I picked up the phone without turning on the light. As expected, it was the sugar trader from our company's Tokyo office. He was calling me from a bar and had a slight slur to his voice. Earlier that day he had sold two cargoes of Thai raw sugar to a local refinery and needed me to hedge the sales by buying an equivalent amount of futures on the London futures exchange. The sugar was for shipment in June so he told me to buy the May futures position.

Now you may say that it is pretty stupid to wake someone up in the middle of the night in Minneapolis to hedge a sale made in Tokyo on the London market, and at 4.30 that morning I would have totally agreed with you. A few months later the company hired a trader in London to "manage the book" from there, but at the time everything was managed from Minneapolis. So I had to do the hedging.

I eased myself out of bed and into the sitting room where I had already set up a home desk. On a scrap of paper I had written down our trading position from the previous night and the telephone numbers of the London brokers. I dialled one of them and a man answered.

"Where's May?" I asked politely down the phone. There was a silence so I repeated the question a bit louder. There was a sort of confused mumbling at the other end of the phone. The guy was wasting my time; I had to get the sales hedged before the market moved. This time I shouted at him, "Where's May?"

"I don't know", he replied.

"What do you mean you don't know", I screamed, " Tell me where May is!"

"I don't know", he repeated. "But she is not here. I haven't seen her, honestly".

I slammed the phone down in embarrassment. I had forgotten to add the international dialling code. Instead of calling London I had dialled a local number, waking some poor bloke up in the middle of the night. I redialled more carefully, got the broker in London and began to hedge the two cargoes. My working day had begun.

Trade houses have traditionally made money in three ways: by physically transporting commodities from areas where they are not needed to areas where they are needed; by buying crops from producers and farmers when they want to sell and storing and financing them until consumers want to buy; by processing commodities in such a way that consumers want to buy them.

All of these operations provide an invaluable function in feeding a hungry world in an efficient and cost effective way. In the jargon of the business the trade houses add significant value to the supply chain. As the world demand for food increases these roles will become ever more crucial. However, the margins that can be made on these operations can at times be wafer-thin.

This raises two questions. The first is, "Can traders continue to make money in this world of instant information and analysis?" The second is, "Do traders abuse their power to manipulate markets and increase their profit margins?" I will try to answer the second question in the next section but the answer to the first question is a qualified "Yes" – at least for some trade houses.

As a general rule if a company is offering a service that adds value to people's lives then that company will be paid enough to keep it in business and to continue to offer that service. The same can be said on a wider level: if a sector adds value then that sector will also continue to exist, even if competition within the sector means that no one participant makes a lot of money. However it does not mean that every company in that sector will make money.

There are exceptions to that rule: a company may be willing to lose money on one activity (or on one product) if it helps to generate bigger profits on another activity or product. A supermarket may discount the price of – and lose money on- its barbeques if the promotion attracts customers to their stores. The supermarket may make more money on selling food to its customers than it loses on selling barbeques. In the jargon of the trade, the barbeques are "loss leaders".

I mentioned earlier that by participating in the physical flow of commodities trade house gain valuable information that helps them to analyse the markets and to predict future price movements. Trade houses are often willing to take a loss on the transportation of physical sugar around the globe in the hope that it will give them valuable insight that will help them make more money elsewhere.

For example, in recent years the trade houses that are most active in the Central American sugar market have had a significant information advantage over the trade houses that aren't. By buying most of the sugar produced in the Central American region they know better than others how much sugar is available for delivery against the futures markets in New York and London. Only they know how much sugar has been sold to destination and how much is still available for delivery against the futures market – and they can decide which futures month against which to deliver.

Central American sugar tends to be the only raw sugar available in the Western Hemisphere during the first half of each calendar year. Centre South Brazil is between harvests during this period and Central American sugar tends to "punch above its weight" in its effect on the futures markets.

Local knowledge can help in other areas as well. To give a recent example, local insight helped one international trade house make a significant profit on the expiry of the October 2014 sugar futures position.

Due to a global surplus and low world sugar prices Thailand's sugar producers had been reluctant sellers throughout 2014 and the country had built up significant stocks. However no one was sure how much sugar the Thai mills were holding in their warehouses; nor were they sure as to the quality of that sugar and whether it had deteriorated since the end of the harvest. This uncertainty kept the October 2014 futures contract under pressure; no one wanted to take delivery of an unspecified quantity of Thai raw sugar that, because of quality issues, they might not be able to find buyers for.

One trade house, because of their local contacts, knew both the quantity and quality of the Thai raw sugar that was available. This knowledge enabled them to sell the sugar to the Dubai refinery. Once it had been sold into Dubai it could no longer be delivered against the October futures and the market rallied strongly, making the trade house an excellent profit in the process. This is not market manipulation: the trading house simply used an information advantage that they created themselves by selling the Thai sugar to Dubai.

"Isn't all this insider trading?" you might ask. "Didn't the trade house concerned take advantage of information that only they had?"

In the equity markets it is usual for employees working within a particular company to have inside information as to how their company is doing – and it would be possible for those "insiders" to use that information to their advantage and to the disadvantage of others. It is therefore right and proper that tough laws exist to "level the playing field" and prevent those insiders taking advantage of their privileged information.

However the concept of insider trading does not exist in the commodity markets. In theory farmers might know before anyone else that their crop is doing badly; they may as a result buy futures (or not sell them, which is more likely) in expectation of an increase in prices. In a way you could say that knowing how your crop is doing could be classed as inside information, but in reality anyone can track the weather patterns and wander around the fields to check how the crops are looking. Similarly, anyone can make estimates as to how much sugar a particular country is likely to import or export and be able to track the shipments.

As for the trade houses that are doing the exporting and importing it would be impossible for each trade house to publicly announce how much sugar it has bought and sold – and to whom – each time that it made a transaction. Sales and purchases have to be hedged on the futures markets; it would be commercial suicide for a trade house to announce a transaction before they had hedged it.

Also, as we have seen above, trade houses do not buy from producers or exporters at the same time as they sell to importers or consumers. Sometimes trade houses have to buy a crop from a farmer months before they can sell it on; if they had to announce that they had bought the crop – were long of it unsold – their competitors might be able to take advantage of them.

Sugar trade houses have in the past tried to create an edge for themselves in other ways. One way that was popular in the 1990s was to make a lot of physical sugar sales to end destination countries and then take delivery of the sugar through the futures market. The sugar delivered against the futures market is traditionally "the lowest common denominator", in other words the cheapest: it is the worst quality sugar in the least convenient port. As a result, other sugars tended to trade at premiums to the futures markets.

However by sourcing sugar exclusively through the futures markets trade houses were able to push the owners of the better quality sugars either to deliver them against the futures (at no premium) or to roll forward their short hedges to the next futures delivery month. If they decided to do the latter they would buy back their short hedges in, say, July futures and resell them in October futures. This would often have the effect of strengthening the July futures position both in terms of the flat price and relative to the October futures.

By taking delivery of a big enough tonnage a trade house could receive premium sugar without having to pay the premium. More importantly, the trade house could also make a profit by owning more sugar than they needed and selling out the surplus when prices rose.

Although successful for a while, this type of futures play has recently fallen out of favour. This is partly because of increased vigilance by the futures exchanges looking to ensure an orderly market. However, it is mainly because of competition among the trade houses themselves. Too many traders ended up trying to do the same thing – and they were all competing against each other to make enough sales to end destination in order to take delivery of the futures. In the end trade houses were selling physical sugar at a significant loss – and the losses on the physicals more than offset any possible profits on the futures.

Competition between the trade houses is ferocious. If one trade house is suspected of trying to push prices higher another trade house will quickly call their bluff and sell into the other one's buying. No single trade house is in a sufficiently dominant position to be able to push a market around, at least for very long. It is this competition that prevents any one trader from manipulating the market.

"But", you may ask, "Can't traders join forces to create a dominant position in a particular market that they can then abuse?" This is effectively what happened in the recent LIBOR and FOREX scandals where traders at the big banks got together to manipulate interest and foreign exchange rates.

However, this is a more a question of competition policy and surveillance than a "trader issue". Economic history is cluttered with cartels where participants in a particular industry have got together to fix prices and manipulate their particular market. This can happen locally, for example when construction companies get together to decide who should bid on what project and at what price. Or it can happen nationally or internationally, for example when two producers of washing powder get together to divide up a market and agree prices.

When they get caught they are (usually and rightly) severely punished. And in the commodity and financial markets, that are more transparent and controlled than others, they get caught more often.

7.3   Ralph Potter – mentor to the sugar trade

Ralph Potter is an ex-Green Beret, the American equivalent of the British Special Forces. For the past forty years he has been an active trader and broker on the world sugar markets and he has mentored many of the sugar market's most successful traders. I met up with him at his local pub in Surrey England and asked him how he had got into the sugar business.

"I got into the sugar club by accident," he replied. "I had returned from the Vietnam War and was attending the University of Illinois. I had some money to invest. My grandfather was a farmer and when I was a boy I used to go with him to talk to farmers about the price of corn. I learned at an early age that the price would go up and down.

"While at university I seconded myself to a small grain and feed merchant. I first noticed them because their parking lot was full of Cadillac's, Mercedes and Porches – and even an AC Cobra. That was in 1971, a very auspicious time to learn to trade grains. They paid me something but not much. I worked with a rag in one hand and a chalk in the other: a girl would call out the prices from the telex ticker tape and I would erase the old price and mark up the new price on the board.

"The room was half the size of a tennis court with eight desks. At each desk was a grain merchant with an assistant; all on several phones to various clients, farmers, elevator operators, chick feed buyers, that sort of stuff. It was largely for corn, soymeal and beans. They taught me a method that I have used for 44 years, with a few improvements. The heart of the method is technical analysis and management of the position.

"After a few months I was short of two contracts of soybean oil. At the weekend I went out to play soccer and there was frost all over the ground - it was 9th September. That cost me half of my trading account. It was an expensive lesson.

"There was a guy I met in a bar at that time who had inherited $8,000 from his grandmother. He bought copper. His trading account went from $8,000 to $60,000. Remember that at that time you could buy a house for $14,000. He ended up with a debit of $4,000. He had no system of money management. That was a lesson I learned from someone else's' bad habit.

"When I left College I ended up at Merrill Lynch as a registered commodity broker but I struggled to get clients in the grains. I was too young; it felt that you had to be at least ninety to be respected in the grain markets!

"By some accident I ended up with ADM's sugar account; no one else in the office wanted it. I knew nothing about sugar, but ADM gave me a chance. Once I had one sugar client I concentrated on the sugar market and found it easier to win other sugar clients.

"What lessons did you learn at that time?" I

asked.

"Being in the military taught me two things. The first was that a bad plan poorly executed is better than no plan. The second was that reserves should only be committed to exploit and consolidate victory, never to salvage defeat. Another way of saying that is, "Don't throw good money after bad".

"I once asked a friend how he traded. He replied that he tossed a coin to decide whether to buy or sell. "That's it?" I asked. "That's your trading system?"

"Yes," he replied. "But I also have a rule never to take a losing position home over night."

"It's not the trigger that gets you into the market that's important. It's about how you manage that position once you have put it on.

"There is a famous story about a speculator at EF Hutton who got his trading recommendations through a Coke bottle wrapped in tin foil; a coat hanger acted as an aerial that he claimed picked up trading recommendations from outer space. Of course everyone ridiculed him.

"At that time people didn't have their own screens so they would come in to their broker's office and sit and watch the prices on the clacking electronic quote boards at the front of the room. When they wanted to trade they would walk up to the order clerk and hand them their order on a slip of paper.

"Most of these people lost money but this guy was a rare success. He had been trading for a number of years. He would receive a signal from his Coke bottle to, say, buy corn. If he were winning on his position he would lord it over everyone else. He really enjoyed that. The net result was that he would let his profits run and not snatch them. But when he was losing, the others ridiculed him so much that he quickly exited any losing positions.

"And when a winning position gave back a certain percentage he would quickly get out, for the same reasons. So money management worked even for a crazy person - someone who was getting his trading signals from outer space.

"Can you explain briefly how you trade?" I asked.

"I don't really want to explain it in detail but it is basically all about managing the position and taking the whipsaws. A whipsaw is when the market moves through a certain price point, you put on a position but then the market reverses again and you have to reverse that position. This is the way floor traders used to trade.

"Most people try to trade in a way so as to avoid whipsaws. The average trader would rather lose money than get whipsawed. I embrace whipsaws. It is like trying to be a boxer without getting punched. No one likes getting punched, but you have to let your opponent hit you on your forearms or on your shoulders or on your gloves - a glancing blow. You avoid being smacked on the head but take the smaller hits.

"What is the biggest mistake that traders make?" I asked

"The biggest mistake traders make is snatching profits. There is a saying that no one ever went broke taking a profit but that is a lie; people do go broke snatching small profits that don't offset their losses. People often snatch profits expecting to get back into the market again at a better price. They may do, but more often than not the market runs away and they either have to chase it or they don't get back in.

"The best thing to do if you have a winning position in the commodity markets is to take partial profits in a non-emotional manner. You reduce your position but you hold on to the core position. Trimming, or reducing, a position provides you with a psychological way of holding on to your core position.

"What is a trader's greatest enemy? I asked.

"A trader's greatest enemy is lack of discipline and succumbing to hubris - that moment when you think you know more than the market, usually because you have been lucky or because you have been a success at using your trading method.

"The worst thing that can happen is when a trader thinks he knows something and disregards his own rules. Or when he has invested so much of his credibility and so much of his personality into putting on a position it makes it hard to exit that position. It's hard to change your mind. That's why you have to have a risk point.

"What makes a good trader?" I asked.

"The best traders are the ones who have unconventional vision and self-belief: to stick your neck out and have the guts to say "I am going to commit this company's money - or my investors' money - to make this trade. It takes someone with exceptional self-belief. Most traders on a desk just want to keep their heads down.

"But you have to take the risk. You have to have the guts to trade. You also have to have an absolute disdain for the opinions of other people. You don't have to tell everybody you think they are full of it; you just can't we swayed by other people's opinions.

And, to be a success in the markets you have to have a well-developed sense of fear: it will keep you in business longer than brilliance. Brilliance can desert you in critical moments. Some traders are naturals but if they aren't trained properly then they blow themselves up and take everyone else with them."

"You talk about risk management but don't you think that most companies have taken risk management too far?" I asked.

"No I don't. But I do think they have taken the process too far. Over recent years some of the bigger trading companies have cashed in and gone public. As public companies they find that they have to comply with thousands of new regulations. All of a sudden the management of these companies is totally swamped with compliance and HR issues.

"Unfortunately a good trader is no longer seen as an asset, he is considered more as a liability - a risk. The creative guys get swamped with compliance, process and management issues.

"I could never work for a big company these days, I would be sacked within a year.

"So you have been happier as a sole trader?"

"I have traded big positions for ACLI sugar, Marc Rich sugar and for a couple hedge funds, but I never aspired to be a multimillionaire. I don't have the temperament or the drive. Every time I wanted something like a car or a yacht, I got it but then I was happy with that. The excess money I made I largely gave away to people that needed it more than me. I think I have enough money, but my wife says I don't. I like being part of the sugar club, part of the team. That was and is more important to me.

"What I really enjoy now is teaching. I am 66

years old and happy to give something back to the sugar business; to teach young people about markets. I try to show them a way to use technical tools and position management in combination with their fundamental trading strategies. Remember, the trade houses' primary role is to move the food around efficiently. If I can help them to do that profitably then I am happy.

"Lastly, and most importantly," I asked, "Do traders manipulate markets?"

"Good traders don't need to manipulate markets, they can make money on their own abilities. Weak traders may try to manipulate markets but it seldom ever works, or if it works it only works for a very short time. The ceiling quickly falls in on them.

"But what if traders get together," I insisted. "Could that give them the market power to do it?"

"Maybe for a while, but price has a habit of going where it wants to go. You may stop it for a while but you will never stop it for long. If you push prices up, extra supply will come out. If you push prices down supply will dry up. Traders who try and push price away from where it should be invariably lose money. I have seen some pretty big companies try and fail spectacularly.

"It is very difficult to manipulate a market. It is much easier to manipulate a government, but then you don't have to be a trader to do that. Everyone can manipulate a government; it's called democracy."

"Thank you Ralph for your time."

The sugar companies

8.1   Can producers manipulate prices?

At a recent industry event I asked the audience where the largest sugar-producing company by volume was headquartered. The answer is "Germany", but very few of the otherwise well-informed audience got the answer right. I then asked the audience how many of the ten biggest sugar-producing companies in the world are European beet producers. The answer is "four". Again very few in the audience got the answer right.

Out of those beet producers, only two also produce sugar from cane; the other two produce sugar exclusively from beet. This is surprising when you consider that less than a fifth of all the sugar produced globally each year comes from beet; the other 80% comes from cane. This made me wonder: why do European beet sugar companies dominate the rankings? What has enabled them to get so big?

At the same industry event I asked a senior official of one of the companies concerned if he had an answer. He looked a little surprised at the question but soon recovered his exposure to answer,

"Three of those four European beet producers are cooperatives. Farmers own us. They understand what it takes to grow sugar. Also, the cooperative model allows us to plan long term - we do not have to worry about quarterly results. This allows us to absorb the bad weather years without questioning our growth strategy.

"Family ownership is the traditional model for the cane

sector and it is often difficult to expand or grow a family business. There are often rivalries within families, particularly when an older generation passes the baton to a new one. But there are also inter-family rivalries: it can be difficult for one family-owned cane mill to take over a neighbouring family-owned mill. There is often bad blood if the two families have been competing for cane for generations; it becomes more than money.

"Being based in Europe helped us to expand internationally. We have had easy access to finance at a low price. We have strong, well-trained management. And we have solid accounting and auditing practices. Companies in developing countries may not have any of those advantages – or may not have all of them."

The circumstances did not allow me to pursue the conversation but the one thing that he failed to mention was the high domestic price in Europe. Set by the European Commission, this high price has allowed the European sugar companies to earn what economists call an "economic rent" on their production quotas. Wikipedia defines economic rent as

"Any payment to a factor of production in excess of the cost needed to bring that factor into production. In classical economics, economic rent is any payment made … for assets formed by creating official privilege over natural opportunities (e.g., patents). In neoclassical economics, economic rent also includes income gained by beneficiaries of other contrived exclusivity, such as labour guilds and unofficial corruption. Economic rent should be viewed as unearned revenue, whereas economic profit is a narrower term describing surplus income greater than the next best risk-adjusted alternative."

In the case of sugar the European Commission

grants European sugar producing companies specific production quotas. Because of the high price of sugar in the EU the owners of these quotas can obtain above normal profits, an economic rent. These high profits have given EU based sugar companies the cash flow and the capital to expand.

It has also helped that (up until recently at least) the EU sugar companies have been able to plan ahead, knowing that the sugar price next year will be similar to the sugar price this year. Very few other producers have had the luxury of being able to predict, subject to weather, their profits and their cash flow in advance. (I will take a more detailed look at the EU sugar regime in Chapter Nine.)

Equally surprising is that out of the world's top ten sugar producing companies only four produce sugar in more than one country. Sugar producing is still a local business. In an age of globalization I find this is rather odd. Why aren't sugar companies more international? I put this question to Jamal Al Ghurair, founder and Managing Director of Al Khaleej Sugar, the world's largest, and first, standalone end-destination, sugar refinery. He answered,

"A number of international companies have made a big mistake in investing in the cane milling sector in Brazil. Some people say that it is because traders don't make good millers but producers in other countries have also invested and they have not done well either. It is really because cane milling is a local business. You have to know the local culture, the local laws, the local weather – and you have to have a strong management presence on the ground. It is not something you can run by sitting in an office in another country".

On a global level, the business of producing

sugar is far from concentrated. According to FO Licht (a leading sugar analyst), the top ten largest sugar producers in the world produced around 32 million tonnes of sugar in 2014: that's about 18% of total global production. However, if you look at that industry structure on a regional basis the figures change somewhat. In the USA the top five companies have 90% of the market share. In the EU the top five have 55% while in Brazil the top five have only 25%.

With only 25% of the domestic market, I doubt that any one of the top five sugar producing companies in Brazil has the market power to set the sugar price higher than it would otherwise be. But could the bigger Brazilian sugar producing companies be colluding together to achieve that aim?

There is a very simple rule of thumb that you can use to see whether producers in an exporting country are colluding. As it costs more to move sugar to the ports and load it on to a ship than it does to sell the sugar locally, the domestic sugar price in an exporting country should always be lower than the world price. If the domestic market pays more than the world market any producer acting alone should sell as much as they can into the domestic market. If all producers acted rationally then they would sell their sugar to the domestic market rather than export it. The domestic price would then fall to a level where it was below the world price (once you take into account the extra costs of exporting). At that point it would become more profitable to sell the sugar to the world market.

However if the local sugar companies collude and agree to limit their sales to the domestic market so as to keep the price high, then the relationship between the world and domestic prices can become inverted.

Brazil is one of the few sugar exporting countries in the world where the domestic price is lower than the world price. This strongly suggests that competition in the Brazilian domestic market is strong and that the producers there are not colluding to push prices higher.

But what about in the US and in the EU: are the local sugar industries so concentrated that producers can abuse their market power in a way to increase prices or exclude competition? As both are net importers of sugar, rather than exporters, you cannot apply the same test as in Brazil. In addition, both have government-set regulations that support domestic agriculture by fixing minimum prices (more on this in the chapter on government intervention).

The top five sugar producing companies in the US may have 90% of the domestic market for sugar but their ability to set prices is limited by competition from domestically-produced HFCS (High Fructose Corn Sweetener), as well as from sugar imports from Mexico.

In 2013 the US consumed about 20.3 million tons of calorific sweeteners: of that quantity 10.75 million tons came from sugar and 9.3 million from corn. (The rest came from honey and other edible syrups.) So although the top five US sugar producers may have 90% of the domestic sugar market, they have less than 50% of the total sweetener market. There is no love lost between the corn and sugar sectors in the US and it is unlikely that they are colluding to raise prices.

Mexican imports have played a role in preventing US domestic producers from abusing their market power. According to figures from the USDA, the US imported more than 1.9 million tons of Mexican sugar in both the 2012 and 2013 crop years (measured on an October / September basis.) These imports led to the US government imposing provisional anti-dumping and anti-subsidy duties on Mexican sugar imports following a petition from the US producers. A minimum FOB mill-selling price was agreed for Mexican imports at 22.25 c/lb for raw sugar and 26.00 c/lb for refined sugar.

So have the US sugar producers used their political clout to eliminate a lower priced competitor? Why do you need a cartel to fix prices when you can get the government to do it for you? And does that mean US consumers are paying more for their sugar as a result? Some commentators certainly argue that way.

It probably goes without question that EU consumers have for years been paying more for their sugar than they should have been. But is that a consequence of the EU sugar policy of minimum prices, production quotas and high import tariffs? Or is it a result of anti-competitive actions by the EU sugar producers? Or is one the consequence of the other? These are questions that the European Commission has been asking itself for the past quarter of a century in an effort to prevent the region's sugar producers from taking advantage of EU sugar policy to raise prices.

Way back in May 1997 the European Commission fined Irish Sugar PLC 8.8 million ECUs (European Currency Units, a forerunner of the Euro) for abusing its dominant position on the Irish domestic sugar market. At the time Irish Sugar had a share of around 95% of the sugar market within Ireland.

In October 1998 the European Commission fined UK sugar producers British Sugar and Tate & Lyle, as well as sugar merchants Napier Brown and James Budgett, a total of 50.3 million ECUs for violating EU competition law. The Commission found that the companies had restricted competition through a co-ordination of their pricing policy on the white granulated sugar market in Great Britain.

However proving anti-competitive action is not easy. In July 2002 the Swedish Competition Authority wrote in a report (1)

"Firms in the (EU) sugar market are able to charge higher prices through so-called tacit collusion. The most important feature of tacit collusion is that firms can succeed in charging a price that far exceeds marginal cost, as long as other firms in the market do the same.

"Tacit collusion need not involve any explicit communication between the firms. Tacit collusion poses a problem for competition authorities since it arises in markets in which there are only a few operators who, by virtue of the characteristics of the market, are able to behave in a parallel manner and derive benefits from their collective market power without necessarily infringing the EU or national competition regulations. The rules prohibiting anti-competitive agreements require concerted practices or explicit agreements, which are not always present under tacit collusion.

The CMO (Common Market Organisation) Sugar has increased firms' ability to sustain tacit collusion in a number of ways. Regulation has blocked non-preferential imports from outside the Union and has prevented both entry of new firms, and the competing product isoglucose, by assigning quotas to incumbent firms.

By assigning fixed production quotas on a national level, the CMO Sugar has consolidated national markets, which has helped firms to separate markets geographically.

In order for tacit collusion to be sustainable, there must be a credible retaliatory mechanism. By subsidising excess production and exports, the CMO Sugar provides a retaliatory mechanism enabling firms to use the threat of shifting quantities from exports to sales within the Union."

In the most recent example, in February 2014, the German Federal Cartel Office (Bundeskartellamt) imposed fines totalling around €280 million on the three major German sugar manufacturers for fixing prices, setting quotas and sharing markets. The infringements took place over several years dating back to the mid 1990s until the Bundeskartellamt started investigations in 2009.

The German competition authorities ruled that their country's sugar producers had formed a "territorial cartel" and for many years had agreed to generally limit their sales of sugar in Germany to their respective sales areas instead of competing in one another's territories. The companies than exported the sugar they were not selling in one another's' territories.

Interestingly, aside from the territorial cartel, the Bundeskartellamt found that the sugar producers had used the European quota regime, the minimum price guarantee and the resulting high market transparency for price coordination. This price co-ordination further limited competition in the market.

In a statement at the time the European Commission said it would end its investigation into the EU sugar industry following the German fines. However a spokeswoman added:

"The Commission does not exclude that it may re-investigate the sugar sector at a later stage on the basis of new elements."

At the time of writing, however, that seems

unlikely. A price war broke out between Germany's producers after the fines were imposed and domestic EU sugar prices collapsed. (As might be expected, the profits of the EU sugar companies also collapsed.) Some commentators argued that the fall in prices was a function of EU sugar reform and the end of production quotas, planned for September 2017. However it seems odd that prices should fall two years in advance of those reforms; increased competition seems a better explanation.

8.2 The world's top sugar companies

For the purposes of this chapter I use the list published by FO Licht for 2014 that I mentioned in the previous section. But first a warning: the list is controversial. Which companies are on the list – and in what order– partly depends on the weather: companies produce more sugar in some years than in others. What's more, the order in which a company appears on the list will depend on whether you count wholly owned or partially owned subsidiary companies. (FO Licht includes subsidiaries that are "controlled" by the parent company.) Finally, the list depends on how you define sugar "production". If you define it to include refining raw sugar, then ASR (American Sugar Refiners) comes out as the leading sugar company in the world; if you don't include refining they don't even appear in the top ten.

American Crystal Sugar, a beet sugar co-operative, is number ten on the FO Licht list: in 2014 the cooperative produced 1.67 million tonnes of sugar. The company is based in Moorhead Minnesota and operates six sugar beet processing plants, four of which are in the Red River Valley, which runs 200 miles south from the Canadian border along the North Dakota and Minnesota border. Three of these factories (East Grand Forks, Moorhead and Crookston) are in Minnesota while two (Drayton and Hillsboro) are in North Dakota. In total they process sugar beets from approximately 425,000 acres.

The company was founded in 1973 by about 2,800 sugar beet growers in the Minnesota and North Dakota areas of the Red River Valley when they acquired the business and assets of the American Crystal Sugar Company, then a publicly held New Jersey corporation in operation since 1899. In 2002 the company bought the Holly Sugar Factory in Montana and renamed it "Sydney Sugars". It processes sugar beet from approximately 30,000 acres.

Biosev, a sister company to Louis Dreyfus Commodities, is the ninth largest sugar producer in the world with a production of 1.7 million tonnes in 2014. The company operates eleven factories in Brazil and has a crushing capacity of 36.4 million tonnes of sugarcane per year; this makes it the second largest cane crusher in the world. The company employs about 17,000 people, manages 340,000 hectares of cane land and works with 1,200 sugarcane suppliers. It is one of the largest producers of energy from bagasse in Brazil with an electricity export capacity of 1,346 GWh per year. The company also has a joint venture with Cargill in the TEAG export terminal in the Port of Guarujá.

Biosev now has an annual production capacity of approximately 2.8 million tonnes of sugar and 1.8 million cubic metres of ethanol. This compares with an actual production in 2014 of 1.7 million tonnes: the company has insufficient cane to feed its mills and operates well below capacity.

We have to travel half way across the world – to Thailand - to find number eight on the list. Thai Roong Ruang Sugar Group (usually known as TRR) has seven mills and produced 1.83 million tonnes of sugar in 2014. The company was founded in May 1946 with a sugar mill on the bank of the Saensaeb canal in Bangkok. Today, the TRR Group is the second largest sugar manufacturer and exporter in Thailand, owning and operating a total of seven sugar factories that produce sugar, molasses, ethanol and electricity. The TRR group also recently launched its own retail brand "Lin" that now has a 20% share of the domestic market, second to Mitr Phol Group with 75% of the domestic market.

If you include the Moroccan sugar producer Cosumar, Wilmar is the seventh largest sugar producer in the world with an output of 2.28 million tonnes in 2014. The company is a relative newcomer to the world of sugar production and its growth has been impressive. Koon Hong Kuok, a nephew of Robert Kuok (see Chapter Four), founded Wilmar International Limited in 1991 with headquarters in Singapore. The company began in palm oil plantations and entered the sugar business in 2010 when it bought Sucrogen for A$1.5 billion. Sucrogen is Australia's largest sugar producer with eight mills that are responsible for more than 50% of the cane crushed and the raw sugar produced in the country.

Wilmar also owns two refineries in Indonesia, located near Cigading Port in West Java. They are licensed to import raw sugar and supply refined sugar to the food and beverage manufacturing industry. The group produces about 700,000 tonnes of refined sugar per year in Indonesia, representing a market share of around 20% and ranking amongst the top two sugar operators in the country. In 2013, Wilmar acquired a controlling 27.5% stake in Cosumar. The company is based in Casablanca and is the only sugar producing company in Morocco. It has one refinery in Casablanca and seven sugar beet/cane mills. Cosumar is the third largest sugar producer in the African continent and the second largest refiner. Cosumar is an unusual company in that it produces sugar from both sugar beet and sugar cane in the same country.

A year later, in 2014 Wilmar acquired a 27.5% (joint-controlling) stake in India's Shree Renuka Sugars. SRS operates seven sugar mills in India with a total crushing capacity of 7.1 million tonnes of cane per year as well as two port based sugar refineries with a capacity to refine 1.7 million tonnes of raw sugar per year. The company also has significant presence in South Brazil through Renuka Vale do Ivai and Renuka do Brasil.

Renuka Vale do Ivai is 100% owned while Renuka do Brasil is 59.4% owned. The combined crushing capacity of the Brazilian subsidiary companies is 13.6 million tonnes per year. SRS is an unusual company in that it is the only cane sugar producer globally with year round crushing due to complementary seasons in India and Brazil. The company's eleven mills have a total crushing capacity of 20.7 million tonnes of cane per year. In 2014 Renuka produced about one million tonnes of sugar from cane (not including the refineries): 560,000 tonnes in India and 440,000 tonnes in Brazil. (The Brazil number is slightly lower than in previous years as they produced more ethanol.) Because Shree Renuka Sugars is still managed by its founding team, Shree Renuka's production is not included in Wilmar's total production.

Germany's Nordzucker is the sixth largest sugar producer in the world and the second-largest sugar producer in the EU with a market share of more than 15%. In 2014, the company produced around 2.69 million tonnes of sugar from sugar beet at 13 sites in seven European countries. The company was created in 1997 through a merger of North Germany's sugar producers; shareholders are to large extent also active beet suppliers. Nordzucker AG is not quoted on the stock exchange.

Nordzucker operates five sugar factories in Germany. The plants, in Lower Saxony and Saxony-Anhalt produce around one million tonnes of quota sugar a year for customers in the food and food retail industries – primarily for the German market. In addition, the company holds a majority stake in two liquid sugar factories the country. In Northern Europe, Copenhagen-based Nordic Sugar produces and processes sugar in five factories and two refineries in Denmark, Sweden, Finland and Lithuania. In Eastern Europe Nordzucker owns two sugar factories in Poland, one of which is also used as a sugar refinery, and one in Slovakia. In addition, Nordzucker has a 35 per cent stake in Tereos TTD, a sugar producer in the Czech Republic.

Tereos is the fifth largest producer in the world, having produced close to 4.0 million tonnes in 2014. The company is a co-operative owned by 12,000 French sugar beet producers and has operations in the EU, Brazil, Africa, the Indian Ocean and China. It now employs around 24,000 people worldwide and operates 42 industrial facilities that process crops from one million hectares of farmland. In addition to sugar,

Tereos produces close to 2 million tonnes of starch products and 1.5 million cubic metres of alcohol.

The Tereos Group traces its origins back to 1932 with the setting up of a cooperative distillery in Origny, a small town about 65 km north east of Dijon, France. At the time, the majority of sugar beet cooperatives were using their crops to produce only alcohol, which was already being used as a fuel. It was only in 1956 that the first sugar factory was built in Origny, led by Jean Duval, the grandfather of the company's current CEO.

In 2001 the company acquired the Bourbon Group's sugar plants in Reunion, a French Overseas Territory in the Indian Ocean. In 2002 it acquired Béghin-Say's sugar plants and beet growers. In 2003 the cooperative adopted the Tereos name and acquired the Brazilian company Guarani. In 2006 Tereos merged with the sugar beet cooperative Sucreries et Distilleries des Hauts de France, adding a further three sugar factories in France and also expanded into Mozambique to produce and process sugarcane. In 2010 Tereos acquired the Réunion-based assets of Quartier Français making the company the only sugar producer on the island.

Mitr Phol Sugar Corp is the fourth largest sugar producer in the world with a production of 4.3 million tonnes in 2014. It was founded in 1946 as a small household industry producing syrup that it sold to a nearby sugar mill. A decade later, in 1956, the company built its first sugar factory. The company remains family owned and is Asia's biggest sugar and bioenergy producer. Within Thailand, Mitr Phol has six sugar mills with a total daily production capacity of 130,500 tonnes of sugar cane. All mills have refineries attached and produce white sugar. Taken together the mills have the capacity to process 20 million tonnes of cane per year, producing approximately 2 million tonnes of sugar.

Mitr Phol is Thailand's largest ethanol producer with four ethanol plants and a total capacity of 1,100,000 litres per day, all from molasses. Mitr Phol runs several power plants that are attached to the sugar mills and burn bagasse to power steam turbines to generate all the power needed for the mill. Excess electricity is produced and sold to the national power grid. The company manufactures particleboards and medium density fibreboard from bagasse and rubber wood chips.

Mitr Phol group now has seven sugar factories in China with total crushing capacities of 87,000 tonnes of cane per day. The group has also expanded to Lao's People Democratic Republic; their factory there can produce 60,000 tonnes of sugar per year, most of which is exported to European Union.

In 2012, Mitr Phol acquired MSF Sugar Limited, Australia's third largest sugar producer behind Sucrogen and Mackay. MSF was established in 1886 in the Maryborough District, Queensland. The company currently runs four sugar mills with a total cane crushing capacity of 4.7 million tonnes of cane per year, buying cane from 600 contracted growers. The four mills produce around 500,000 tonnes of raw sugar a year.

AB Sugar is the third largest sugar producer in the world, employing around 40,000 people and operating in 10 countries. In 2014 the company produced close to 4.5 million tonnes of sugar but has the capacity to produce over 5.0 million tonnes in a good weather year. In addition to the UK the company has sugar operations in Africa, Spain and China. AB Sugar has majority control in five cane sugar factories in Guangxi Province, China where annual production has risen to around 500,000 tonnes per year. AB Sugar also operates four sugar beet factories in northern China that produce around 200,000 tonnes of sugar each year.

AB Sugar's Spanish business, Azucarera, operates three sugar beet factories in northern Spain and one in the south of Spain, where the company has also constructed a refinery to process imported cane raw sugar. In the UK, British Sugar processes the entire UK sugar beet crop to produce more than a million tonnes of sugar annually in its four beet factories.

In 2006 AB Sugar acquired 51% of Illovo Sugar Limited, the largest cane sugar producer in Africa. Ilovo has operations in Malawi, Zambia, Swaziland, Tanzania and Mozambique. In 2012/13 it produced around 6.5 million tonnes of cane on its own cane estates and manufactured just under 1.8 million tonnes of sugar in its factories.

Raízen is the second largest sugar producing company in the world by tonnage. It is also the third largest Brazilian energy company by revenue and the fifth largest company in Brazil. It is a joint venture formed in 2010 from the merger of the assets of sugar, fuel and ethanol derived from sugar from Cosan and Royal Dutch Shell in Brazil. The company has a market value of approximately US$15 billion and revenue of about US$26 billion. The company traces its origins back to 1936 with the foundation of the Costa Pinto sugar mill in Piracicaba in Sao Paulo State.

Raízen has 23 sugar mills that in the 2014 season produced 4.62 million tonnes of sugar. The company has an annual cane crushing capacity of 62 million tonnes and has 900 megawatts of installed capacity of electric power production from sugarcane bagasse. In 2014 Raízen announced that returns on capital from the company's sugar and ethanol operations had fallen to below 10 per cent, insufficient to justify further investment in the sector. Instead the company said it would look to expand its gasoline and natural gas distribution, service stations and railroads.

In January 2015 Raízen announced that it would stop production at its Bom Retiro mill in south-eastern Brazil for two years because of a shortage of cane. The company plans to use nearby mills in the interior of Sao Paulo state to crush cane that would normally be processed at Bom Retiro.

Along with their joint venture partner Iogen, Raízen began production in December 2014 of cellulosic ethanol at the company's US$100 million expansion at the Costa Pinto sugar cane mill in Piracicaba, São Paulo. The new facility converts sugar cane bagasse and straw into 40 million litres per year of advanced, second-generation cellulosic biofuel. If the technology lives up to expectations Raízen intends to spend up to US $1 billion on further second-generation ethanol plants.

And now the winner is…!

Südzucker AG, based in Germany, is the largest sugar producer in the world with an annual production of around 4.8 million tonnes. The company was formed in 1926 and now has 18,500 employees working in 29 sugar factories and 3 refineries with € 7.7 billion annual revenues. Sugar beet farmers hold 52% of the company's share capital. In addition to sugar the company is involved in ethanol production (from grains as well as from sugar beet), fruit processing and packaging and pizza manufacturing.

Südzucker has nine beet-processing factories in Germany and five in Poland. Südzucker Moldova has two factories that process beets from around 17,100 hectares. Through Raffinerie Tirlemontoise the company owns two factories in Belgium with a combined capacity of around 27,500 tonnes per day. The Südzucker Group bought the French Saint Louis Sucre in 2001. The company runs four sugar beet plants, four packaging plants and one cane sugar refinery. It also has a shareholding participation in one other sugar factory.

Through Agrana the company runs two sugar factories in Austria, two in the Czech Republic, one in Hungary, one in Romania, one in Slovakia as well as one refinery in Bosnia-Herzegovina and one in Romania. Südzucker also owns 25% minus one share of ED&F Man Holdings Ltd. The trade house was founded in 1783 and currently has over 3,400 employees in 60 countries. With headquarters in London ED&F Man trades coffee, molasses, biofuels, edible oils as well as shipping and financial services.

So much for the top ten; what about the other contenders?

Bunge, a publically quoted company on the NYSE, entered the sugar market as a trader in 2006 and now owns and operates eight mills in Brazil with a combined cane crushing capacity of over 20 million tonnes. The company grows about two thirds of its sugar cane itself and buys the rest from other sources.

Bunge bought Santa Juliana (MG), its first sugar mill in Brazil in 2007 and three years later sold its Brazilian fertilizer operations to Vale SA and acquired five sugar mills from the Moema Group. The following year Bunge opened its first Greenfield cane crushing plant in Pedro Afonso (TO), a joint venture between Bunge and Itochu, a Japanese trading company. Itochu is also a partner in the Bunge plant in Santa Juliana, in Minas Gerais.

Bunge has been hit by a shortage of cane as a result of the bad weather in the past few years. The company crushed 20 million tonnes of cane in 2014, up from 17 million tonnes in 2012 and 13 million tonnes in 2011; this compares to an estimated total capacity of 21 million tonnes. In 2014 Bunge produced about 1.0 million tonnes of sugar; out of their eight mills two produce only ethanol.

In October 2013 Bunge's chief executive suggested that the company was launching "a thoughtful comprehensive review" of its Brazilian milling operations. He estimated the replacement value of its milling assets at more than $3 billion but admitted that it had been challenging for Bunge to transfer its strengths in other agribusiness areas such as grains and soybeans to sugar.

Among the other contenders Turkiye Seker Fabrikalari, otherwise known as Turkseker, deserves a mention. The company has an annual sugar output of around 1.34 million tonnes. It is state-owned and operates 25 sugar factories with a nominal daily beet processing capacity of 105,000 tonnes and a theoretical maximum sugar production of just over two million tonnes. The company employs 25,000 people and is one of the largest state-owned companies in the country.

Turkey's first beet modern factory started operations in 1923 and a second factory opened in 1926; a further two followed a couple of years later.

The four factories merged in 1935 to form Turkseker. In 1950 the government launched an expansion plan for the industry with the opening of eleven new factories in the period 1951-1956. Over the years, and as domestic consumption climbed, further factories were added.

In total there are 33 beet factories in Turkey; the eight that are not owned by Turkseker are privately run by six independent companies and produce the other one million tonnes of sugar that make the country largely self-sufficient.

But not necessarily efficient: some analysts estimate that it costs Turkseker $1,000 to produce one tonne of sugar; this compares to the estimated $350 that it costs Turkey's private companies to produce one tonne. Turkey's domestic sugar price is set at a level that covers Turkseker's costs so it is unsurprising that the private companies are making a considerable margin on their own production. Unsurprisingly, government-set quotas limit the amount that they are allowed to produce

At the time of writing the Turkish government is looking to liberalise the industry and privatise Turkseker, possibly as early as 2017. This will not be easy given the size of the company's payroll and its high production costs: a large proportion of those 25,000 employees may find themselves out of a job. It will also not be easy because Turkseker plays a major agricultural role in the country, providing guaranteed off take for the country's farmers. Turkseker estimates that the company contributes about US$ 500-550 million each year to the national economy in terms of added value.

Finally, no league table of top global sugar companies would be complete without mentioning

ASR. The company owns nine refineries in five countries with a capacity of more than six million tonnes of sugar, making it the largest cane sugar refiner in the world. ASR also owns and operates sugar mills in the United States, Mexico and Belize. In 2007 the company expanded into Canada when it bought Redpath Sugar and into Mexico by acquiring the San Nicolas mill and refinery. In 2010 ASR acquired Tate & Lyle's European sugar operations in Portugal and the UK, including the Thames Refinery that has been in continuous operation since 1878. In 2012 ASR Group acquired the majority interest in Belize Sugar Industries Ltd.

ASR Group was formed in 1998 when two Florida sugar companies – Florida Crystals Corporation and Sugar Cane Growers Cooperative of Florida - partnered to acquire the sugar refinery in Yonkers, NY. Two years later ASR bought Domino Sugar on the U.S. East Coast and in 2005 the company acquired C&H Sugar on the U.S. West Coast.

The Fanjul family founded Florida Crystals Corporation in 1960. The family had been producing sugar in Cuba since 1850. Today, the company owns 155,000 acres, two sugar mills, a sugar refinery, and a packaging and distribution centre in Florida. In its most recent harvest, Florida Crystals processed 5.7 million tons of sugarcane on 152,000 acres, yielding 676,000 tons of raw sugar.

In 1960, less than 10 miles away, another group of family farmers joined together to begin the construction of a sugar mill in Belle Glade, Florida. Today, the Sugar Cane Growers Cooperative of Florida is comprised of 46 small-to-medium size sugarcane farmers in South Florida. During the last harvest season, the Cooperative processed 3 million tons of sugarcane grown on 68,000 acres, yielding 374,000 tons of raw sugar.

ASR Group and its shareholders now farm 450,000 acres of sugar cane fields in North America, Central America and the Caribbean. In addition the company annually acquires over 5 million tons of raw and direct consumption sugar from suppliers located in over 40 countries.

Governments

9.1 Why governments intervene

According to the FAO and World Bank,

"The international sugar market is one of the most highly distorted agricultural commodity markets." (1)

Sugar has also often been called "the most political of all commodities". This is partly because of the political lobbying power of sugar beet and cane farmers around the world – and their willingness to vote. But it is also partly because of the "sweetness" of sugar and the role that it plays in the modern diet. Although consumers pay little attention to the price of sugar they do get upset when the shelves are empty and they can't buy it.

In a freely functioning market, supply and demand is in theory at least matched by price. If demand increases or supply falls, prices rise to encourage supply while at the same time reducing demand. If supply increases or demand drops then prices fall, sending a signal to producers to reduce output or to consumers to increase demand.

This process is what is often described as the *"invisible hand"*, the unobservable market force that helps the demand and supply of goods in a free market to reach equilibrium automatically. Adam Smith introduced the phrase in 1759 in reference to income distribution and then used it again in *"The Wealth of Nations"* in 1776. He argued that an economy works best in a free market scenario where everyone works for his or her own interest – and where the government leaves people to buy and sell freely among themselves.

The American baseball player Yogi Berra once said that in theory there is no difference between theory and practice – but in practice there is.

In practice, markets may not always be efficient and governments may need to interfere to correct those inefficiencies. This might happen if producers club together into a cartel to raise prices, requiring the government to intervene to break up the cartel. But even without a cartel a sugar mill might be so big in a particularly region that it could in its own right be a monopoly employer or buyer of cane, forcing down wages and cane prices, or a monopoly seller, forcing sugar prices higher.

In addition, sugar producers might not correctly price what economists call "collective goods": these could be the environmental costs of factory pollution or heavy traffic on the roads at harvest time. Individual producers might not also correctly value the benefits of research into new cane varieties or of infrastructure investment such as railways or ports. On a wider scale governments rather than markets may better provide collective goods such as education and health services.

Inefficiencies sometimes creep into markets due to a lack of information. To counter that a government could encourage the setting up of commodity exchanges to facilitate trade and improve price transparency.

But governments also interfere in markets, not to correct market inefficiencies, but to obtain specific policy objectives such as the alleviation of poverty or a fairer distribution of wealth. Interfering in the market in this way can however have a cost: it can create price distortions that prevent the most productive and efficient allocation of resources. This "economic loss" has to be measured against the "social gain", say, of a more equal income distribution.

Governments may also interfere in markets for diplomatic reasons, for example by applying a lower import tariff on sugar from one country compared to sugar from another. Lower import tariffs might be applied to curry favour from a neighbour or in exchange for lower tariffs on other goods within the framework of a Free Trade Area (FTA). Altruistic governments may also reduce or remove import tariffs on sugar imports as part of a policy to promote growth in developing countries. Such an example would be the EU's "Everything But Arms" agreement (discussed in more detail below).

In the agricultural markets some governments, in particular China, may try to keep cane prices high in order to maintain rural incomes and to slow down the migration of the population to the cities. Other governments (or more correctly politicians) may try to keep cane prices high for less altruistic reasons: to win political votes. India is an obvious example of this; perhaps Thailand is a less obvious example.

Governments may also often interfere in markets to maintain employment. It would certainly be more cost efficient, say, for Bangladesh to close down their few remaining sugar mills and import the sugar they need from Brazil or Thailand. (The same also applies, but on a much larger scale, to China.) However, closing factories can result in a politically unacceptable increase in unemployment. Sugar industry employees in Bangladesh and China might be better off making something else other than sugar but a reallocation of that sort takes time. It would involve short-term hardship for the employees concerned and would be a difficult "political sell" in the short term. And everyone knows that politicians operate in the short term: their time frame is the next election.

While farmers are an important source of votes in most democracies, mill and factory owners can be useful sources of political campaign funds. Politicians don't just need votes to get elected; they also need money. The sugar industries in both developed and developing countries are often strongly connected politically; their voices can be heard.

The most famous, or rather infamous, example of this occurred on Presidents' Day in 1996 when President Bill Clinton was, according to the Starr Report, in a conversation with Monica Lewinsky in the Oval Office, looking to break off the relationship. That obviously important conversation was interrupted when the President received a phone call from Mr Alfonso Fanjul Jr., the Chairman and Chief Executive Officer of Florida Crystals Corporation.

Why did Mr Fanjul call the Oval Office on a federal holiday?

The answer may have been that a few hours earlier, Vice President Al Gore had announced in Everglades National Park a plan to levy a penny-a-pound tax on Florida sugar growers. The money raised would go toward a $1.5 billion effort to clean up the Everglades. Florida was set to be a key battleground in the upcoming presidential race, and according to one poll, most Floridians wanted to make sugar growers help pay for the Everglades clean up.

But why did the President take the call on a

federal holiday? Alfonso Fanjul Jr served as co-chairman of Bill Clinton's Florida campaign in 1992 and is still a major contributor and fundraiser for the Democratic Party. His brother Pepe contributes to the Republican Party.

Political power in the sugar market is skewed in favour of millers and farmers and against consumers. Sugar makes up a small part of the weekly family budget and most consumers would not be able to say how much they paid for their last bag of sugar at the supermarket.

And although most sugar these days is bought by food manufacturers, and sold on in products, sugar is still a relatively small part of their budget compared to marketing, branding and distribution. Sugar growers can sometimes protest noisily when prices are low. With the exception of India, sugar consumers almost never take to the streets when prices are high.

Consumers do protest noisily, however, when the supermarkets run out of sugar. This rarely happens but shortages did occur in various countries in 2011 at the height of the recent bull market in sugar. Supermarket shelves were bare in a number of countries, most notably in Portugal, but also in Egypt and the importing countries of West Africa. This provoked wide media coverage and prompted questions from politicians.

When sugar prices rise too much or shortages develop, politicians usually look to pass the blame on to someone else. Just as Louis Renault did in the film "Casablanca", they "round up the usual suspects". Speculators are the "usual suspects" in the case of rising prices; "hoarders" in the case of shortages.

In an attempt to limit speculation governments

will sometimes impose position limits in the futures markets, limiting the quantity of sugar futures that any individual or company can hold. In extreme cases, as happened in India in the 1990s, the government can even close the futures markets, a perfect example of "shooting the messenger".

Governments have in the past arrested (and sometimes even executed) anyone that they thought was trying to push prices higher by holding sugar off the market. They have also confiscated stocks, even if those stocks were "normal working stocks" – the stocks that a drink processor or sugar miller would hold in the normal operation of their businesses.

And if all else fails politicians will blame "foreign interference" for the shortages. This has happened recently when the Venezuelan government blamed the US for a shortage of food, toilet paper and washing powder. Of course blaming other people or confiscating stocks does little to resolve the problem, but it does deflect attention.

Governments and politicians will intervene in markets to correct perceived inefficiencies or to achieve certain policy objectives. However governments will also intervene for philosophical reasons, believing that they can do a better job than the free market at balancing supply and demand at a "fair price". Politicians often argue that food is too important to be left to the vagaries of the free market and to the laws of supply and of demand.

The EU's Common Agricultural Policy (CAP) has in the past tried to balance supply and demand through complex systems of import, export and production quotas. The tricky bit is trying to work out where to set the price. Set it too low and production can fall short of the quotas. (In Soviet times the government solved this problem by punishing producers who failed to meet their quotas.) Set the price too high and you will end up with Butter Mountains and Wine Lakes; both were features of the CAP in the 1970s and 1980s.

Set the price too high and the producers will earn a "rent" on their quotas. When that happens the quotas can become valuable commodities in themselves. And if production quotas do become valuable how do you decide who should get them and who shouldn't. The same dilemma arises, incidentally, with any quotas, whether they are on production, imports or exports.

Another problem is that the committees that set the prices tend to be inflexible and slow to react. A weather problem somewhere might significantly reduce the prospects for production. In addition the committee might not necessarily have all the relevant information to make informed decisions. Committees are generally vulnerable to political lobbying and may be corruptible. Of course, most committees are comprised of well meaning individuals that are trying to do their best at solving whatever problem they have to solve. It is just that commodity prices are so complex that no committee could ever solve them correctly.

In sugar the cane crop cycle means that the market can be particularly slow to balance supply and demand. Cane is expensive to plant and once it is in the ground it costs relatively little to harvest and crush it in following years. As years pass each stick of cane will yield less sucrose but the cane can economically be kept in the ground for years without replanting. Just how long it stays in the ground varies from country to country: two years in India and four years in Thailand and Brazil. Cane is not only expensive to plant but it is also expensive to grub up and replace with an alternative crop: once cane is in the ground it tends to stay there even if sugar prices fall significantly.

As long as the sugar price is high enough to cover the marginal cost of cutting and processing the cane the mills will keep on crushing it. The farmer may cut back on field inputs such as fertiliser, herbicides and pesticides but it is only when the farmer or the mill is faced with a decision as to whether or not to replant the cane that the sugar price seriously begins to impact production. This results in a long time lag between the price signal and the supply response.

Beet sugar has an annual production cycle and a much faster price response. However most beet sugar is grown in countries where prices are fixed or production is subsidised. As a result beet sugar rarely responds in world price signals.

9.2   How governments intervene

Governments have a market intervention toolbox so full the lid won't close. Some tools are designed for controlling imports; others for encouraging (or discouraging) exports, production or consumption. Let's start with imports.

Import restrictions can take the form of outright bans, tariffs and/or quotas. They can also take the form of non-tariff barriers that restrict imports through bureaucratic delays or quality restrictions. Barriers can also be created by "non-action", for example by not taking any action against a cartel of sugar importers that might agree to quietly limit imports.

Although nearly all countries control sugar imports in one way or another, few countries ban them outright. When a country does ban imports completely the measure is usually temporary, to deal with a short-term problem. Iran banned all sugar imports in 2014 to allow time for excessive stocks to be worked off and to conserve foreign exchange in response to low oil prices.

India has occasionally banned sugar imports for short periods, but then India has at one time or another pretty much tried everything in terms of sugar policy; they have used every tool in the box. These tools have included import tariffs; export subsidies; a complex mill licensing system, controls on the amount of sugar each mill can sell (at times on a yearly, quarterly or monthly basis), and a requirement that each mill sell a percentage of their production at below market prices to the poor through the Public Distribution System.

Most of these mechanisms were abolished when sugar was finally "decontrolled" in 2013 but one important mechanism remains: minimum cane prices. At present, mills are required by law to pay growers a "Fair and Representative Price" (FRP) for their cane. The FRP is set each year by the central government and stands at Rps 2,300 per tonne of cane for the 2015/16 harvest. Some states set a minimum cane price higher than the FRP. Uttar Pradesh has set its minimum cane price this season at Rps 2,800 per tonne of cane.

Indian mills are required by law to crush all the cane that is delivered to them and mill owners and managers have at times been put in prison for either not paying the full price or for not crushing all the cane.

When sugar prices are low mills end up forced

to pay more for the cane than they can recover when they sell the sugar; margins turn negative and the mills lose money. They try to sidestep this problem by running up what are called "cane arrears" whereby they pay the farmers only a percentage of the minimum cane price and give them an "IOU" for the rest. At the time of writing Indian domestic prices are low and cane arrears are in excess of $1 billion.

Some states, namely Karnataka and Maharashtra, have stopped setting their own cane price and have instead introduced a cane pricing formula where the farmers get 70% of the mills' revenue on sugar and ethanol sales and the mill gets the rest. There is still some argument as to whether this 70% should include revenues on by-products such as electricity – as well as to disputes as to whether there should be a revenue sharing formula at all.

The FRP and the states' minimum cane prices have been set so high that cane farming is by far the most profitable agricultural crop now in India. This has in turn led to an expansion in production that has driven prices even lower.

As a result the central government stepped in to try and help the mills by subsidising bank loans to the sector. This had little impact, as banks grew increasingly reluctant to lend money to the struggling sector. After much wrangling the government introduced an export subsidy of approximately $64/tonne on up to 1.4 million tonnes of raw sugar exports. Unfortunately the measure took so long to work its way through the political and bureaucratic process that by the time it was finalised the world market had fallen so far that the subsidies were insufficient to encourage exports.

The government and the sector are looking now

at alternative policies, but the problem will not go away until the farmers get the price signal to reduce production. By setting cane prices too high the government is encouraging farmers to grow cane that no one wants but that mills are forced to buy. The only real solution is to abolish minimum cane prices – or at least keep them at a level that does not result in over production – and instead widen the use of a revenue sharing scheme.

China also has a long history of managing domestic agricultural commodity prices, either through reserve stocks or import controls. Both have tended to work in unison: import controls can tighten domestic supply to an extent that reserve stocks can be sold off at a profit. However the system has recently begun to come apart at the seams with the Chinese government forced to sell off cotton and other reserve stocks at a loss.

When China joined the World Trade Organisation the country agreed to impose a TRQ (Tariff Rate Quota) of 15% on imports of sugar up to 1.93 million tonnes per year and a 50% tariff on imports on any quantity above that level. The government allocates the quotas among three or four state companies but those companies do not have to use the quotas if there is no money to be made importing.

The fall in world prices in 2014/15 resulted in a flood of raw sugar imports into China at the full 50% import duty. The government slowed this flow by introducing what they called an "automatic licensing scheme" whereby any company looking to import sugar would have to apply for an import licence that would be given "automatically". However the licences are not as "automatic" as the importers would like. The scheme therefore seems to be working in slowing the flow of raw sugar into the country.

Controls on raw sugar imports have led to a surge in white sugar imports: up to 500,000 tonnes of (often Thai) white sugar enter China each year across the border from Vietnam and Laos. Even a government as powerful as China's cannot necessarily control sugar imports.

This inability to control imports is leading to a complete rethink of agricultural policy in China; the government is considering moving towards a system of letting the market set agricultural prices and then providing direct subsidies to farmers if those prices fall too low. However paying farmers to produce sugar that might not be needed would be just another distortion in the market.

Sugar is also a political commodity in Thailand where more than one million farmers depend on it for their livelihood. These one million "votes" are too important to be left to the vagaries of the market and way back in 1984 the government introduced a quota and revenue sharing system that is still in place today. At the beginning of each season the government, millers and farmers jointly estimate how much sugar will be produced and estimate the price it will fetch. From this, they calculate a "preliminary cane price" which millers must pay farmers for their cane as it is delivered to the mills.

The stakeholders meet again after the crop season ends, usually by early October, to agree a final cane price based on how much sugar was produced and at what price it was sold. If the final price is higher than the preliminary price, millers pay farmers the difference.

If it's lower, farmers don't have to pay anything back; the government reimburses millers through the Cane & Sugar Fund (CSF). The government uses the value-added tax collected from domestic sugar sales to repay the Bank for Agriculture and Agricultural Cooperatives (BAAC) for the costs incurred by the state-run Cane and Sugar Fund (CSF). The CSF can be topped up as required by the state budget.

India, China and Thailand are just three examples of how governments in developing countries try to control their domestic sugar markets. But the list is long: nearly every developing country interferes in their domestic sugar market. Indonesia uses an import quota system that allows only raw sugar to be imported and insists that the white sugar that is produced from those imports is only sold to industrial food and beverage manufacturers and not directly to consumers.

Even non-sugar producers restrict imports. For example Nigeria protects its local refining industry by insisting that all sugar sold in the country contains Vitamin A. This is something that is difficult to add in an exporting country but much easier to add in at destination.

But it is not just developing countries that interfere in markets: the developed world is an even worse offender.

The EU sugar market currently operates under an incredibly complex system of import tariffs and quotas. The bloc imposes a standard import tariff of €339 per tonne on raw cane sugar for refining and €419 per tonne on white sugar. Countries that were at one time European colonies can export some sugar duty free to the EU under an import quota. These "so-called" ACP (African, Caribbean and Pacific) countries are even allowed to export their own production to the EU and import sugar to satisfy domestic consumption.

In 2001 the EU introduced what is called "Everything But Arms", a policy that allows LDCs (Less Developed Countries, as defined by the UN) to export, literally, "everything but arms" to the EU duty free. Sugar was included in the list of products although it was only in July 2009 that transitional measures were lifted and full duty free access was given. The EBA programme has today largely been replaced by so-called "Economic Partnership Agreements", negotiated with each individual country.

The EU reformed its sugar policy regime in 2006 following a negative ruling from a WTO (World Trade Organisation) panel in a case brought against it by Australia, Thailand and Brazil. As part of the reforms, the EU reduced the intervention price for white sugar from €631.9 per tonne to €404.4 per tonne – a 36% cut spread over four years. At that level, once you add in the cost of freight for shipping the sugar to the EU, few LDCs can compete cost wise with the large European beet sugar producers.

In addition to ACP and EBA sugars, 334,054 tonnes of Brazilian sugar can be imported into the EU under what is known as the CXL quota at a preferential rate of €98 per tonne. There is also an erga omnes TRQ (a Tariff Rate Quota open for any country to meet) of 253,977 tonnes that is also available at the same duty rate.

Cuba also has a reduced tariff on 68,969 tonnes of imports per year while the Balkan countries also have a reduced tariff rate import quota on 91,506 tonnes. In 2014 the European Commission negotiated a free trade agreement with Central America, Colombia and Peru that allows a limited quantity of sugar imports at a reduced tariff.

Prior to the 2006 reforms the EU paid subsidies on sugar exports, including on sugar exported in processed food and drinks. Since 2008/09, the EU no longer pays export subsidies and, because EU prices are higher than world market prices, EU food processors have had to find another way to compete in the world market. To help them the European Commission introduced something called Inward Processing Relief (IPR) whereby food companies are authorized to import sugar from any origin duty-free on the condition that they export the equivalent tonnage in their processed products.

As well as closely managing imports the EU also controls domestic production through a reference price and a system of production quotas, both of which are due to disappear as of 30th September 2017.

All in all the EU sugar regime is so complicated that if you think you now understand it I haven't explained it properly.

The U.S. sugar industry has enjoyed trade protection since 1789 when Congress enacted the first tariff against foreign sugar. Since then, the U.S. government has continued to provide trade support and protection for its domestic sugar industry. U.S. sugar imports are strictly controlled by Tariff Rate Quotas (TRQs) that fix the amount of sugar that can be imported at a low or zero duty. The United States Department of Agriculture (USDA) establishes the volume of these quotas annually and the U.S. Trade Representative (USTR) allocates the TRQs among countries.

The amount set aside for import under TRQs

must meet US obligations to the World Trade Organization (WTO) – currently a minimum of 1,117,195 tons of raw sugar and 22,000 tons of refined sugar. Sugar that is imported under the TRQs pays a tariff of $0.625 cents/lb. This compares to sugar imported outside the TRQs of $15.36 cents/lb for raw sugar and 16.21 cents/lb for refined sugar.

Although the North American Free Trade Agreement (NAFTA) came into force on 1st January 1994 Mexico only obtained unrestricted tariff-free sugar exports into the US market on 1st January 2008, after a fifteen-year transition period. North American free trade in sugar lasted through to August 2014 when the US government imposed provisional anti-dumping and anti-subsidy duties on Mexican sugar imports following a petition from the US producers.

After negotiation the provisional tariffs were officially suspended in December 2014 in exchange for a system of minimum prices and tonnage limits. Under the so-called "suspension agreements" Mexico agreed to limit sugar exports to the US, using a system of export quotas to be imposed by the Mexican government on individual mills. A minimum ex-mill selling price was agreed for Mexican imports at 22.25 cents/lb for raw sugar and 26.00 cents/lb for refined sugar. In addition it was agreed that no more than 53% of Mexico's total exports to the United States could be refined sugar.

However US sugar policy is not just limited to managing imports; the country also operates a system of production allotments (quotas) and price support. The USDA provides loans to sugarcane and sugar beet producers and processors that guarantee a minimum price regardless of the market price. At the end of the loan term (generally nine months), sugar producers and processors can either turn over to the government the sugar they produced as payment for the loan, or sell their sugar on the market. They will do the latter if the market price is higher than the USDA loan amount. Currently, the loan rate is US$ 18.75 cents/lb for raw cane sugar and US$ 24.09 cents/lb for refined beet sugar.

The USDA also allocates a share of the anticipated U.S. sugar market to sugar producers annually. This allotment determines the amount of sugar an individual company is allowed to sell that year. There allotments are often adjusted based on harvest conditions. If companies produce sugar in excess of their allotments, they must store it at their expense until they have permission to sell in the future. The 2008 Farm Bill requires that these allotments be at least 85% of domestic sugar demand.

Under another provision of the 2008 Farm Bill, the U.S. government can sell sugar forfeited under the loan programme to ethanol producers. Over the past couple of years the USDA has indeed done that, locking in a significant loss.

US sugar policy is not only complicated, it is also controversial. According to the USDA, only 4,600 out of the 2.2 million farms in the U.S produce sugar beets or sugarcane. According to a report from the Heritage Foundation (2) each sugar farm in 2013 received on average an additional $310,000 thanks to the sugar programme.

Governments have not limited their ambitions to interfering in their domestic markets, they have also at times tried to control the world sugar market – or at least stabilize prices. They have done this through a series of international sugar agreements.

Their first attempt was the Brussels Convention of 1902, signed by the Austro-Hungarian Empire, Belgium, France, Germany, Italy, the Netherlands, Norway, Spain, Sweden and the United Kingdom. The parties undertook to promote consumption and effectively abolish subsidies on the production and export of both beet and cane sugar. The Brussels Convention legally expired in 1920 but had effectively already ceased to operate six years earlier with the outbreak of the First World War.

Attempts to negotiate a new comprehensive international price stabilization agreement were made during the 1920s and early 1930s and an agreement was finally reached in 1937. It was signed by both exporters and importers and was intended to take into account the interests of both. However the Second World War made the agreement unworkable.

A series of new agreements were negotiated in 1953, 1958, 1968 and 1977, all using adjustable export quotas to try and stabilize world prices. These export quotas were increased or suspended when world market prices rose towards the ceiling price; they were reduced, within limits, when prices fell.

The last International Sugar Agreement with economic clauses was signed in 1977 and lasted from 1978 to 1984. Quotas were strengthened by "special stocks" of 2.5 million tonnes, which at that time were more than 10% of world net-exports to the free market. The stocks were financed by a transaction tax on every tonne of sugar traded.

None of the international agreements, except arguably the 1953 one, succeeded in their price objectives. None were flexible enough to deal with structural changes that occurred in the world sugar economy. The 1958 agreement failed to handle the aftermath of the Cuban Revolution and the US embargo, when the US sought imports from non-Cuban sources and drove up the world market price abruptly. The 1968 agreement was unable to cope with the spike in prices in 1974 while the 1977 agreement failed to prevent the 1980 price boom, or the subsequent price collapse.

There have been no further agreements with economic clauses since the 1977 one expired at the end of 1984, and none is in prospect. Since 1985 the International Sugar Organization has existed through administrative agreements without economic clauses, with the objective of fostering international cooperation in sugar matters through providing information, statistics and analysis on world sweeteners markets and a forum for intergovernmental policy discussion.

Markets are far from perfect; they can be volatile and price can over-shoot in both directions. But however flawed, markets are powerful things: once you start to mess with them the law of unintended consequences quickly kicks in.

The success of production and import quotas depends on correctly estimating demand. Even if you get demand right, quotas need to be effectively policed. Sugar can sometimes be "sold out the back door".

Quotas also need to be priced correctly. If they are priced incorrectly then either the quota holders earn excessive profits (in the form of rent on their quota) or they are not motivated to use them. The former results in an excessive distribution of wealth from consumers to producers; the latter results in commodity shortages.

As for export subsidies, the recent example of

India shows how ineffective they can be. In February 2015 the Indian government introduced an export subsidy of about $64 per tonne on 1.4 million tonnes of raw sugar. The world didn't need that sugar and world price did what it always does in such a situation – it ran away from it. World sugar prices fell to a level where Indian exports were no longer economically viable even with the subsidy.

But as a number of commentators pointed out at the time, if the subsidised sugar had been exported it would have resulted in a transfer of wealth from the Indian government to the consumers of that sugar in the importing countries. That may not have been exactly what the Indian government had in mind.

Commodity prices are blunt instruments when it comes to social policy. The Chinese and Indian governments have tried to maintain rural incomes through high sugar cane prices. This has resulted first in excessive domestic production and, in the case of China, as world prices fell, excessive imports.

If governments really want to improve rural incomes they have more efficient tools in their toolbox than the price of sugar. One efficient tool is to provide direct payments to poor families. This is what Brazil's government has done with *Bolsa Família*; payments are dependent on the families making sure that their children attend school and are vaccinated against disease. Accompanied by investment in education, these payments can do more to alleviate poverty than artificially high commodity prices.

Unfortunately, giving taxpayers' money to poor people in the form of direct payments is usually too visible a method of income distribution – and therefore politically less acceptable. Governments often prefer to redistribute wealth by stealth, by keeping food prices high and transferring wealth from the consumer to the producer. This is an "invisible" tax on the consumer.

9.3   Institutionalised corruption

After spending two years as a futures trader in Minneapolis, my company transferred me back to London with a brief to develop new markets in the Middle East and North Africa. The company's agent in an African country (I won't say which one) contacted me to say that they had a surplus of sugar that year and the government would like to export a couple of cargoes to earn much needed foreign exchange. The minister who was handling the sale was coming to London the following week. Could I meet him?

Despite being only 25 years old at the time I met the minister and took him to a swanky restaurant. We had an excellent meal, discussed the sugar market and tried to estimate the price for the particular grade of sugar the country was exporting. As we were leaving the restaurant I was surprised when the minister suggested that we dine again the following evening. I agreed but wondered what we had left to talk about.

At dinner the next evening the minister slipped me a shopping list of electronic items that he would like to take back with him from London. There were only four items on the list: a television, a radio, a stereo system and (bizarrely) an electric iron. He asked if I could help him obtain these items. I wasn't quite sure if he was asking me to go with him to the shops to help him choose the items or if he was asking me to buy the items and give them to him for free. And if it was the latter I was surprised at how little it took to bribe a government minister.

The next day I told my boss what had happened. I thought it was a bit of a joke but he took it seriously, advising me to go back to the minister to politely explain that company policy meant that we couldn't help with his request but that we would still like to buy his sugar and that we would be very competitive on the price. I did as instructed and was not surprised to hear a week later that one of our competitors had bought the two cargos of sugar. I calculated they had probably made a profit of $250,000 on the deal and I compared that to the couple of hundred dollars that it would have cost to buy the items on the minister's shopping list.

I mentioned this to my boss who told me angrily that I should never ever think about paying a bribe to anyone, no matter how much money was at stake. He called it "selling your soul to the devil" and argued that even if a television may not cost much it was "the thin edge of the wedge. And from a business point of view", he added, "It makes no sense.

"First it will give your client a hold over you. Second, if everyone does the same thing you will end up competing against each other in the amount of bribes that you pay." He called it "competitive corruption" and said that paying a bribe would be ineffective if your competitor paid more. Of course he was right. However his advice proved unnecessary. That was the only time in my 37-year career in the sugar business that I was ever asked for a bribe.

Governments have largely got out of the business of buying and selling sugar; and those that are still in the business are far more transparent than they were 30 years ago. When business is in private hands producers or buyers have little interested in receiving bribes – what they are interested in is the price and the terms.

But governments set sugar policy. They impose import restrictions and subsidise exports. They negotiate duty-free import quotas for some exporters but not for others. They allocate production quotas to domestic millers and farmers. They fix minimum prices and give interest free loans. They buy surplus stocks and store them to maintain domestic prices. They give away taxpayer funds for research and development, as well as for infrastructure projects such as roads and rails. And finally they can influence demand through consumption taxes on sugar or legally enforceable mandates on ethanol. All this can make a huge difference; it can determine whether an industry flourishes, thrives or fails.

If you are the CEO of a sugar producing company and have an hour to spare should you spend that hour talking to your cane or beet growers, to your employees or to your customers? The answer is probably "none of the above". You would be better off spending that marginal hour lobbying the government to intervene on your behalf in the markets.

If you are Brazilian you might want to lobby the government to increase the mandated quantity of ethanol in gasoline. If you are Indian you might want to lobby for production or export subsidies or reserve stocks. If you are European you might want to lobby your national government to use some (or in some cases, "more") of the CAP (Common Agricultural Policy) discretionary funds on subsidies to beet growers. If you are American you might want to call your Congressman and remind him to veto any legislation that might weaken the US sugar policy.

Government intervention in the sugar market is often both distorting and inefficient but governments will nevertheless continue to interfere. As long as they do, the sugar industries across the world will continue to lobby their governments for favourable policies. Payments to political parties can "buy" favourable policies but this institutionalised corruption is unfortunately the way that modern democracy works. And as long as politicians gain from the system they have little interest in changing it.

Consumers

10.1   Are we eating more or less sugar?

My old Economics professor always used to tell me that if I was stuck on a problem I should always return to the data. Although that is probably sound advice, data on sugar consumption is not easy to find – and when you do find it, you can't rely on it.

One of the problems that sugar statisticians face is that sugar consumption is what you have left over once you have accounted for production, imports and exports. This is what we call "apparent consumption", an "implied" number that cannot be measured directly.

But even production, imports and exports can be difficult to track. Sugar production data is usually fairly reliable because each mill has to prepare accounts and pay taxes. However in certain countries, for example in Northern India, some production is never declared. It is sold, literally, out of the back door of the sugar mill. (Rather oddly, it is called "black sugar".) No one knows how much sugar is sold in this way.

Sugar import and export statistics are also usually pretty accurate but some trade flows do get missed. This can be intentionally when sugar is smuggled into or out of a country to avoid paying duties. Sugar smuggling is common in SE Asia; an estimated 500,000 tonnes move illegally (or semi-legally) each year across the borders into China from Laos and Vietnam. Smuggled sugars also find their way from Malaysia to Indonesia and even the Philippines. Sugar is also smuggled both into and within the EU, the latter as part of a VAT fraud that the European Commission is trying to crack down on.

Although it is hard to track imports and exports of sugar it is even harder to keep tabs on the import and export of sugar in food products. In the US, many confectionary manufacturers have moved south of the border to take advantage of Mexico's lower sugar and labour costs and they now export the finished products back north. The prepared, or processed, food industry has also grown in Asia (for the same reasons). Australia, for example, used to be a net exporter of sugar-containing food products to Asia but is now a net importer.

However Australia is still a net exporter of what are called "blends", sugar mixed with sorbitol, cocoa or milk powder (or even salt) that Japanese trading companies import to avoid the country's hefty import tariffs on sugar. Both Australian and Japanese Customs figures may under-estimate these flows.

It is not only Customs Officers who have difficulty in working out the quantity of sugar in food products; we all do. We all expect to find sugar in breakfast cereals or cookies but sugar is also "hidden" in a lot of places where we don't expect to find it, such as pasta and barbeque sauces, salad dressings and "low fat" diet products, particularly yoghurts. Sugar is also hidden in white bread; it is what turns white bread that appetising brown colour when it is toasted. So if you ask people how much sugar they consume they usually have no idea.

The other problem is that people lie, whether intentionally or not, about what they eat. Most people underestimate their food intake, forgetting that cookie they had at work or the leftover children's dinner that they finished off before their partner came home from the office. Some researchers have tried to get a better idea of what people eat by asking them to conserve all their shop and supermarket till receipts, but you still don't know whether they "forget" to keep an occasional Starbucks receipt.

You also don't know how much of the food that was bought was thrown away before it was eaten. Remember that the FAO estimates that about a third of all food is wasted between farm and fork; the USDA estimates that 11% of all sugar is "lost" between the retail outlet and the customer while a further 34% is "lost" by the customer. And although those figures seem high, remember that sugar goes into a lot of perishable food items such as yogurts, cakes etc.

All this means that we don't really know for sure how much sugar – or even any other foodstuff – people consume. The statistics can be obscure and contradictory and the consumer surveys unreliable. With such unclear data it is relatively easy for lobbyists to find sugar consumption estimates that support the point of view that they want to put across. Lobbyists use sugar statistics like a drunken man uses a lamppost: for support rather than for illumination.

Having got the disclaimers out of the way, what does the limited data that we have tell us about the amount of sugar we are consuming?

But before I try and answer that question, take a moment to try and answer that question yourself. I imagine that your reply will be that we are all eating more prepared foods than we used to – and that because so much sugar is hidden from sight in those prepared foods - we must all be eating way more sugar than we, or our parents, did thirty years ago. If you did answer that way you will not be alone: a casual survey of the Internet will support the view that sugar consumption has rocketed and we are getting fat – and ill – because of it.

Fortunately both your answer and the conventional wisdom of the Internet are wrong. People will consume about the same quantity of sugar this year, or in some cases significantly less sugar, than they or their parents consumed thirty or even forty years ago. Let's look at some numbers in Australia, the UK and the US.

Australia's Bureau of Statistics stopped publishing data on sugar consumption in 1999 but Greenpool, a consultancy company, published a report in 2012 (1) that found that the country's annual per capita sugar consumption had fallen from 57 kg in 1951 to around 42 kg in 2011.

The report caused a heated media storm. Some commentators dismissed the report outright, arguing that it contradicted other data from ABARE (Australian Bureau of Agricultural Economics). Others criticised the methodology: in particular they argued that the report underestimated the amount of sugar Australia imports in processed food products. Others argued that the report did not take into account fructose consumption and that HFCS consumption had increased even if sugar consumption had fallen. Others simply could not believe that sugar consumption had fallen so much given the growth in the country's obesity rates.

However the authors stood their ground, arguing that: the ABARE data did not include exports and was never intended to be used to measure domestic consumption; that they had correctly assessed imports of sugar-containing food products; and that Australia does not produce HFCS and very little, if any, of it is imported into the country.

The Australian Health Survey (AHS) for 2011/12 (published in 2014) may support the study's conclusions. (2) The AHS was conducted by the Australian Bureau of Statistics, which also conducted Australia's last national dietary survey of adults and children in 1995. The survey showed a surprising result: over the period Australians had reduced their daily consumption of calories. In the 1995 survey, average daily energy intake was 2,641 calories for men and 1,787 calories for women. By 2012 the reported average energy intake had fallen to 2,306 calories for males and 1,768 calories for females.

Carbohydrates, of which sugar is one, contributed the largest proportion of energy intake for men (45%) and women (46%) in both surveys. The contribution of fat to energy intake remained constant, at approximately 32-34% for men and women, in all age groups. Australians are apparently eating less of everything than they were thirty years ago, but still eating roughly the same percentage of carbohydrates, fat and protein.

Sugar consumption has been a touchy subject in Australia for quite a while. In a study published in 2011 Jennie Brand-Miller and Alan Barclay argued that sugar consumption was falling; they coined the term "Australian Paradox" to describe what they claim were diverging trends in sugar consumption and obesity rates in Australia. (3) The study raised a storm amid accusations that the authors had used incorrect or inappropriate statistics. An academic investigation subsequently cleared the authors of misconduct and the authors stand by their conclusions (4). However the storm is still raging. (5)

But let's return to the Australian Health Survey for 2011/12. The survey found that on average Australian adults spent 33 minutes per day doing physical activity. However the distribution within that average was highly skewed with 60% of adults doing less than 30 minutes, and fewer than 20% doing an hour or more per day on average. In contrast, sedentary leisure occupied just over 4 hours a day on average, with almost 30% of the adult population reporting more than 5 hours of sedentary leisure activity each day.

This importance of physical activity was taken up in a 2014 paper published by the Institute of Economic Affairs in the United Kingdom. (6) Christopher Snowdon, the author of that report, blamed the rise in obesity in the UK over the past forty years on a decline in physical activity at home and in the workplace, not on an increase in sugar, fat or calorie consumption.

The paper argued that per capita consumption of sugar, salt, fat and calories has been falling in Britain for decades: per capita sugar consumption had fallen by 16 per cent since 1992 and per capita calorie consumption has fallen by 21 per cent since 1974. Since 2002, the average body weight of English adults has increased by two kilograms. This has coincided with a decline in calorie consumption of 4.1 per cent and a decline in sugar consumption of 7.4 per cent.

Mr Snowdon is not alone in this surprising conclusion. According to the British Heart Foundation,

'Overall intake of calories, fat and saturated fat has

decreased since the 1970s. This trend is accompanied by a decrease in sugar and salt intake, and an increase in fibre and fruit and vegetable intake.'

It is worth quoting the IEA report in more length:

The Department for Environment, Food and Rural Affairs (DEFRA) has carried out annual surveys of the British diet since 1974. These surveys are based on diet diaries compiled by a cross-section of the public and are supported by till receipts...These data indicate a significant decline in daily per capita calorie consumption in the last forty years, from 2,534 in 1974 to 1,990 in 2012. This represents a decline in energy consumption of 21.5 per cent.

The survey also ... shows a decline in the consumption of 'total sugars' of sixteen per cent since 1992 and a decline in saturated fat consumption of 41 per cent since 1974. Consumption of protein, cholesterol, sodium and carbohydrates (of which sugar is one) have all declined since 1974. Indeed, the consumption of almost all of the nutrients in the British diet have either declined or held steady since the DEFRA study was initiated. Overall, fat consumption declined from 111 gms per day in 1974 to 81 gms per day in 2012...

All of these figures relate to food and drink consumed in the home, which accounts for 85-90 per cent of total consumption, but DEFRA also holds information on food and drink consumed outside the home. These 'eating out' figures only go back to 2001/02, but they show a significant decline in daily calories consumed, from 310 in 2001/02 to 219 in 2012. At a time when sugary snacks and fast food outlets are being blamed for fuelling obesity, it is worth noting that the evidence shows a decline in sugar consumption (from 14 gms per day in 2001/02 to 8 gms in 2012) and a decline in saturated fat consumption (from

4.2 gms per day in 2001/02 to 3.0 gms in 2012) outside the home....

The trends discussed above are corroborated by the National Diet and Nutrition Survey (NDNS), which began in the 1990s, the results of which can be compared to the Dietary and Nutritional Survey of British Adults, which holds data for 1986/87. These surveys collect data for food and drink consumed inside and outside the home.... They indicate that average calorie consumption has fallen by 9.8 per cent for 19-64 year olds since 1986/87. This is close to the 12 per cent reduction reported by DEFRA in the same period for the whole population.

But if we are eating less, why are we getting fatter? The answer, according to the IEA report, is that although we may be eating less, we are doing even less physical activity.

The transition from manual labour to office work saw jobs in agriculture decline from eleven to two per cent of employment in the twentieth century while manufacturing jobs declined from 28 to 14 per cent of employment. Britons are walking less (from 255 miles per year in 1976 to 179 miles in 2010) and cycling less (from 51 miles per year in 1976 to 42 miles in 2010). Only 18 per cent of adults report doing any moderate or vigorous physical activity at work while 63 per cent never climb stairs at work and 40 per cent spend no time walking at work.

Outside of work, 63 per cent report spending less than ten minutes a day walking and 53 per cent do no sports or exercise whatsoever. Add to this the ubiquity of labour-saving devices and it is clear that Britons today have less need, and fewer opportunities, for physical activity both in the workplace and at home. Put simply, they have reduced the number of calories they consume, but they have reduced the amount they move around even more".

The view that we are eating less sugar now than we used to is supported by research carried out by Czarnikow (a sugar trader and consultant) in May 2014. (7) Czarnikow wrote that we all eat less sugar as we become richer and that once basic needs are met, we become relatively indifferent towards sugar.

We may eat more sugar in processed foods but we eat less sugar directly (only 20% of sugar usage in the UK today is in table-top form). Czarnikow's consumption records show that UK sugar consumption peaked at 53 kg/head in 1957, dropped to 48.5 kg/head by 1970 and has since fallen to 35kg/head.

According to FAO figures (8) consumption in Europe as a whole has remained stable for over 40 years at an average of 33 kg per capita per year between 1970 and 2011. The FAO figures are "apparent consumption" numbers, the amount of sugar that is available based on the sugar supply. Once wastage is taken into account, the actual amount consumed could be as low as 25 kg per capita.

But what about in the US: are Americans also eating less sugar than they used to? Data from the USDA shows that unlike Australians or Europeans, Americans are eating more than they used to.

According to the loss-adjusted food availability data, (9) Americans are consuming more calories per day than they did 40 years ago. In 1970, Americans consumed an estimated 2,109 calories per person per day; in 2010 they consumed an estimated 2,568 calories. Of this 459-calorie increase, grains (mainly refined grains) accounted for 180 calories; added fats & oils, 225 calories; added sugar & sweeteners, 21 calories;

dairy fats, 19 calories; fruits and vegetables, 12 calories; and meats, eggs, and nuts, 16 calories. Only dairy products declined (13 calories) during the time period.

The average American is eating 459 calories more each day today than he, or his parents, were eating in 1970. Although it varies from individual to individual, an excess of 500 calories per day will result in a weight gain of about 1 pound per week. Keep that up for a year and you will have gained 52 pounds or 23.5 kilos. That is if you keep the same lifestyle. If you slow down your level of activity you will gain even more weight.

Let's look a bit closer at the sugar numbers. According to the USDA the average per capita consumption of refined cane and beet sugar declined by about one third between 1970 and 2014: from 17.8 teaspoons per day to 11.9 teaspoons per day in 2014.

Over the same period average per capita consumption of corn sweeteners increased from virtually nothing in 1970 to 7.9 teaspoons per day in 2014, but off from a peak of 11.4 teaspoons per day reached in 1999. Per capita consumption of edible syrups and honey has been steady over the same period at around three teaspoons per day. (10)

So even though Americans are consuming more calories, they are consuming a relatively smaller proportion of sugar in their diets. It is worth repeating that over a 40-year period from 1970 to 2010 daily US per capita calorific sweetener intake only increased by 21 calories; one teaspoon of sugar contains 16 calories.

Taking all this together it is easy to understand why the sugar industry is so surprised – and upset - that their product is being blamed for the obesity epidemic.

However there is a caveat. Obesity rates are not

spread out evenly among income groups. Obesity is higher among lower income groups in developed countries and among higher income groups in developing countries. The consumption figures reported above show "average" consumption. Over the past decades there has been a conscious shift among richer people to eat better. There has been a boom in the sales of health foods and gym memberships and this has probably led to a decline in sugar consumption among richer people.

This could mean that although rich people are eating less, and better, than they used to, poor people may be eating more and worse than they used to. Anecdotal evidence may support this view. Junk food is often cheaper than food cooked at home. And many poor neighbourhoods, particularly in the US, are now classified as "food deserts"; areas where you can't buy fresh food even if you want to. The shops only sell soda, confectionary and potato chips.

This might also explain the higher obesity rates among rich people in poorer countries. As the poor get richer they can afford to eat more junk food and confectionary. Not only that, but as the poorer rural population move to the cities they may no longer have access to the fresh food that they used to grow on their farms.

More research needs to be done on this but in the meantime obesity campaigners pin the blame on the processed food companies, arguing that they are not only pushing fresh food off the shelves but also pushing the poor, particularly the American poor, to over-consume.

10.2   The role of the food industry

In his book "*Sugar Salt Fat*" the Pulitzer Prize winning Michael Moss describes the way that the food industry has used science to get the taste and "mouth feel" of their products just right. Key to that process is the "bliss point", a term that is believed to have been coined in the 1970s by a Hungarian-born mathematician named Joseph L Balintfy.

As Michael Moss explains, when you add sugar to a food product, that product tastes better only up to a certain point. Add too much sugar to the product and it becomes "sickly". The percentage of sugar in any product forms an inverted U-curve, the top of which is the high point of satisfaction that consumers get from sugar. For children it can be as high as 36 per cent; for adults it is probably below 20 per cent, but that depends on the product.

Rather surprisingly there is no "bliss point" for fat; there is no level at which fat becomes "sickening". You can keep on adding fat to a product and people keep on liking it more. This could help to explain why calorie intake of fat in the US has increased more than that of sugar. Fat has on average 9 calories per gram, twice that for sugar or protein: a teaspoonful (4.2 grams) of sugar contains 16 calories while a teaspoon of olive oil contains 40 calories.

Food company scientists have found exactly how much sugar, salt and fat to use in a product to make you want to eat more of it. But remember that sugar is a carbohydrate that is treated by the body in the same way as any other carbohydrate. As Michael Moss points out (10),

"We don't have to eat sugar to feel its allure. Pizza will do, or any other refined starch, which the body converts to sugar — starting right in the mouth, with an enzyme called amylase."

He quotes Danielle Reed, a Yale-trained scientist and an expert on the matter, as saying

"The faster the starch becomes sugar, the quicker our brain gets the reward for it. We like the highly refined things because they bring us immediate pleasure, associated with high sugar, but obviously there are consequences. It's sort of like if you drink alcohol really fast, you get drunk really fast. When you break down sugar really fast your body gets flooded with sugar more than it can handle, whereas with whole grain it is more gradual and you can digest it in a more orderly fashion".

People "crave" foods that give them this high, this sudden rush. But it is not just sugar that people crave; they also crave pizzas and potato chips. And if you doubt that, just ask your children.

Cutting back on refined foods can reduce your cravings for them. After reading Michael Moss's book I tried a simple test on myself that you can also, safely, do in your own home. The next time you are sitting around at home on a Sunday afternoon and you feel a little hungry, go grab a cookie. I can almost guarantee that you will want another one. The following Sunday when the same thing happens, eat an apple instead. You won't want a second apple. The next Sunday try eating a couple of sugar cubes; you won't want any more.

The apple and the sugar cubes contained the same amount of sugar as the cookie. It was not the sugar in the cookie that made you want another one; it was the perfect mixture of sugar, salt and fat that the cookie contained that gave you a craving to eat another one – or even the whole packet.

Progress in food technology over the past forty years has allowed processed food manufacturers to use sugar more efficiently and to find that perfect mixture that encourages you to eat more than you would have done in the past. But as I said above, table sugar, or sucrose, is just one source of sugar: the refined flour in pizza is one source and the humble potato is another.

A study published in the New England Journal of Medicine in 2011 (and quoted by Michael Moss) followed the eating and exercise habits of 120,877 people since 1986. The study found, (11)

Every four years since 1986 the participants have exercised less, watched TV more, and gained an extra 3.35 pounds.... The top contributors to the weight gain included red meat, sugar-sweetened beverages, and potatoes, including mashed and French fries.

But far and away, the largest weight-inducing food, outstripping all others, was the potato chip. The chip, at about 160 calories an ounce, led to a 1.69-pound gain in weight in each of the four-year study periods. By comparison, sweets and deserts accounted for less than half a pound."

Potato chips are irresistible: they are loaded with fat and covered by salt, creating

"a mouth feel... that the brain rewards with an instant feeling of pleasure...Potato chips are also loaded with sugar...the kind of sugar that the body gets from the starch in the potatoes. Starch is considered a carbohydrate, but more precisely, it is made of glucose, the same kind of glucose that you have in blood".

Michael Moss quotes one of the authors of the study, Eric Rimm, an associate professor at the Harvard School of Public Health as saying,

"The starch is readily absorbed. More quickly even than a similar amount of sugar. The starch in turn causes the glucose levels in blood to spike, and this is a concern, in relation to obesity…. Recent research suggests glucose spikes will cause people to crave more food, as long as four hours after they've eaten whatever caused the blood glucose to spike. Eat chips one hour. Crave more the next".

The food industry has, through extensive research and testing, developed products that make us all crave for more. By using exactly the right proportion of sugar in their products, food manufacturers achieve a "bliss point" that creates a craving and encourages us to eat more. But sugar doesn't do it alone, fat and salt play important roles in creating these cravings. Indeed, as the humble potato chip shows, sucrose is not the only source of glucose; starch can do the job just as well.

This craving sensation has led some commentators to argue that glucose (whether from a cookie or from a pizza or a potato chip) is different from other food products in that it is addictive. They argue that it is like sex, drugs and socialising (yes, socialising) in that it activates the reward mechanism of the brain. And the brain tells you *"Hey, that was great, let's do it again".* You may have heard one of your friends describe a cookie or an ice cream as *"better than sex".* Now you know why. It has the same effect on the brain.

Dopamine is the major currency of our reward system and pushes us to repeat whatever it was that we did to produce it in the first place. And sugar's critics argue that because a body builds up a tolerance to whatever it was that produced the dopamine in the first place you have to consume more and more sugar, drugs or sex to maintain the same amount of dopamine in the brain. The more you have the more you need.

However, most people do not get addicted to sex (I repeat, "most people".) Most drug users do not become addicts. Most social drinkers do not become alcoholics. Most people do not get addicted to sugar. Some may do, but I'd guess it's only a tiny percentage.

Even so there have been calls for sugar to be controlled in the same way that drugs (particularly alcohol and tobacco) are controlled. There are already countries that have imposed taxes on sugar-containing soft drinks and some commentators are calling for a total ban on the sale of them to children.

The taxes that have been imposed have been shown to be effective in curtailing consumption. Mexico imposed an extra 10% tax on sweetened beverages at the start of 2014 that over the course of the first year resulted in a 6% decline in sales. (13) Purchases of untaxed beverages increased by 4% compared to the previous year. Others are following Mexico's example: Berkeley, California, became the first U.S. city to pass a soda tax similar to Mexico's.

Opponents of extra taxes on calorific soft drinks agree that encouraging overweight children to reduce their calorie intake is a good thing. However they say that the means do not justify the end if you deprive normal weight children the pleasure of a soft drink from time to time – or make them pay more for it. They ask why the majority should suffer for the minority.

In addition, bearing in mind that pizzas and potato chips have the same effect, opponents argue that it is wrong to single out sugar. If you are going to tax sugar-containing soft drinks you should also tax pizzas and potato chips. Indeed, in fighting obesity taxing pizzas and chips may be more effective than taxing sodas.

Civil liberty campaigners meanwhile question whether it is the role of government to interfere at this level; they argue that it should be left to the family or the individual to determine what they eat. They add that it is the role of the parent, rather than the government, to tell a child what he should or should not be consuming.

In addition, drinking less soda may not help you to lose weight if you compensate, or over compensate, by eating more of other foodstuffs. As I mentioned in the Preface, my friend gave up sugar three years ago but has put on 15 kilos. As he was no longer eating sugar he felt justified in eating more of other things.

To fight childhood obesity it might in any case be more efficient to tax video games rather than sodas. It would encourage children to go outside more to play physical games rather than to sit indoors, turning them into couch potatoes before they are even 10 years old.

Having said that, there is still much scientific research to be done regarding the way that the body processes sugar, particularly the way it copes with a sudden inflow of glucose and fructose that is contained, say, in a soft drink or a glass of fruit juice. If a soda is drunk quickly, and let's be honest, most are, its rapid digestion can lead to a surge in blood glucose that may upset the body's equilibrium. That's the reason why the American Diabetes Association recommends that people avoid sugar-sweetened beverages to help prevent them from contracting diabetes.

But it is not just the glucose in the sugar that worries obesity campaigners, some argue that dumping a whole load of fructose in the body can over-load the liver; taken to excess they argue this may even lead to sclerosis of the liver. (14) When you eat an apple it takes time for your stomach to break down the fibre in the apple to extract the fructose; when you drink a sugar-containing soft drink that work has already been done for you. Some argue that the "rush" of fructose in a soft drink may overload your liver and encourage it to turn it into fat (but more on that in the next chapter).

There is another issue regarding calorific soft drinks: some researchers have raised the question as to whether the mind registers the calories contained in liquids. In the Bible (Exodus 33.3) the Promised Land is described as one of "flowing with milk and honey" – at that time milk and honey were the only two liquids that contained calories. For nearly all of man's existence, most if not all calories came from solid food. It is only in recent history that humans have obtained significant calories from liquids. It would not be surprising therefore if the human brain was not hardwired to recognise this new phenomenon of calorie-containing liquids.

You can try a simple test at home. One 8 oz (250 ml) glass of apple juice contains the juice – and approximately 175 calories – from three to four apples. This evening before dinner drink a glass of apple juice and see if it reduces your appetite. You will find it won't. Tomorrow evening eat three and a half apples before sitting down at the dinner table. Even though you have consumed the same number of calories as the previous evening you will find that you are far less hungry. Your stomach will feel full, giving you a sensation of "satiety" that will result in you eating less for dinner.

However that may depend on when you eat your dinner. Most nutritionists argue that when you are eating it takes around 20 minutes for the stomach to send a message to the brain to say, *"Hey, I am full; stop eating!"* This means that the slower you eat the less you eat. Many nutritionists recommend that you should wait at least 20 minutes before serving yourself a second helping or a desert. And of course this casts a whole shadow over the whole concept of "fast food": you can eat a lot more of it before the body says, "STOP!"

That 20-minute time delay probably didn't matter when we got our sugars from fruit and our oils/fats from vegetables and meat. It took a while for our stomachs to break down the food into glucose that we could burn in our bodies. Now the commodity industry does the hard work that our stomachs used to do. Huge factories take the vegetable oil out of vegetables (mainly corn) and the sugar out of cane or beet. This means that not only do our bodies use less energy processing the food that we eat but also that we absorb the calories more quickly; as a result our stomach may now be too slow to send a signal to the brain to tell us to stop eating.

The role of fibre (or bulk) is therefore very important. Some friends of ours like to start each day with a "smoothie" that they blend themselves from whatever fruit they have at hand. A lot of fruit goes into each one. However, juicing fruit removes the fibre but not the calories. Just as the sugar or vegetable oil companies use factories to do the work that your stomach used to do, the blender in your kitchen does the same thing. It breaks down the fibre and lets you consume more calories more quickly and more easily.

Just as an aside, some less scrupulous processed food manufacturers are reacting to the anti-sugar lobby by replacing cane or beet sugar with concentrated fruit juice. This has the advantage of enabling the manufacturers to put "Contains real fruit" and "No added sugar" on the packet. The problem is that "concentrated fruit juice" is sugar. It is made from fruit rather than sugarcane or beet but it is still the same. As far as the product is concerned the manufacturers may just as well have left the sugar in the product and put "Contains concentrated sugar cane juice" on the label.

Actions such as this have sometimes led to food company executives being presented in the media as Blofeld-like characters, evilly stroking a cat on their lap as they think up new ways to poison the human race. But food company executives are just like you and me; they have kids and families and want to do good and not evil in the world. The food companies have no interest in poisoning anyone; they need to keep their clients alive and well.

Most food companies have tried to respond responsibly to the obesity epidemic and have introduced what they call "product extensions", versions of a product that contain less sugar, salt or fat than the originals. Unfortunately that hasn't worked out too well, for two reasons.

The first is if you reduce the fat in a product you often have to increase the amount of sugar in it to make it palatable. That's why so many "low-fat" products contain more sugar than their full-fat versions. (But remember that sugar contains much fewer calories than fat.) The second reason is that the full fat, sugar and salt versions taste much better; as a result consumers continue to buy them. If one food company reduces the amount of fat, salt and sugar in their products they risk losing market share to their competitors. For a successful outcome, all food companies have to do the same thing.

That's why some health advocates have argued that governments should intervene and force the processed food manufacturers to make healthier products. Critics of the food industry argue that governments forced car manufacturers to make safer cars so why can't they force food manufacturers to make healthier food? Admittedly there are more food companies than car manufacturers so policing the new laws would be harder, but it would not be impossible.

Rather than using laws or taxes to force the food companies to make healthier products, governments generally are opting for a softer approach via the consumer, educating him or her to make healthier choices. This is being done through advertising campaigns and better labelling on food products. And it is working. We already understand that cigarettes are bad for us and we are now beginning to understand that high fat, high sugar and high salt processed foods are bad for us. But we also all need to understand the importance of physical activity.

Health

11.1   Professor Luc Tappy: scientist

While I was researching the health and obesity aspect of this book I kept coming across the name of Dr Luc Tappy, Professor of Physiology at the Faculty of Medicine and Biology at the University of Lausanne. Professor Tappy has published a number of scientific papers (with often intimidating titles) but one paper that caught my eye was *"Q&A: 'Toxic' effects of sugar: should we be afraid of fructose?"* (1)

Some in the sugar business have argued that obesity is caused by HFCS (High Fructose Corn Syrup) and not by "natural" cane or beet sugar. Fructose corn syrup is a relative newcomer to our diet and only began to take market share from sugar in the USA in the 1980s, about the time that the obesity epidemic took off. There is a strong correlation between US consumption of HFCS and US obesity levels. However there is also a strong correlation between sales of bottled water and obesity levels and no one is pretending that bottled water causes obesity.

There are two reasons to suspect that HFCS is not to blame for obesity. The first is that obesity levels have also risen in the parts of the world with insignificant HFCS use. The second is that sugar and HFCS have pretty much the same chemical composition. As Dr Tappy writes in his Q&A:

"The most commonly used form of HFCS contains

about 55% fructose, 42% glucose, and 3% other sugars, and hence is associated with similar total fructose and glucose intakes as with sugar. Furthermore, sucrose is hydrolyzed in the gut and absorbed into the blood as free glucose and fructose, so one would expect HFCS and sucrose to have the same metabolic consequences. In short, there is currently no evidence to support the hypothesis that HFCS makes a significant contribution to metabolic disease independently of the rise in total fructose consumption."

The last sentence requires further explanation. The "metabolic disease" that Dr Tappy refers to is of course obesity. The second part of the sentence is key: it means that there is nothing in the chemical composition of fructose that is in itself responsible for obesity, but that increased consumption of fructose could play a role.

Some opponents of HFCS argue that fructose is the reason that Americans eat more than they used to. As Dr Tappy explains, rodents that are given access to as much fructose or sucrose as they want, eat more than if they were given free access to other foods. No one is sure why this should be the case. He writes,

"This may be due to a stimulation of sweet receptors in the mouth activating reward pathways within the brain. Alternatively, ingestion of fructose or sucrose may elicit lower satiety responses than other nutrients. Satiety is a process through which eating sends signals that activate specific brain pathways that in turn regulate appetite. Protein and carbohydrate have long been known to elicit a robust satiety response, mediated in part by an increase in insulin. Some observations suggest that fructose or sugar exert less satiating effects than starch or glucose, possibly due to a lower insulin response.

"It is not clear whether fructose consumption leads to increased total energy intake and obesity. To address this question further studies focusing on the effects of fructose on food intake control will be needed, and the possibility that fructose may increase energy intake through mechanisms related to addiction will need to be assessed."

"Given the substantial consumption of fructose in our diet, mainly from sweetened beverages, sweet snacks, and cereal products with added sugar, and the fact that fructose is an entirely dispensable nutrient, it appears sound to limit consumption of sugar as part of any weight loss program and in individuals at high risk of developing metabolic diseases. There is no evidence, however, that fructose is the sole, or even the main factor in the development of these diseases, nor that it is deleterious to everybody, and public health initiatives should therefore broadly focus on the promotion of healthy lifestyles generally, with restriction of both sugar and saturated fat intakes, and consumption of whole grains, fresh fruits and vegetables rather than focusing exclusively on reduction of sugar intake."

I caught up with Dr Tappy at his office at the CHUV, Le Centre Hospitalier Universitaire Vaudois, in Lausanne where he teaches. As we walked to a nearby sandwich shop I told him, "We in the sugar business argue that sugar is a calorie like any other and that obesity is a result of excessive calorie intake. We believe that it is wrong to single out any particular food product as the cause of obesity."

"And you want to know if that is true," he replied.

"Yes," I said. "I also want to know if sugar causes diabetes?"

"No," replied Dr Tappy. "Obesity causes diabetes. But excessive sugar consumption can contribute to obesity."

"Is there any difference in the way that beet or cane sugar is treated by the body compared to corn fructose?" I asked.

"HFCS and "table sugar", as I call it, are more or less the same in a chemical sense. They both contain about the same proportions of fructose and glucose. There is a difference in the way that the body deals with these two. The body absorbs glucose directly into the blood stream but treats fructose through the liver. It is the fructose that isn't necessarily good for the body. The name "High Fructose Corn Syrup" confuses people. HFCS doesn't contain any more fructose than table sugar."

"So it's hardly surprising that the HFCS producers tried to change the name of HFCS to "corn sugars", I added encouragingly. "But they failed. The sugar industry blocked them."

"Chemically they are more or less the same," Dr Tappy continued. "Honey and fruits have provided man with small amounts of glucose and fructose but grains and other starchy food have been the sole source of carbohydrate for most of man's time on this planet. We lived without sugar for most of our history; this means that we can live without it now. It is what I would call a "non-essential dietary element."

"It may be non essential but is sugar necessarily bad?" I asked, suddenly alarmed.

"Sugar has two undesirable consequences", Dr Tappy replied. "The first is that, because of its rapid digestion, it leads to surges in blood glucose that may place some stress on the body's ability to maintain a stable equilibrium mediated by insulin."

"And the second?" I asked, still concerned.

"By eating sucrose we take in fructose which we do not need. And when we eat too much fructose we place an important metabolic burden on the liver."

"So sugar is bad for you because it contains fructose?"

"Excessive consumption of sugar can be bad for you but when eaten in moderate amounts as part of a balanced diet it is OK. It is for this reason that the FAO and others suggest that we should all limit our sugar consumption."

"There is a lot in the media about sugar being as addictive as cocaine," I prompted. "Would you agree?"

"It certainly stimulates the brain's reward networks in the same way and as such you could say it is addictive, but probably not as much as cocaine."

"What about the idea of sugar being "toxic"? Sugar at the moment is being blamed for a whole host of ailments from cancer to Alzheimer's. Is that possible?"

"It has become fashionable to blame sugar for many evils and this helps to sell books, but there is no scientific proof that any of it is true. Please note that I am not saying that it is not true. I am saying that there is currently no proof that it is true: more work needs to be done."

"What about the issue of satiety: is it possible that the body does not register the calories absorbed as sugar?"

"This is possible and some earlier studies on rats shows that could be the case. However there is as yet no proof of that for humans."

"There is also an argument that the body does not register calories absorbed in liquids. Could that explain why people, particularly Americans, are consuming more calories than in the past?" I asked.

"Some people suggest that that is the case but it is difficult to prove scientifically. More research needs to be done on the issue."

"Why is it that Americans are eating and drinking more calories now than they used to?" I asked.

Dr Tappy shrugged. "Maybe it is because food is more readily available – and cheaper – than in the past. My guess is that the fast food industry has been a big contributor to that. But it's not necessarily all bad: more plentiful and cheaper food on a global basis is actually a good thing."

"Do you mean that the spectrum has shifted a little?" I asked, suddenly warming to the debate. "Calories are more freely availably than in the past," I continued, "so fewer people go hungry. But at the other end of the scale more people eat too much."

"This presents something of a moral issue," replied Dr Tappy, also warming to the discussion. "In the past those that went to bed hungry had no choice; they either had no access to food or they couldn't afford it. But now their situation has improved. At the other end of the scale as you call it the rich world has a choice as to whether or not to over eat. I think the world should accept that having a small percentage of people over-weight is better than having a small percentage of people going hungry."

"Is there any final comment you would like to make?" I asked Dr Tappy.

"Yes," he replied. "You should be aware that if you ask other "experts" the same questions you would get entirely different answers. There is a lot that we don't know and much more research has to be done."

11.2   Is sugar toxic?

A few years back I underwent a medical examination at the request of my insurance company. I failed one element of the test: the level of Gamma-GT in my liver was above the maximum allowed. Gamma-GT is a hormone that is a useful marker for alcohol abuse or liver disease. As diplomatically as he could, my doctor told me to reduce my alcohol consumption generally and in particular for the next couple of weeks. He said he would then redo the test and, once my Gamma-GT levels had fallen back to acceptable levels, he would submit the results to the insurance company.

The problem was that at that time I had not had any alcohol for at least six months. (I was training for a marathon.) I tried to explain this to my doctor but it was obvious that he didn't believe me. We agreed that I would come back again in two weeks time. When I did, my Gamma-GT level was even higher. I hadn't drunk any alcohol during those two weeks but again my doctor did not believe me.

We repeated this the following two fortnights; each time my level of Gamma-GT was higher than the previous fortnight and my doctor was becoming alarmed. I somehow managed to convince him that I really wasn't drinking any alcohol and he asked me to write down everything that I ate and drank every day for the next two weeks. Something was poisoning my liver and killing me; he had to find out what it was.

Two weeks later I went to see him again but before I could show him the list of everything that I had consumed he asked me if I drank green tea. I replied that yes I did; lots of it. I had read that green tea was good for my health and I had assumed that the more I drank of it the better. That was a mistake, at least in my case.

Green tea was indeed good for me in small quantities but was toxic in large quantities. It was poisoning my liver and killing me. I stopped drinking green tea completely and within two weeks my Gamma-GT measurement had fallen back to a normal level. The doctor sent off my results and the insurance company was happy.

When my wife was pregnant (admittedly over 25 years ago) with our first child I was shocked when our (French) doctor recommended that she drink a glass of red wine a day. Although it is unthinkable now that a doctor should recommend that an expectant mother should drink alcohol, he believed at the time that red wine was a good source of iron and would help relax her.

Nowadays some scientists suggest that one glass of wine per day may be beneficial to health (as long as you are not pregnant). Drink a second glass however and it will undo any of the (possible) beneficial effects of the first. A cup of green tea a day may have been beneficial to my health but a litre of it wasn't.

I have friends who drink a lot of green tea without any problems. We are all different. Everyone "knows" that smoking is bad for you but my father smoked forty cigarettes a day until he was fifty and then twenty small cigarillos a day until he died – at the age of 102. What may have a negative effect on some people may have no effect on other people.

The other point is that science is always progressing. We are learning more about how our bodies work and, because of that progress, recommendations change. If you are over forty years old you will remember how we all gave up butter for margarine; now we are doing the reverse.

However, as a general rule, anything that we consume in excessive quantities can be toxic for our health, even water. But is it possible that sugar, even in small quantities, is killing us?

A causal look at any health magazine or Internet site will show you that sugar is not only being blamed for obesity – and hence diabetes – but also for a whole range of other ailments including strokes, heart disease, Alzheimer's and even cancer. (2) Some medical professionals argue that even a small amount of sugar is toxic.

In 1674 Dr Thomas Willis published *"Phamaceutice rationalis"* in which he identified the sweet flavour in the urine of patients suffering from diabetes; history does not relate what possessed him to taste the urine. In any case he nicknamed the disease the "Pissing Evil", a name that stuck for at least a couple of centuries. (3) The supposed connection between sugar consumption and diabetes continued in people's minds for even longer and still continues today. However, the connection between sugar consumption and diabetes is not a direct one: excess sugar consumption can lead to obesity, which can in turn lead to diabetes.

Just as my liver could not cope with excessive quantities of green tea, there is some suggestion that a liver cannot cope with the surge in fructose that comes, say, from the consummation of a soft drink.

Dr Robert H. Lustig is an American paediatric endocrinologist at the University of California, San Francisco where he is a professor of clinical paediatrics. He first came to public attention when he claimed that fructose in sugar can be bad for you if consumed in too large amounts. In 2009 he delivered a lecture called "Sugar: The Bitter Truth" (4) which was posted on YouTube. The video" went viral" with some 5.7 million viewings. Dr Lustig calls fructose a "poison" and equates its metabolic effects with those of ethanol.

Remember that both HFCS and table sugar are more or less the same thing, they both contain about the same amount of glucose and fructose. The glucose is absorbed directly into the blood stream (and activates the reward system in the brain) but the fructose first has to be processed by the liver. If the liver receives too much fructose in one go it converts some of it to fat. And not just fat, but the bad fat: "small dense LOC" (according to Dr Lustig). This type of fat lodges in the blood vessels and forms plaques that are associated with heart disease.

Dr Lustig argues that drinking a sweetened drink is just as bad for you as eating a fatty hamburger. He adds that the American health authorities have made a huge mistake in encouraging people to consume less fat. If you reduce the amount of fat in a food product it doesn't taste as good. To make it taste better you have to increase the amount of sugar. Dr Lustig argues that it is the sugar that is making us obese, not the fat.

Dr Lustig's arguments sound plausible, but they are simply not supported by the data. Per capita sugar consumption has been falling in most developed countries and been more or less steady in others since the obesity took off in the 1970s. Even in the US consumers are not eating more sugar instead of fat. In fact the opposite has occurred; they are eating more fat and relatively less sugar.

But as I pointed out in the previous chapter

those are average figures; some people may be consuming way above average quantities of sugar, both in soft drinks and in food, and damaging their health in the process.

Some sugar critics argue that sugar causes cancer, that when we consume sugar it causes a spike in our insulin levels and this acts as a catalyst for certain types of cancer. Breast and colon cancers have insulin receptors on the surface of their cells and when insulin hits these receptors they signal the cancer cells to start consuming glucose – tumours need glucose to grow.

More research needs to be done on this subject but in the meantime is in everyone's interest to keep insulin levels as constant as possible.

Some people also blame an increased incidence of Alzheimer's disease on the growth of sugar consumption - or at least on the modern western diet, characterised by high intakes of red meat, sugary foods, high-fat foods, and refined grains.

But there again, to blame an increased incidence of Alzheimer's disease on sugar needs sugar consumption to have increased – and it hasn't. It may therefore be more a function of an aging population - or more readiness to put a medical name to Aunt Agatha's forgetfulness.

What about the tooth decay – is that still an issue? When I was growing up in the 1960s I hated going to the dentist; I always seemed to end up having an enormous hole drilled in one of my teeth and having it filled with lead.

When my own children were growing up they seemed to eat far more sweets and candies than I ever did - but all four of them reached adulthood without a single filling. They even looked forward to their visits to the dentist; they had an opportunity to catch up on the latest comics in the patient waiting room.

The reason for this inter-generational shift is of course due to the fact that in France, where we lived at the time, the government added fluoride to the tap water. Tooth decay had as a result become less of an issue.

My own dentist told me that potato chips were now the number one tooth public enemy; they stick to your teeth while sugar doesn't. However drinking sugar-containing soft drinks and fruit juices between meals also means that the PH level in your mouth stays high throughout the day, favouring tooth decay.

The best solution is to brush your teeth at least twice a day, particularly before bedtime and, if possible, use sugar-free chewing gum after each meal. It helps to restore the PH level in your mouth and can significantly reduce tooth decay.

Although tooth decay is a recognised and real problem, child hyperactivity is not. Here the medical profession has an apology to make to all those children who were brought up during the 1980s and 1990s and who had to endure sugar-rationed birthday parties. We now know that sugar does not cause hyper-activity; being a child causes hyperactivity. Until a child is old enough to "hang out" he will only have two speeds: "flat out" or "stop".

The conclusion has to be that consumed in excessive quantities sugar is toxic but then everything else is too. Consumed in moderation, sugar adds sweetness and pleasure to the lives of billions of people.

11.3 The sugar trader's diet

Lose weight and lead a healthier, happier life by following the "Sugar Trader's Diet".

All the recommendations in the "Sugar Trader's Diet" have been scientifically proven to work and personal testimonials can be found on my website.

Well, actually I don't have a website. But that is not the only thing that is wrong with the above (spoof) publicity. The first thing that is wrong is that it assumes that you will be healthier if you shed a few pounds. If you are only slightly overweight then losing a couple of pounds probably won't make any significant difference to your health.

Another thing that is wrong is that it equates being happy with being thin. I know a lot of fat people who are happy and a lot of thin people who are unhappy. Losing a few pounds won't alter your life much; you won't suddenly find the partner of your dreams or suddenly make new friends. (It is partly for this reason that diets don't work; the weight lost is usually regained when the dieter realises that their life hasn't, as they had hoped, changed for the better.)

Another thing that is wrong is "the scientifically proven part". A couple of years ago two enterprising German journalists carried out a "scientific" study that "proved" that eating chocolate helps you to lose weight. They managed to get the study published in a scientific journal and sent out press releases to all the media. Within a week it was on the front page of all the newspapers (5). None of those newspapers verified the story or checked on how vigorous and exhaustive the study was; they based their stories entirely on the press release.

We all like to believe in science but unfortunately there is "good" and "bad" science. And even the good scientists can disagree strongly in their opinions and recommendations. Remember Professor Tappy's parting words, "If you ask another scientist exactly the same questions you will get entirely different answers". At the time I thought he was joking, but he was not.

Nutrition is an inexact science. It is not possible to isolate the different elements or to establish the causality of any correlation. One test group may lose weight when they eat bananas, but that does not mean that they lose weight because they eat bananas. They could, because they were taking part in the study, have focused more than usual on their health and taken more exercise.

Another point is that in the German study the test group that ate chocolate did lose weight, but the sample size (4 people) was too small to be significant. And as for the "testimonials", you can get anyone to say pretty much anything if you pay them to say it. After all, that's what actors do.

The biggest problem, however, is that we now know that diets don't work; you may lose weight for a while but you invariably put the weight back on – and more – within a year or two. As a result, many nutritionists focus now on "healthy" eating: eating a healthy balanced diet coupled with physical exercise will do you a lot more good than short term calorie deprivation.

While researching for this book I came up with a few simple health rules that I now apply to myself. I admit that most of the science behind them is both unproven and controversial, but none of the rules will actually do you any harm. So here goes:

Moderate the moderation: We in the sugar industry believe that sugar is a calorie like any other. The evidence supports that view but you still need to eat a balanced diet and not eat too much of one thing. If you drink three litres of sweetened sodas a day then you are likely to have health problems. Drink a couple of cans a week and you probably won't. Sugar is not a poison but as with my green tea example earlier, excessive sugar consumption may be unhealthy.

Some people have given up sugar completely; they lose weight initially but eventually put it back on by making up the calories elsewhere. My friend who gave up sugar compensated for his lack of deserts by eating cheese instead. According to the USDA, 100g of American cheese contain 371 calories. Add that to the butter and the biscuits that he ate with the cheese and my friend would have been better off eating a sugar-containing desert.

My grandmother used to say, "A little bit of what you fancy does you good"; that is my first rule of healthy eating. So enjoy your food and don't beat yourself up over that occasional cheesecake.

Prepare your plate: We saw earlier that Americans are consuming more calories than they were 30 years ago while consumers in other developed countries are consuming less. Why should that be?

A few years ago I met up with some good

friends for a dinner in an Italian restaurant in Manhattan. We all ordered pasta and I was the first to be served. My bowl of pasta was so big I assumed that it was in fact for everyone. Without thinking I put the bowl in the middle of the table for everyone to share. However my friends were all brought a similar sized bowl. At home my bowl would have been enough for my entire family – and we have four children.

To play the role of Ron Woodroof in the film "Dallas Buyers Club" the actor Matthew McConaughey lost nearly 50 pounds (22 kg). He did it by reducing the quantity of food he ate and by increasing the amount of exercise he did (6). However he also had the occasional glass of wine (see moderate the moderation above). I don't suggest anyone try to follow Matthew McConaughey's extreme example, but it does show that eating less and exercising more works.

So the second rule in the Sugar Trader's Diet is "Prepare your plate" in the kitchen and don't bring seconds to the table (and certainly not to the couch in front of the TV). If your plate looks as if it has too much food on it then it probably does. Immediately throw away one third of it.

Take a hike: Exercise can help you to lose weight but it can be counter-productive if it means that you eat more after a workout. It is perhaps for this reason that many nutritionists recommend walking, especially after a meal, as an excellent way to help you digest. Walking is one exercise that won't leave you ravenously hungry and result in you eating more.

Cash in your chips: Do you remember that long term Harvard study that found that most of the weight gain in America over the past thirty years could be attributed to the humble potato chip? Chips are a perfect mixture of sugar (carbohydrate), salt and fat that makes it almost impossible not to finish the packet once you have opened it. So don't open the packet. Or, better still; leave the packet out of your supermarket trolley in the first place.

Can the cola: I wrote earlier that the human body might not be able to recognise calories in liquids. In addition it might not be able to process the sudden fructose download that each soft drink contains. Neither of these has been scientifically proven but there is sufficient doubt to suggest that you should err on the side of caution. So reduce your consumption of calorific soft drinks and try ice-cold club soda (with a twist of lime) instead. It is delicious.

Banish the blender: A friend of my wife recently completed a "juice week" during which she consumed nothing but vegetable and fruit juice for seven days. She did it to detoxify her body and to lose weight. My wife asked her if she had lost weight and she replied that she hadn't, but she did feel better and enjoyed the challenge of not consuming anything that hadn't first been through a blender.

There are two problems with this. The first is that if you blend fruit you are likely to consume more fruit without feeling full. The second is that the liver may not be able to cope with all fructose that arrives in one go. It may convert some of it to fat.

If you eat the fruit whole, rather than blending it first, you will not only eat less of it but the fructose may be absorbed more slowly into the body and allow your liver more time to process it. (You should notice the use of the word "may"; this is still a controversial point.) So liquidising fruit into smoothies or juice means that you will consume more calories and consume less fibre. Instead of juicing the fruit eat it whole.

See the Sugar: Food manufacturers use sugar in their products to make them taste better. Sugar is cheap compared to other ingredients and is also often used as a "bulking agent". It is also used as a preservative to give the product a longer shelf life.

All this means that most of the sugar you consume is "hidden" sugar – and it is hidden in the most unlikely places. So read the labels and be aware how much sugar is hiding in the product you are buying. The salad dressings that you buy ready-made often contain large amounts of sugar. There is no reason to add sugar to a salad dressing. Make your own instead. They are easy to make and taste better.

Axe the Oil: Most of the extra and unneeded calories that you consume are coming from vegetable oils and not from sugar. A spoonful of oil contains four times the number of calories as a spoonful of sugar. So if you really want to lose weight, stop adding olive oil to your steamed fish. For all the supposed health benefits of olive oil you would be better off sprinkling your food with four teaspoons of sugar rather than one teaspoon of oil.

Spare the Salt: You cannot live without salt but eating too much of it can increase your blood pressure and raise your risk of a heart attack. So go easy on the saltshaker and check the processed foods that you buy to check their salt content.

As salt helps make many processed foods addictive, reducing your salt intake may have the additional benefit of helping you to eat less. So pick up the unsalted cashew nuts rather than the salted peanuts next time you are in the supermarket.

Cut the White Bread: The more refined a product the higher the glycaemic index. The quicker the glucose enters the body the more likely it is that you will feel hungry again shortly afterwards. So eat wholemeal bread rather than white bread – and while you are at it eat brown rice rather than white. Always choose fibre over refined.

There is an old joke about a man who went to see his doctor and asked him what he should do to live to one hundred years old. The doctor replied that he should give up sex, sugar and alcohol and only eat fibrous vegetables mixed with unsweetened porridge.

"If I do that," asked the man, "will I live to be one hundred?"

"No", replied the doctor, "but it will seem like it".

Following the rules above probably won't ensure that you live to be one hundred, but you might live a healthier and more enjoyable life.

Sugar's Green Future

12.1 Sven Sielhorst: towards a modern industry

Solidaridad is an international civil society organisation with more than 45 years of global experience in facilitating the development of socially responsible, ecologically sound, and profitable supply chains.

Sven Sielhorst coordinates Solidaridad's International Sugarcane Programme. He is responsible for ensuring the consistency and strategic relevance of the Solidaridad's activities, in the sector as well as driving the sugarcane agenda and promoting internal learning and exchange. Sven has been working with Solidaridad since 2009. He is based at The Netherlands (Utrecht office) of Solidaridad. Sven is also a member of the Board of Directors of Bonsucro, an international organisation that fosters the sustainability of the sugarcane sector.

"Hello Sven, thank you for taking the time to speak with me. Can you begin by telling me a little bit about Solidaridad?

"Solidaridad is a development organisation that began work in its current form in 1988. It was one of the co-founders of what has become the Fairtrade system. It has always been our belief that we could drive the economic development of communities through the promotion and the inclusion of farmers and growers into the mainstream markets. We started with coffee and over the years it grew into a whole range of commodities. We have been doing sugar since 2008.

"Solidaridad started as a Dutch organisation but it is now a network of ten organisations around the world, each of them have their own legal presence in their country or their region of operation; two in South Asia, three in Africa, three in Central and South America, one in the US and one in Holland.

"Solidaridad currently runs fifteen sugarcane projects around the world. We have a large programme in India that includes seventeen mills and 260,000 growers. We have a project in Pakistan with three mills and 10,000 growers. In Africa we have projects in Malawi, Swaziland, South Africa and Tanzania and we are also busy in Brazil, Bolivia, Colombia and Mexico. Sugarcane grows right across the world."

"What are the main human rights' issues in sugarcane at the moment?" I asked.

"They are related to labour and land conflict. The issues with labour revolve principally around seasonal labour where conditions are often not in line with the core conventions of the ILO (International Labour Organisation), particularly during the harvest. The sugarcane sector has a number of occupational hazards compared to other sectors and a lot of accidents happen during the cutting - and also due to the infield traffic.

"Sometimes general labour conditions can enter into the realm of human rights violations. There are places where child labour is still an issue, particularly in Asia and some pockets of South America and Africa. This is not only in family agriculture but also when migrants follow the harvest. Forced or bonded labour is also prevalent in some places where people enter into a contract that they can't get out of. We don't see forced labour very much any more but every now and then we have a situation where the passport is being withheld, for example.

"We see cases of bonded labour in South America and India; migrants are the most vulnerable group because they are brought into rural areas for the harvest. Sometimes they can only buy stuff in the company shop with coupons; once the harvest is finished those purchases are deducted from their salary. Sometimes the labourers have to repay the contractor for the travel costs from their region of origin to the region of work. We try to do something about it but the position of migrant labourers is often weak because labour unions, local politicians and local society often take little interest in migrant workers.

"Some argue that these cases of forced or child labour are more related to the countries involved and not to the sugarcane industries. Is it wrong to criticise the sugar industry when these practices are prevalent in their countries of operation?" I asked.

"Child or forced labour is a result of the way that society has been structured in those countries and you are right that it is not sugarcane specific. However, I think it is too easy to say that you can't criticise the sugarcane industry for being involved in those practices. The industry can organise itself in such a way to limit the risk of those things happening. It has an obligation to do that. It is no good simply saying that it is a government and not an industry problem: the government is often relatively absent in the places where many sugar mills work. Mills therefore must engage themselves in these issues."

"Solidaridad has also been looking at the issue of workers' health," I prompted.

"Over the past few years it has become clear to us that sugarcane cutters in El Salvador and other Central American countries are heavily affected by "chronic kidney disease of non traditional causes", as it is called. It is over represented in sugar cane workers and that is explained by a couple of factors: chronic dehydration; excessive heat exposure and a process called Rhabdomyolysis. The latter is a breakdown in muscle tissue that is cause by repetitive muscle strain, something that also happens to people who go to the gym too much. These three factors explain a lot but not yet all of the disease; more research needs to be done."

"Is the solution looking after the cane cutters better or is it mechanised harvesting?" I asked.

"It depends on the local context. It is always good to protect workers better in any case. In the long term, mechanisation is the preferred solution for all of the sugarcane industry. In the short term that is, of course, going to create a huge social problem. This means you have to set out a path for what I would call "responsible mechanisation". It should not come as a shock to those communities that rely on sugarcane for their often quite low income. But over time the labour conditions in the sugar cane sector are such that harvest mechanisation is the only option."

"You mentioned the problem of low incomes among sugar cane workers. Is that because sugar prices are often low and the market oversupplied?" I asked. "Or is it because the workers capture too small a portion of the revenue compared to the millers or the landowners?"

Sugarcane is a low value crop but that doesn't

explain the very large differences in wealth between the workers, particularly the seasonal labourers, and the ones owning the sugar or the industry. The wealth divide in sugar is substantial compared to other agricultural crops in the world."

"That is because sugar is an industry that benefits greatly from economies of scale. You get an accumulation of very thin margins that still brings considerable wealth to the industry owners. Admittedly it is also a risky business because of the very sizeable investments that it requires compared to other agricultural crops. However, you can often get quite a lot of protection from governments.

"Industry owners often say: "We are big employers, and we help people to survive – often in areas with low job availability". That's true, but it is not good enough. As an employer, you also have a responsibility for the quality of labour and to provide fair compensation. This is not the situation in many industries. The easy excuse is always that paying better wages would impair their competitive position. My answer to that is: better remuneration and labour circumstances are often possible when you take a good look at labour efficiency, and you let labourers share in efficiency gains. You see huge disparities in terms of efficiency: on average one worker can cut less than 2 tonnes of cane per day in India or the Dominican Republic but 10 tonnes per day in Brazil.

"As soon as cane cutters' wages begin to rise employers start to pay attention as to how to improve the efficiency of the cane cutting process. And there are huge gains to be made. As part of moving the industry towards sustainability you need to start raising salaries while at the same time look at how you can make the process more efficient. Once wages become sufficiently high you want to go towards mechanisation.

"The labour productivity in Brazil is huge but the labour conditions in Brazil are infinitely better than in countries where they cut maybe only two tonnes per day. They have really thought out how they are going to organise the harvest, how they are going to minimise the movements of the workers and so forth. So once workers start to earn relatively good salaries as they do in Brazil and Colombia then you will use that resource as efficiently as possible."

"What are the main issues from the point of view of environmental sustainability?" I asked.

"Water use is always top of my list. Cane is the second thirstiest plant in the world after rice. Cane is very efficient in terms of converting sunlight into energy but because it is such a bulky crop the water use per hectare of cane is very high. This is a problem in water-stressed areas such as in parts of India and Pakistan and some parts of Indonesia and Eastern and Southern Africa. Irrigation is a big issue.

"In southern India you see rapidly declining water levels and the government of Maharashtra for example has recently announced legislation that says that you can't grow sugarcane in 2020 unless you use drip irrigation.

"Cane burning before harvesting, and the resulting air pollution, is a serious health issue for the communities that live around the cane fields. Studies from Brazil have shown that it has a negative impact on peoples' life expectancy and that particularly young children and elderly people have substantially higher levels of respiratory illness.

"In addition, a lot of CO_2 emissions and a lot

of organic matter is lost during burning that could have been used to improve the soil, particularly in areas where they don't do rotation cropping for example. You see that over time the quality of the soil deteriorates quite quickly."

"What about ethanol from sugarcane?" I asked. "Is sugarcane ethanol good or bad for the environment?"

"At Solidaridad we believe that if the sugarcane is grown in the correct way sugarcane ethanol is a very sizeable net gain for the planet in terms of CO_2 reduction when compared with gasoline. Despite all the stories that we are running out of agricultural land I think that is simply not the case. There is enough land available to expand the cultivation of agricultural crops and if you look at those crops, sugarcane is the winner in terms of ethanol production.

"Sugarcane also holds out the big promise that if we can make ethanol from the lignose cellulose part of the plant, which I believe will happen commercially in the next 5-10 years, we can double or triple the productivity of a hectare in terms of ethanol production.

"Is there any other environment issue for sugarcane?" I asked.

"Nothing that really stands out. There are still places in the world where too much fertilizer and too much pesticide are used but there is not a specific sugarcane problem."

"This is my penultimate question," I said. "Is sugar a force for good or is sugar a force for evil? Is it a net contributor to human welfare or a net detractor?"

"That's a difficult call to make, but I believe in the end it is a net contributor The position of some of the people in the supply chain is not where it needs to be, but a lot of people in this world rely on sugar for their livelihood; it is an economic activity that has the right to be around."

"Is there anything else that you would wish to add?"

"The sugar industry is quite inward looking in various aspects, perhaps because it is the only economic activity in some rural areas. But the world is getting smaller. In terms of human rights and sustainability people's expectations of the sugar industry are changing. There is a huge need for the industry to modernise and it can do that if it links up with new actors who can bring in new insights and new processes. The industry has a huge potential for creating all types of products that the world needs, but that really requires a cultural mind shift.

"My hope is that books like yours will help open the industry's doors and the windows onto the world - and open the doors and windows of the world on an industry that is under-valued.

"Sugarcane can play an important part in the replacement of mineral oil in producing fuels, chemicals and plastics and of course it provides us with sugar. Sugarcane has tremendous economic potential and this industry can provide an avenue to improve farmer income and labour conditions for millions of people, but we can only fulfil this promise as the crop of the future if we work together to further improve the way sugarcane is being produced. The question we need to ask is, "How can you change the world with sugarcane?"

12.2   Sugar: a force for good not evil

In the mid-eighties an important fund manager – a big client of our New York office - visited our office in London. Although he wasn't one of my direct clients I was asked to look after him and take him out to lunch.

After lunch we were sitting in the trading room chatting about various trading strategies and techniques. He leaned over and asked me to buy 200 lots (10,000 tonnes) of sugar on the London market.

I called the floor broker, executed the order and gave the fund manager the fill. We continued to chat and a little while later he asked me to sell out the 200 lots. I dutifully did so and gave him the prices. I mentally calculated that he had made nearly $100,000 on the trade, not bad for a casual afternoon chat. Intrigued, I asked what had prompted him to buy.

"I was looking at the price screen behind you", he replied, "and saw the price slowly moving higher. It hit resistance, a level where there seemed to be a lot of selling. The market failed a couple of times to move higher but then broke through the selling. I reckoned that the folks that had been selling the market would want to buy their sales back and I correctly assumed that their buying would push the price higher in the short term."

I turned around and looked at the price screen that he had been watching. It showed the prices for the London rubber market, not the sugar market. He had bought the wrong commodity. I wondered if I should tell him but instead I mentioned something about Napoleon preferring lucky generals to smart ones. He didn't react.

David Spiegelhalter is the Winston Professor for the Public Understanding of Risk at the Cambridge Centre for Mathematical Sciences. He recently wrote,

"Unpredictability is a fact of life. Sometimes we can narrow the odds and take some control, but there's always a margin left over which is not in our control, in any way. If it turns out well people call it luck. Luck is just a retrospective label that people give to unpredictable things that happen to go their way. But as soon as you start talking about luck, people start thinking that's some kind of external force that's guiding things, and I think that's absurd.

"Runs of events happen much more often than is intuitive. If you flip a coin and you get four heads and four tails in a row that seems strange, so people think they are having runs of luck. This is how probability works in the real world – in very unintuitive ways. We are so desperate for a sign, some kind of understanding, that we start giving these labels to things when it's just chance" (1)

Many people in the sugar industry can't help feeling that they are going through a prolonged period of bad luck. A series of bad weather and poor harvests led to a spike in prices that few producers could take advantage of, precisely because they had poor harvests. And those high prices have in turn incited producers to expand their production, leading to oversupply that has once again pushed sugar prices below costs of production.

Meanwhile sugar producers are reviled in the media for allegedly driving peasants off their land and using children for cheap labour. Sugar traders are accused of manipulating markets and speculators are loathed for profiting from food prices. At the same time you can't turn on the television without being told that sugar is poison. The industry is under attack from all angles.

But why is sugar so controversial? And why does it generate such strong emotions?

Perhaps the answer lies in sugar's dark history of slavery and exploitation. But then no one blames modern Germany for the crimes committed under the Nazis; and no one really blames a modern sugar mill owner for the atrocities committed by slave owners two hundred years ago. The answer therefore has to lie elsewhere. And according to some psychiatrists, it lies deep in the realms of human psychology.

Humans develop a taste for sugar during the last three months in their mother's womb. A baby in the womb responds to the presence of a sweet taste in the amniotic fluid, for example when the mother is under a glucose infusion, by rapidly swallowing the liquid. At the same time the facial images of the child show the characteristic smile, the "gusto-facial reflex" that a newborn shows when given something sweet. (2)

This "gusto-facial reflex" is characterized by a relaxation of the face muscles; the lips open in exploration and the baby usually smiles. This same "gusto-facial reflex" is found in many cultures and even in children born with brain damage. The acceptance of a sweet taste is innate; it is present both pre-birth and from birth. The child develops a preference for sweetness in the last weeks of pregnancy and this preference is strengthened with the sweet taste of breast milk.

Strictly speaking, we cannot say with certainty that a newborn (or a foetus) loves sugar. What we do know is that it happily swallows sweet foods while rejecting tart or bitter foods. Getting a smile from a baby is a rewarding experience for nurturer; it encourages them to repeat the behaviour that earned them such a success. In other words, it encourages a parent to feed their baby sweet not bitter foods.

But we are not only programmed to associate sweetness with energy. It has been proved first among new-born laboratory animals (3), then in human infants, that eating something sweet has relaxing properties and can act as a pain killer (4). Young rats that are separated from their mothers soon after birth emit distress cries, but these cries subside when a sugar solution is injected into their mouths. And as Mary Poppins knew, the same applies to humans. Sugar is an analgesic and a stress reducer.

But why are we programmed pre-birth to like sweetness? And why do babies make facial expressions that encourage their nurturers to give them more sweetness?

The answer can be found in terms of natural evolution. In nature, a sweet taste is a property of carbohydrates that are energy sources (5). During the evolution of the species, the attraction and acceptance of sweetness at an early age would have been an adaptive advantage, allowing humans to seek and ingest substances that could feed them. Conversely, an innate rejection of bitter taste stimuli protect infants from sometimes toxic substances to which they might be exposed.

The taste for sweetness continues among most young people during childhood. The two most important factors in determining children's food preferences are the familiarity of the food and its sweetness (6). A child will eat a food if he is familiar with it or, failing that, if it is sweet. As the child grows older the appetite for sweetness tends to fade but it does not disappear completely. And the parents who reward a child's good behaviour with sweet food or drink often reinforce it.

Rewarding a child with a dessert for eating vegetables may lead to the child hating vegetables and strengthen their appetite for dessert. In the same context, recent studies have shown that the strict prohibition of food by parents lead the child to focus on this food, to seek and consume it as soon as possible, even when they are not hungry. Two opposite attitudes (the strict prohibition and use as rewards) lead to the same result: the exacerbation of taste for these products (7).

Taste for sweetness is innate; it is present at birth and is almost certainly the result of genetic factors selected by natural evolution. And there is nothing you can do about it. You have no control; you are pre-programmed to like sweetness.

It is perhaps this lack of control that generates a feeling of guilt when you eat sugar: it may make some people "hate" sugar. They hate it because they can't control it – and the only way they can try to control it is to hate it even more. They try to convince themselves that the food itself is poison and that the industry that produces it is evil. Sugar has an emotional value that is a class apart from other foodstuffs.

Some argue that our relationship with sugar is even more complex, that it goes even deeper than a lack of self-control. In his book The Homnivore, the sociologist Claude Fischler notes that morality has always looked disapprovingly at sugar and at whoever eats it. He writes,

"This is due to its borders with sexuality, that link the pleasure, whether assumed or prohibited, guilt or enjoyable. But while sexual pleasure has been legitimized, becoming a component of personal development, attraction to sugar is increasingly misjudged. It has replaced sex in guilt, especially if the sweet treat is lived alone. Some attacks against sugar remind us how we talked about masturbation in the last century."

When we were children we were rewarded for good behaviour with a sweet reward. When we behaved badly we were punished by sweet-deprivation. However somewhere along the line when we were growing up we began to feel guilty about eating sugar, a deep emotional response that we try to rationalise by demonising sugar.

But sugar is not a demon and the sugar industry is not evil. Sugar provides much needed energy and is a source of pleasure and sweetness to billions of people. The sugar industry provides employment and a livelihood to tens of millions of people. And traders enable this by efficiently moving sugar around the world, generating the correct price signals that make sure that there is enough sugar in the right places to meet the needs of a hungry population.

Yes, sugar can be bad for your health if consumed in excessive quantities, but that applies to everything, including red wine and green tea. Yes, sugar can spike your blood sugar levels but so too do other foods. Yes, sugar is bad for your teeth but so too is any carbohydrate; the negative effects can be offset by regular brushing and government policies on fluoride.

And no, contrary to public opinion, sugar does not cause diabetes. Nor can sugar be blamed for the world's obesity epidemic. As I have shown, average per capita sugar consumption has been steady or falling for the past forty years in most developed countries. Admittedly, within those averages some people will be eating more sugar and some will be eating less, but those eating more are still not eating anywhere close to the quantity their parents were eating forty years ago.

A small number of sugar producers need to improve on their sustainability and human rights but the issues are being taken seriously and progress is steadily being made. The world is becoming a smaller place and there is less room for "bad practitioners" to hide. The same applies to the trading community; there will always be some traders who try to manipulate markets but market policing has improved. Besides, attempting to manipulate markets almost never works.

As we have also seen, we are all speculators in one way or another. Speculators play a key role in the markets in assuming some of the risk that producers, consumers and traders might not want to take, and they help price signals get more quickly to those that need them. If in the process speculators push prices too high or too low then the markets respond, prices revert to their correct fundamental value and speculators lose money. It is a messy process, but no one has found any better solution than a market to balance supply and demand.

Governments have a role in policing the markets and to make sure that they operate efficiently, but governments also have a responsibility not to distort the markets, no matter how well meaning their intervention. Using the price of sugar as a tool of social policy has never worked well and never will. Similarly, subsidizing farmers to grow crops, only to see those crops rot in state warehouses, is immoral and inefficient. It would be much better to use the billions of dollars that are currently being spent each year on agricultural subsidies on health, education and infrastructure.

We will need a lot of energy to feed, heat and cool the nine billion people expected to inhabit our world by 2050. We will need to do that without damaging the planet on which we all live. Sugarcane and sugar beet have an important role to play in the sustainability of human life on earth in terms of providing both food and fuel. This will require massive investment not only in growing the crops but also in the logistics to move those crops to hungry mouths.

These are challenging goals and the world will only achieve them with the support of public opinion. Love sugar. Don't demonise it.

Notes for Chapter One

1   I have used three main sources for this section (and the later section on slavery). If you are interested in learning more about the history of sugar I strong recommend:

"Bittersweet, The story of Sugar" by Peter Macinnis;
"Sugar, A bittersweet history" by Elizabeth Abbott;
"Sweetness and Power: The Place of Sugar in Modern History" by Sidney Mintz".

All three are excellent books. I have tried to credit all references to them in my text but if by error I have omitted any I apologise. If you are interested in even further reading, try to borrow a copy of *"The History of Sugar"* by Noël Deere 1949/50. It is now out of print.

2   I could have used other popular lyrics to begin the book. The chorus from Lou Reed's "Walk on the Wild Side" was one possibility (*They said, hey Sugar, take a walk on the wild side, I said, hey babe, take a walk on the wild side, alright, huh*) but "sugar" in this case referred to drugs, particularly speed; and not sucrose.

I did think of using the Rolling Stones "Brown Sugar"; the song is about slavery but brown sugar in this case refers to heroin.

The last choice was "Sugar Sugar" by the Archers; it topped the charts in 1969 but is such an annoying song I thought I would spare you the pain of reliving it. And once you start singing it you can't get it out of your head for days. Ooops, sorry.

3   Abbott "Sugar" p. 20

4   Quoted in Abbott "Sugar" p. 55

5   Mead W.E. "The English medieval feast" 1967 quoted in Mintz p 81

6   Quoted in Abbott "Sugar" p. 20

7   Abbott "Sugar" p. 20 and p. 21

8   Abbott "Sugar" p. 44

9   Macinnis "Bittersweet" p. 45

10 An Audience with Queen Elizabeth I, 1597," www.eyewitnesstohistory.com (2004)

11 Macinnis "Bittersweet" p XV111

12 Macinnis "Bittersweet" p. 2

13 Abbott "Sugar" p. 18

14 Macinnis "Bittersweet" p. 22

15 Abbott "Sugar" p. 47

16 Abbott "Sugar" p. 51

17 http://www.queensroyalsurreys.org.uk/queen_
of_reg/catherine.html

18 Deerr, The History of Sugar, vol 2 p 532 as
quoted in Abbott p. 63

19 Burnett, Plenty and Want pp 14-15, quoted in
Abbott p. 66

20 Abbott p. 68

21 Sweetness and Power p. 172 Mintz

22 All quantities in this book are expressed in what
sugar statisticians call "white value". When raw
sugar is refined into white sugar it loses between
4% and 8% of its weight. Also all quantities in
this book are approximate; production can vary
between seasons.

23 http://www.who.int/mediacentre/news/releas
es/2015/sugar-guideline/en/

24 Interview with Dr Tappy see Chapter 11

25 http://www.worldobesity.org/aboutobesity/wo
rld-map-obesity/

26 India has 550 sugar mills, each with between
10,000 and 20,000 farmers. On average there
are five people in each family. Each of the 550
mills has direct and indirect employment of
around 2,500 people, including harvesting
labour.

27 For a fun look at various spurious correlations see http://www.tylervigen.com/spurious-correlations I think the best one is the almost perfect correlation between per capita cheese consumption and the number of people who die entangled in their bed clothes. (But then cheese is said to give you nightmares!)

28 http://www.ers.usda.gov/data-products/sugar-and-sweeteners-yearbook-tables.aspx Table 56 Mexico: Sugar production and supply, and sugar and HFCS utilization

Notes for Chapter Two

1. Macinnis "Bittersweet" p. 36

2. Macinnis "Bittersweet" p. 36

3. Macinnis "Bittersweet" p 40 42

4. Macinnis "Bittersweet" p 42

5. Abbott "Sugar" p. 89

6. Abbott "Sugar" p. 92

7. Macinnis "Bittersweet" p. 34

8. Macinnis "Bittersweet" p. 114

9. Macinnis "Bittersweet" p. 116 -118

10. Macinnis "Bittersweet" p. 150

11. I was a non-executive board member of Shree Renuka Sugars from 2006 to 2012

12. http://www.dol.gov/ilab/reports/child-labor/list-of-products/index-country.htm
13. https://www.cambodiadaily.com/news/thai-rights-body-censures-firm-over-koh-kong-sugar-plantations-84968/
14. http://www.inclusivedevelopment.net/wp-content/uploads/2013/10/Bittersweet_Harvest_web-version.pdf
15. https://www.oxfam.org/sites/www.oxfam.org/files/bn-sugar-rush-land-supply-chains-food-beverage-companies-021013-en_1.pdf
16. http://www.theguardian.com/world/2013/jul/09/cambodia-sugar-land-grab-claims

Notes for Chapter Three

1. Jenkins, Beth, Piya Baptista, and Marli Porth. 2015. "Collaborating for Change in Sugar Production: Building Blocks for Sustainability at Scale." Cambridge, MA: The CSR Initiative at the Harvard Kennedy School and Business Fights Poverty. http://reports.businessfightspoverty.org/wp-content/uploads/sites/49/2015/02/CSRI-BFP-Building-Blocks-for-Sustainable-Sugar-FINAL.pdf

2. http://www.fao.org/docrep/018/i3347e/i3347e.pdf

3. https://www.iisd.org/sd/

4. http://sugarcane.org/sustainability/preserving-biodiversity-and-precious-resources

5. https://en.wikipedia.org/wiki/Tragedy_of_the
   _commons

6. http://www.wwf.org.br/informacoes/english/?
   40932/Certification-of-sugarcane-production-
   increases-productivity-and-income

7. http://www.canegrowers.com.au/page/Industr
   y_Centre/advocacy/environment-reports/

8. Quoted in Jenkins, Beth, Piya Baptista, and
   Marli Porth. 2015.

9. http://www.ifc.org/wps/wcm/connect/region
   __ext_content/regions/south+asia/news/the+
   sweet+taste+of+success

10. http://sugarcane.org/internal/images/presenta
    tion-eduardo-leao-de-souza-expo-milano-2015

11. http://sugarcane.org/sugarcane-
    benefits/greenhouse-gas-reductions

12. This section is based on prepared comments
    and a panel discussion during the Kingsman
    Dubai Sugar Conference in 2013. I have
    reedited it in the form of an interview for ease
    of reading.

Notes for Chapter Four

1. In order to reduce price volatility, futures exchanges sometimes limit the amount that a price can move up or down in a day. If a market is "limit up" it means that price cannot move any higher during that trading session. Some exchanges now prefer what they call "circuit breakers" that suspend trading for a certain time (sometimes only 20 minutes) when a price has moved too far too fast.

Notes for Chapter Five

1.http://fic.wharton.upenn.edu/fic/papers/06/0607.pdf

2. Speculative influences on commodity futures prices 2006–2008 Christopher L. Gilbert No. 197 March 2010
http://unctad.org/en/Docs/osgdp20101_en.pdf

3.http://faculty.som.yale.edu/garygorton/documents/FactsandFantasiesaboutCommodity.pdf

4. June 3, 2015 The Financial Times, Investment: Revaluing commodities by Gregory Meyer and John Authers
http://www.ft.com/intl/cms/s/0/a6ff2818-094c-11e5-8534-00144feabdc0.html#slide0

5.http://www.fao.org/worldfoodsituation/foodpricesindex/en/

Notes for Chapter Six

1. For a fuller discussion see "The Economics of Trading Firms" by Craig Pirrong, Professor of Finance at Bauer College of Business, University of Houston. It can be found on http://www.trafigura.com/media/1364/economics-commodity-trading-firms.pdf

2. This section is based on prepared remarks and a discussion at the Dubai Sugar Conference in 2013. I have reedited it (with Chris' permission) into a more readable format.

Notes for Chapter Eight

1. Sweet Fifteen: The Competition on the EU Sugar Markets
http://www.konkurrensverket.se/globalassets/english/publications-and-decisions/sweet-fifteen-the-competition-on-the-eu-sugar-markets.pdf

Notes for Chapter Nine

1. Nyberg, Jennifer. No date. "Sugar International Market Profile." Background Paper for the World Bank's Competitive Commercial Agriculture in Sub- Saharan Africa Study.
http://siteresources.worldbank.org/INTAFRICA/Resources/257994-1215457178567/Sugar_Profile.pdf (Page 2.)

2. http://www.heritage.org/research/reports/201
4/06/us-trade-policy-gouges-american-sugar-
consumers

Notes for Chapter Ten

1. Sugar Consumption in Australia: A statistical update
4 October 2012
http://greenpoolcommodities.com/files/8113/493
2/3223/121004_Sugar_Consumption_in_Australia
_-_A_Statistical_Update_-
_Public_Release_Document.pdf

2. http://www.abs.gov.au/ausstats/abs@.nsf/Looku
p/by%20Subject/4364.0.55.007~2011-
12~Main%20Features~Key%20Findings~1

3. Barclay AW, Brand-Miller J (April 2011). "The
Australian paradox: a substantial decline in sugars
intake over the same timeframe that overweight and
obesity have increased". Nutrients 3
http://www.mdpi.com/2072-6643/3/4/491

4. http://www.theaustralianparadox.com.au/

5. https://en.wikipedia.org/wiki/Australian_paradox

6. Briefing 14:03 The Fat Lie by Christopher
Snowdon August 2014
http://www.iea.org.uk/sites/default/files/in-the-
media/files/Briefing_The%20Fat%20Lie.pdf

7. The Inconvenient Truth about Sugar Consumption (it's not what you think) Czarnikow May 2014 http://www.czarnikow.com/news/01-05-14/inconvenient-truth-about-sugar-consumption-it-s-not-what-you-think

8. http://www.comitesucre.org/site/about-sugar/sugars-role-in-food-and-nutrition/

9. http://www.ers.usda.gov/data-products/food-availability-(per-capita)-data-system/summary-findings.aspx

10. All figures are available from the USDA website http://www.ers.usda.gov/data-products/sugar-and-sweeteners-yearbook-tables.aspx#25512

11. Salt Sugar Fat p. 10

12. Salt Sugar Fat p 328

13. A coordinated study by the Mexican National Institute of Public Health and the University of North Carolina quoted in The International Business Times http://www.ibtimes.com/heres-how-much-sugary-beverage-tax-dropped-consumption-sugar-sweetened-drinks-mexico-1970091

14. Ma, J; Fox, CS; Jacques, PF; Speliotes, EK; Hoffmann, U; Smith, CE; Saltzman, E; and McKeown, NM. "Sugar-Sweetened Beverage, Diet Soda, and Fatty Liver Disease in the

Framingham Study Cohorts." Journal of Hepatology. June 5, 2015. http://dx.doi.org/10.1016/j.jhep.2015.03.032 http://now.tufts.edu/news-releases/daily-sugar-sweetened-beverage-habit-linked-non-alcoholic-fatty-liver-disease#sthash.ttNuzC1W.dpuf

Notes for Chapter Eleven

(1) Published in BMC Biology http://www.biomedcentral.com/1741-7007/10/42

(2) http://nancyappleton.com/141-reasons-sugar-ruins-your-health/

(3) Abbott Sugar p. 54

(4) https://www.youtube.com/watch?v=dBnniua6-oM

(5) http://www.bodyandsoul.com.au/nutrition/nutrition+tips/can+eating+chocolate+help+you+lose+weightr,17367

(6) http://www.accesshollywood.com/matthew-mcconaughey-reveals-diet-for-extreme-dallas-buyers-club-weight-loss_article_84533

Notes for Chapter Twelve

1. Quoted in Cambridge Alumni Magazine Issue 66 Easter 2012

2. France BELLISLE, Université Laval, Québec - XXIIèmes Entretiens de Nutrition de l'Institut Pasteur de Lille - 03 juin 2010 http://www.i-dietetique.com/articles/preference-pour-le-sucre-innee-ou-acquise/8168.html

3. Blass, EM, Shide DJ. Some comparisons among the calming and pain-relieving effects of sucrose, glucose, fructose and lactose in infant rats. Chem Senses 1984,19, 239-249.

4. Blass EM, Shah A. Pain-reducing properties of sucrose in human newborns. Chem Senses, 1995, 20, 29-35.

5. Menella JA, Pepino Y, Reed DR. Genetic and environmental determinants of bitter perception and sweet preferences. Paediatrics 2005, 115, e216-e222.

6. Sullivan SA, Birch LL. Pass the Sugar, Pass the Salt: Experience dictates preference. Devel Psychol 1990, 26, 546-551.

7. Fisher JO, Birch LL. Restricting access to a palatable food affects children's behavioural response, food selection and intake. Am J Clin Nutr 1999, 69, 1264-1272.

Sugar Lexicon

Anhydrous ethanol: ethanol with less than one per cent water content that can be mixed with gasoline (up to 25 per cent in Brazil) and burnt in unmodified cars.

Arbitrage: buying a product in one market and selling it in another, hopefully at a higher price. The transactions must occur simultaneously to avoid exposure to market risk (the risk that prices may change on one market before both transactions are complete).

Arbitration: a legal technique for the resolution of disputes outside the courts, where the parties to a dispute refer it to one or more persons (the "arbitrators), by whose decision (the "award") they agree to be bound. It is a settlement technique in which a third party reviews the case and imposes a decision that is legally binding for both sides.

Average cost: the average cost of all units produced.

Average price: the average price of all that you have bought or sold for a particular quality or shipment.

Backwardation: a market condition in which a futures price is lower in the distant delivery months than in the near delivery months.

Basis: a grain trading term for the physical premium or discount relative to the futures.

Basis Risk: the variation between the spot price of a commodity and the price of the futures contract.

Bear market: a market where prices are falling.

Bear: someone who thinks prices will fall.

Buffalo: someone who thinks that prices will stay in a range.

Bull market: a market where prices are rising.

Bull: someone who thinks prices will rise.

Call option: the right to buy something sometime in the future at a predetermined price.

Carrying charge: a market structure where sugar for nearby shipment is less expensive than for later shipment. This is also known as Contango.

CFR or CNF – Cost and Freight (named destination port): seller must pay the costs and freight to bring the goods to the port of destination. However, risk is transferred to the buyer once the goods have crossed the ship's rail. Insurance is at the Cost of the Buyer.

Charter-party: the contract between the owner of a vessel and the charterer for the use of that vessel. The charterer takes over the vessel for either a certain amount of time (a time charter) or for a certain point-to-point voyage (a voyage charter).

CIF – Cost, Insurance and Freight (named destination port): the same as CFR except that the seller must in addition procure and pay for insurance for the buyer.

Collar: a protective options strategy that is usually implemented after a long position has experienced substantial gains. It is created by purchasing an out of the money put option while simultaneously writing an out of the money call option.

Contango: a term used in the futures market to describe an upward sloping forward curve (as in the normal yield curve).

Convergence: as a futures month expiry approaches the futures and the physicals converge in price. At the expiry the futures and the physicals that are delivered are worth the same.

Crop year: a period of 12 months during which all of a country's production is included in statistics. Crop years may vary from country to country and from statistician to statistician. For example, the crop year in CS Brazil is April / March but for NNE Brazil it is October / September.

Default: a situation where one party to a contract fails to fulfil their contractual obligations.

Demurrage: the charges that the charterer pays to the ship owner (or the fobs seller pays to the buyer) for the extra use of a vessel after the period normally allowed to load and unload cargo (laytime). Officially, demurrage is a form of liquidated damages for breaching the laytime set out in the charter party.

Despatch: the opposite of demurrage. If the charterer requires the use of the vessel for less time than the laytime allowed, the charter party may require the ship owner to pay despatch for the time saved.

Ethanol parity: the sugar price below which Brazilian producers will switch to making ethanol rather than sugar (but their switch ability may be limited for technical reasons).

EXW – Ex Works (named place): the seller makes the goods available at his premises. The buyer is responsible for all charges.

Flat price (or outright price): the price of sugar, usually expressed in US$/tonne for white sugar and in US cents per pound (c/lb) for raw sugar. To convert c/lb into $/tonne multiply by 22.0462.

Flexfuel car: one that can run on either gasoline or ethanol or any mix of the two.

FOB – Free on board (named loading port): the seller must load the goods on board the ship nominated by the buyer, cost and risk being divided at ship's rail. The seller must clear the goods for export. It is not used for sea transport in containers.

Forward market: an over-the-counter physical market in contracts for future delivery. Forward contracts are personalized between parties (i.e., delivery time and amount are determined between seller and customer). The forward market is a general term used to describe the informal market by which these contracts are entered into. Standardized forward contracts are called futures contracts and traded on a futures exchange.

Futures market: a futures exchange or derivatives exchange is a central financial exchange where people can trade standardized futures contracts; that is, a contract to buy specific quantities of a commodity or financial instrument at a specified price with delivery set at a specified time in the future.

Hydrous ethanol: ethanol with 5 per cent water content burnt in modified or "flex-fuel" cars.

Import margin (expressed as either positive or negative): the amount of money per tonne that an importer will earn or lose by importing sugar from the world market to a local market, after having paid all import duties and logistics costs.

Limit down: When a futures market has hit the lower price limit for the session imposed by the Exchange.

Limit up: When a market has hit the upper price limit for the session imposed by the Exchange.

Long position: an uncovered contractual obligation that will make money if prices rise.

Long: someone who has bought sugar and is holding it in expectation that price will rise and he can sell it out at a higher price later.

Marginal cost: the cost of producing one more unit.

Marginal price: the price that you would have to pay to buy one more unit. The price of sugar that is quoted and traded is the marginal price.

Notice period: When you buy fobs you have to give your seller notice in advance as to when your vessel will arrive. The notice period refers to how long in advance you have to inform your seller of the vessel's arrival date; it may vary from contract to contract.

OTC - Over the Counter: A non-exchange-traded bilateral contract in which two parties agree on how a particular trade or agreement is to be settled in the future. Forwards and swaps are prime examples of such contracts.

Physical Premium/Discount: the premium/discount to the futures price that is being paid for a particular grade or origin of sugar compared to the futures market. Normally expressed in c/lb for FOB purchases and $/ton for CIF purchases.

Polarisation: the quality of raw sugar as measured by the way that it refracts light when it is dissolved in solution.

Put option: the right to sell something sometime in the future at a predetermined price.

Ratoon: a new shoot or sprout springing from the base of a crop plant, especially sugar cane, after cropping

Ratoon crop: one that is grown from ratoons and is not newly planted.

Raw sugar: sugar that has been produced directly from crystallisation of sugar cane juice but that has not been refined or whitened by chemical process.

Raw value: On average 4-8% of weight is lost during the refining process. To convert a white sugar tonnage figure into raw value the standard is to multiply it by 1.08.

Shipment period: on a FOB contract this refers to the dates within which the buyer must present his vessel. For example, if a trader buys June shipment he can present his vessel to load right up to 30th June (provided he has given the contractual notice); it does not matter when the vessel actually finishes loading. On a Cost and Freight contract, the vessel must have finished loading by the end of the shipment period.

Shipping documents: the documents that must be completed before the seller can get paid for his sugar. These will always include the Bill of Lading, but may also include quality and health certificates.

Short position: an uncovered commitment that will make money if prices fall.

Short: someone who has sold sugar for forward shipment in expectation that price will fall and that he can buy it back at a lower price later.

Spot price: the price of sugar for prompt or immediate arrival or shipment.

Spot shipment/arrival: sugar for prompt or immediate (usually within one month) shipment/arrival. "Spot" is not a legal term and exact dates should always be specified.

Spread: (or time spread) the difference in price between sugar for one shipment period (or futures contract) and another.

Squeeze: usually refers to a situation where someone is short of a physical commodity or a futures contract and is forced to cover his commitment, usually at an uncomfortable loss.

Strangle: An options strategy involving the purchase or sale of both call and put options of different strike prices that allows the holder to profit based on how much the price of the underlying security moves, with relatively minimal exposure to the direction of price movement. The purchase of a call and a put is known as a long strangle, while the sale of a call and a put is known as a short strangle.

Straddle: an options strategy where you hold a position in both a call and put with the same strike price and expiration date.

Terminal (futures market): sometimes used to describe a futures market.

Terminal (port): a facility for the loading of bagged or bulk sugar onto a vessel.

White sugar: raw sugar that has been processed (whitened) but not necessarily refined.

INDEX